Finance for Non-Fin

Finance is key to every business organisation as well as outside. This book makes sense of the finance world from a non-finance perspective. It introduces, explains and demystifies essential ideas of business finance to those who do not have financial background or training. Lucid, accessible, yet comprehensive, the book delineates the financial workings of businesses and offers an overview of corporate finance in the global context. The volume:

- Contains effective tools for financial communication, monitoring, analysis and resource allocation;
- Provides important learning aids such as figures, tables, illustrations and case studies;
- Highlights fundamental concepts and applications of finance;
- Surveys global corporate practices, recent trends and current data.

This updated second edition contains new sections on Tax Planning, including Income Tax and Goods and Services Tax in India. A guide to building financial acumen, this book will be a useful resource for executive and management development programmes (EDPs & MDPs) oriented towards business managers, including MBA programmes. It will benefit business executives, corporate heads, entrepreneurs, government officials, teachers, researchers, and students of management and business, as well as those who deal with finance or financial matters in their daily lives.

Sandeep Goel is Associate Professor of Accounting and Finance at Management Development Institute (MDI) Gurgaon, India. He holds two doctorates, one in Finance; and another in Accounting from the Faculty of Management Studies, University of Delhi. He completed his bachelor's and master's degrees in commerce from Shri Ram College of Commerce, and the Department of Commerce, University of Delhi, respectively. He has over two decades of industry and academic experience across various organisations and institutions, including the Shri Ram Group, the University of Delhi and MDI. He is a management trainer and consultant to top business organisations and has conducted over 200 programmes dealing with financial skills and consultancy assignments on financial management, accounting application and corporate governance. His areas of teaching and research interests are financial reporting and analysis, corporate finance, forensic accounting and corporate governance. He has authored ten books, including *Financial Management Practices in India* (2016) and *Financial Statements Analysis: Cases from Corporate India* (2014), and over 75 articles in journals, as well as being the financial columnist for *Purchase*.

Finance for Non-Finance People

Second Edition

Sandeep Goel

Routledge
Taylor & Francis Group

LONDON AND NEW YORK

Second edition published 2019
by Routledge
2 Park Square, Milton Park, Abingdon, Oxon, OX14 4RN

and by Routledge
52 Vanderbilt Avenue, New York, NY 10017

Routledge is an imprint of the Taylor & Francis Group, an informa business

© 2019 Sandeep Goel

First edition published by Routledge 2017

British Library Cataloguing-in-Publication Data
A catalogue record for this book is available from the British Library

Library of Congress Cataloging-in-Publication Data
Names: Goel, Sandeep, 1975– author.
Title: Finance for non-finance people / Sandeep Goel.
Description: Second edition. | Abingdon, Oxon ; New York, NY :
    Routledge, 2019. | Includes bibliographical references and index.
Identifiers: LCCN 2018056439 | ISBN 9780367076849 (hardback : alk. paper) |
    ISBN 9780367185084 (pbk. : alk. paper) | ISBN 9780429196669 (e-book)
Subjects: LCSH: Business enterprises—Finance. | Corporations—Finance.
Classification: LCC HG4026 .G6228 2019 | DDC 658.15—dc23
LC record available at https://lccn.loc.gov/2018056439

ISBN: 978-0-367-07684-9 (hbk)
ISBN: 978-0-367-18508-4 (pbk)
ISBN: 978-0-429-19666-9 (ebk)

Typeset in Sabon
by Apex CoVantage, LLC

Printed and bound in Great Britain by
TJ International Ltd, Padstow, Cornwall

Contents

Figures

Tables

Preface

The second edition

I take this opportunity to thank everyone for the overwhelming response to the first edition of this book. This has motivated me to bring out the second edition. New material has been added for the enrichment of the book. The basic organisational structure, topical coverage, readability, and useful instructional cases and examples that marked the success of the first edition have been retained.

Specifically, a new Part on 'Tax planning' has been added – it has two chapters:

Chapter 25: Direct taxation: income tax
Chapter 26: Indirect taxation: Goods and Services Tax (GST)

Further, all chapters have been thoroughly updated to reflect the cutting edge of current trends and practices in the finance domain. The book provides helpful new approaches, expanded coverage, and enhanced pedagogy anchored by a state-of-the-art integrated learning process. I hope that these enhancements will offer increased value to the book.

■

Understanding your organisation's financial health is the fundamental aspect of managerial decision-making and control. A good manager is one who is able to (i) analyse financial performance trends and (ii) make a suitable decision in time and adjust planned and forecasted amounts to avoid various risks. This is where 'financial proficiency and efficiency' becomes essential at all levels of business and in all types of organisations across the globe.

Imagine a northwest regional sales head's reaction on being asked budgets for his region for the next quarter by his country head. Please remember that he comes from the humanities side of academics! Till now, he was relying on his immediate assistant, but unfortunately this time he was on leave. He was asking himself, 'How does one make a budget?'

Explore another situation faced by the director of operations in a multinational company (MNC) where he has been promoted as the CEO. But he was not happy. To date, he was just concerned with the technical side of the business. All of a sudden, he was finding himself in an alien land because now he has to make all types of decisions and for the entire company, including the financial decisions. One thing which he has been running away from all his life was 'Finance'.

In both these situations, one thing is common, that 'finance is an inevitable part of business'. Finance is not only essential but an exciting area of management that every executive wants to discover and explore in depth.

Objective

The book will help to develop not only an understanding of the concepts of accounting and finance, but most importantly to enable the managers to use it as an effective tool for financial communication, monitoring, analysis and resource allocation.

It helps to answer questions, like:

- What are the accounting nuances of managing a business organisation?
- What financial statements are prepared and analysed as a part of financial reporting?
- How is the cost of a product or service ascertained and controlled?
- How is cost accounting information utilised for managerial decision-making and control?
- How should the firm be managed to increase the wealth of shareholders?
- What is the nitty-gritty involved in financial decision-making, such as launching a new product, buying a new asset, acquiring another company, and financing the firm's investments?
- What decisions must managers make to manage the business operations for value-based management?
- What could be the financial implications of your decisions?
- How can the firms be managed to ensure sound corporate governance?

Features

Various aids like figures, tables, illustrations and case studies have been included in the book to facilitate learning. Real world organisations' cases have been analysed and discussed from diverge sectors. These companies have global operations, so they will be of immense use to international readers. All these features will make the book more interesting and useful to readers.

The book is a thoroughly updated edition containing current concepts, corporate practices, recent trends and current data. An attempt has been made to cover every possible aspect of the finance in depth.

Highlights

- Thoroughly updated comprehensive chapters
- Self-contained chapters
- Global concepts and practices
- Corporate case studies
- Updated current data
- Solved problems
- Summary points
- Key terms.

Target audience

'Almost everything boils down to finance', as the adage goes. In light of the universal requirement of finance, the present book is an attempt to meet the needs of all the people out there, including business executives, corporate heads, entrepreneurs, government officers, teachers, researchers, and of course students and everyone who has to deal with finance, and financial matters in the daily course of their work. In nutshell, this book is for everyone who is not a finance expert but wants to learn finance, and also for people with finance background who would like to refresh and revive their concepts and apply them better for much more meaningful decision-making in various walks of life. This book is one single platform wherein you will find answers to all your queries.

- It is for everyone who wants to learn finance.
- This book is equally useful to people with a finance background for advanced learning.
- The book is perfectly designed for basic courses in accounting and finance at graduate and undergraduate level in B-schools and universities.

- The book can be a good substitute for, or a helpful complement to, the main textbook in advanced courses in finance.
- It is tailor-made key resource book for executive and management development programs (EDPs and MDPs) oriented towards business managers, including MBA programs.
- This book will provide a solution in finance to all those students and learners who are struggling to enhance their financial knowledge for advanced finance courses, the managers who are having sleepless nights to mind the numbers on account of lack of financial acumen, the entrepreneurs who have to bear the tantrums of their accountant for every accounting need and the potential investors who dream of investing in stocks one day. This book is an attempt to improve that financial acumen and communication.

Organisation of the book

The book has been divided into eight parts. It has been logically sequenced to facilitate better connectivity and learning among the readers. Most chapters are self-contained and can be read independently of the others.

Part I, 'Introduction', gives an overview of different forms of business organisations and accounting fundamentals and principles. Recognising that executives often approach financial problems from a financial accounting perspective, Part II, 'Financial statements and analysis', discusses corporate financial statements and various accounting tools like ratio analysis, which are used for analysing the financial performance of a business.

Part III, 'Cost accounting and management', discusses the cost accounting concepts and techniques for cost ascertainment, control and managerial decision-making in an organisation. Part IV, 'Financial system', discusses the financial markets in India, their constituents and the international financial management where currency and country risks must be taken into account.

Part V, 'Financial management', is a complete manual on the financial management process of a business organisation. It demonstrates how managers should make sound financial decisions to maximise the firm's value. It builds on the concepts of compounding and discounting and covers the key areas of financial management, such as capital budgeting, sources of finance, working capital management and dividend policy.

Part VI, 'Value-based management', discusses making value-creating business decisions. Part VII, 'Strategic finance', concludes with two chapters on the strategic issues in finance of corporate restructuring and corporate governance.

Part VIII, 'Tax planning', deals with the taxation part of an individual and business. It covers both direct and indirect taxation, in particular income tax and Goods and Services Tax (GST).

This book will build up your finance acumen, which is essential for your professional growth and success. This is a perfect blend of theory with practice. An attempt has been to keep the book simple in nature yet comprehensive in approach. I am confident that the readers will find this book truly valuable in terms of its quality and presentation. Any constructive comments and suggestions for future improvement of the book are highly appreciated and welcome (sandeepgoel18@rediffmail.com).

Happy learning!

Acknowledgements

This book has come out of decades of rich experience of imparting financial knowledge and skills to thousands of students and participants at different levels of corporates and organisations. At this moment, I take the opportunity to express my gratitude to each one of those whose inspiring queries and questions have motivated me to pen down this single-window 'book' where they can quench their thirst about finance.

I wish to thank God Almighty for everything in life! The work would be incomplete if I do not acknowledge my parents' contribution. They have been a constant source of inspiration for me and have always stood by me through thick and thin. My wife provided her unstinted support and encouragement in completing the book. My little daughter Maanya is my soul whose smile always keeps me going in life.

Last but not least, I am thankful to Dr. Shashank Sinha and the entire team at Routledge, New Delhi, for their tremendous support and wholehearted cooperation at all stages of publication of this book.

Abbreviations

ACP	Average collection period
AD	Authorised dealer
ADR	American depositary receipt
AHP	Average holding period
AICPA	American Institute of Certified Public Accountants
AMC	Asset management companies
AMFI	Association of Mutual Funds in India
AMT	Alternate minimum tax
A/P	Accounts payable
APP	Average payment period
A/R	Accounts receivable
ARR	Accounting rate of return
ASB	Accounting Standards Board
ATR	Assets turnover ratio
BC	Benefit-cost ratio
BEL	Bharat Electronics Ltd.
BHEL	Bharat Heavy Electricals Limited
BIS	Bank for International Settlements
BoP	Balance of payments
BSE	Bombay Stock Exchange
BV	Book value per share
CA/FA	Current assets/fixed assets ratio
CAR	Capital adequacy ratio
CASA	Current and saving accounts ratio
CBDT	Central Board of Direct Taxes
CBIC	Central Board of Indirect Taxes & Customs
CCIL	Clearing Corporation of India Ltd.
CFF	Net cash flow from financing activities
CFI	Net cash flow from investing activities
CFO	Net cash flow from operating activities

CGST	Central Goods and Services Tax
CII	Confederation of Indian Industry
CIMA	Chartered Institute of Management Accountants
COCE	Cost of capital employed
COD	Certificate of deposit
COGS	Cost of goods sold
CP	Commercial paper
CRR	Cash reserve ratio
C/S	Contribution/sales ratio
CSR	Corporate social responsibility
CTR	Creditors turnover ratio
CVP	Cost-volume-profit analysis
CWIP	Capital work in progress
DCF	Discounted cash flow
D/E	Debt-equity ratio
DFL	Degree of financial leverage
DOL	Degree of operating leverage
D/P	Dividend pay-out ratio
DPS	Dividend per share
DR	Depositary receipt
DSCR	Debt service coverage ratio
D/Y	Dividend yield ratio
DTC	Delhi Transport Corporation
DTR	Debtors turnover ratio
EBIT	Earnings before interest and tax
EBITDA	Earnings before interest, tax and depreciation and amortisation
EBIT-EPS	Earnings before interest and tax – earnings per share
EBT	Earnings before taxes
EIL	Engineers India Ltd.
ELSS	Equity linked saving schemes
EPS	Earnings per share
ESIC	Employees' State Insurance Corporation
EVA	Economic value added
FASB	Financial Accounting Standards Board
FDI	Foreign direct investment
FEDAI	Foreign Exchange Dealers' Association of India
FEMA	Foreign Exchange Management Act
FERA	Foreign Exchange Regulation Act
FII	Foreign institutional investors
FMC	Forward Markets Commission
FMCG	Fast-moving consumer goods

FOREX	Foreign exchange
FV	Future value
GAAP	Generally accepted accounting principles
GAIL	Gas Authority of India Limited
GCPL	Godrej Consumer Products Ltd.
GDR	Global depositary receipts
G-Secs	Government securities
GSFC	Gujarat State Fertilisers and Chemicals Ltd. (formerly Gujarat State Fertiliser Company)
GSM	Global system for mobile communication
GST	Goods and Services Tax
GSTIN	GST identification
GSTN	Goods and Services Tax Network
HCC	Hindustan Construction Company Ltd.
HRA	Human resource accounting
HRV	Human resource valuation
HUF	Hindu undivided family
HUL	Hindustan Unilever Ltd.
IASB	International Accounting Standards Board
ICD	Inter-corporate deposit
ICR	Interest coverage ratio
IDBI	Industrial Development Bank of India
IFFCO	Indian Farmers Fertilisers Cooperative Limited
IFRS	International financial reporting standards
IGST	Integrated Goods and Services Tax
Ind AS	Indian accounting standard
IPO	Initial public offering
IRDA	Insurance Regulatory and Development Authority
IRR	Internal rate of return
ITR	Inventory turnover ratio
JV	Joint venture
Kwh/kWh	Kilowatt hour
L&T	Larsen and Toubro Ltd.
LIC	Life Insurance Corporation of India
LLP	Limited liability partnership
M&A	Mergers and acquisitions
MAT	Minimum alternate tax
MCA	Ministry of Corporate Affairs
MD	Managing director
MNC	Multinational corporations
MSIL	Maruti Suzuki India Ltd.
MV	Market value

MVA	Market value added
NAPA	National Anti-Profiteering Authority
NAV	Net asset value
NIM	New issue market
NOPAT	Net operating profit after tax
NPA	Non-performing asset
NPV	Net present value
NSE	National Stock Exchange of India Limited
OECD	Organisation for Economic Co-operation and Development
OFR	Operational and financial review
OPC	One-person company
OTC	Over-the-counter
PAN	Permanent account number
PAT	Profit after taxes
P/B	Price to book ratio
PBDT	Profit before depreciation and tax
PBP	Payback period
PBT	Profit before taxes
P/E	Price to earnings ratio
PFRDA	Pension Fund Regulatory and Development Authority
PGCIL	Power Grid Corporation of India Ltd.
PI	Profitability index
PSU	Public sector undertaking
PV	Present value
P/V	Profit volume ratio
RBI	Reserve Bank of India
RCA	Rupee cost averaging
RIL	Reliance Industries Ltd.
ROCE	Return on capital employed
ROE	Return on equity
ROI	Return on investment
RONW	Return on net worth
SAIL	Steel Authority of India Limited
SBI	State Bank of India
SEBI	Securities and Exchange Board of India
SENSEX	Sensitive index
SFC	State finance corporations
SGST	State Goods and Services Tax
SIDBI	Small Industries Development Bank of India
SIP	Systematic investment plan
SLM	Straight-line method

SLR	Statutory liquidity ratio
SOX	Sarbanes-Oxley Act
SWIFT	Society for Worldwide Interbank Financial Telecommunications
SWM	Shareholders' wealth maximisation
TAN	Tax deduction and collection account number
T-Bill	Treasury bill
TVM	Time value of money
UTGST	Union Territory Goods and Services Tax
UTI	Unit Trust of India
VAT	Value-added tax
WACC	Weighted average cost of capital
WCTR	Working capital turnover ratio
WDM	Wholesale debt market
WDV	Written-down value method
WTD	Whole time director
ZBB	Zero-based budgeting

Part I
Introduction

1   Business organisations

Business organisations operate for the production of goods or rendering of services to society. The scale of their activities is vast and has an enormous impact on the life of the community. The activities include providing essential goods and services to ultra-luxury and luxury. Every individual comes into contact with business organisations practically at every turn in his or her daily life. Undoubtedly, these business enterprises are inevitable to the growth of the economy and a part of every individual's daily life directly or indirectly.

Meaning of business organisation

A business organisation (also known as business enterprise, business undertaking, business firm or business concern) is an organisation which is engaged in some business or commercial activity. It may be owned and controlled by a single individual or by a group of individuals. So business organisation can be defined as 'an enterprise which produces, distributes or provides any product or service needed by the members of the community for a price'.

Types of business organisations

Business organisations may be classified into three broad categories as depicted in Figure 1.1.

Figure 1.1 Classification of business organisations

I. Private sector enterprise

A private sector enterprise is owned, managed and controlled exclusively by private businessman. There is no participation by the central or state governments in the establishment and ownership of a private enterprise. The main motive of a private enterprise is to earn profit. *Examples: Reliance Industries Ltd. (RIL), Infosys Ltd., Parle Products Pvt. Ltd., etc.*

II. Public sector enterprise

A public sector enterprise is defined as an enterprise which may be (a) owned by the state, (b) managed by the state, or (c) owned and managed by the state. According to Prof. A. H. Hanson, 'Public enterprise means state ownership and operation of industrial, agricultural, financial and commercial undertakings'.[1] The basic purpose of such undertakings is to render service to society. *Examples: Life Insurance Corporation of India (LIC), Steel Authority of India Limited (SAIL), Engineers India Ltd. (EIL), Delhi Transport Corporation (DTC).*

III. Joint sector enterprise

Joint sector enterprises consist of those business undertakings wherein the ownership, management and control are shared jointly by the government, private entrepreneurs and the public. Joint sector enterprises have been designed as an effective instrument for exercising social control over industry. *Example: Gujarat State Fertilisers and Chemicals Ltd. (GSFC) incorporated in 1962 as Gujarat State Fertiliser Company (GSFC), a joint sector enterprise set up by the Government of Gujarat. Its equity structure consisted of 49% of state government and the rest of public and financial institutions.*[2]

Joint sector enterprise is not same as 'Joint Venture' (JV), though in both the arrangements, two or more parties agree to pool their resources for the purpose of accomplishing a specific task. The basic difference between them is that 'A business relationship is needed for a joint venture but not for a joint enterprise'.

Types of private sector enterprises

1. Sole proprietorship

In this form of a business enterprise, a single person provides the entire capital, bears all the risks and manages the business. The proprietor is personally liable for all the debts of the firm. Thus, a sole proprietorship is a 'one-man army'. It is the simplest form of business to getting started. *Small-scale businesses, like grocery stores and chemist's shops operate as sole proprietorships.*

2. Joint Hindu family business

It may be defined as a form of business organisation in which all the male members of a Hindu undivided family carry on business under the management and control of the head of the family called 'Karta'. It is found only in India and is the result of the Hindu undivided family system followed in India.

3. Partnership

In this form of ownership, two or more persons enter into a contract to carry on some lawful activity jointly and to share its profits. Section 4 of the Indian Partnership Act, 1932 defines partnership as 'the relation between persons who have agreed to share the profits of a business carried on by all or any of them acting for all'.[3] Each partner is considered as the agent of the firm and of its partners. The firm has no separate legal entity from that of the partners. Each partner is jointly and individually liable for the debts of the firm to an unlimited extent.

To form a partnership, the number of members (partners) required for a banking business is 2 to 10, and for a non-banking business it is 2 to 20 members.

4. Cooperative organisation

A cooperative society is a voluntary association of ten or more persons who join hands together to carry on economic activity of common need. It is based on the principles of mutual trust, equality, democracy and freedom. As an incorporated association of persons, it enjoys perpetual life. It has a distinct entity and the liability of its members is limited. IFFCO *(Indian Farmers Fertilisers Cooperative Limited) is an example of a cooperative.*

5. Joint stock company

A joint stock company is an association of persons having a separate legal existence, perpetual succession and common seal. A company is an incorporated association of persons under the Companies Act, 2013 or Companies Act, 1956. Its capital is generally divided into shares which are transferable subject to certain conditions. Its management and control lies in the hands of the board of directors consisting of the elected representatives of the members. A joint stock company in the private sector could be either a private company or a public company.

(a) Private company

According to Section 2 (68) of the Companies Act, 2013, a private company is one which has the following features:

i.   The minimum paid-up share capital is Rs. 1 lakh
ii. The company restricts the right to transfer its shares
iii. The minimum number of members is two
iv. The maximum number of members is 200
v.   It is prohibited from issuing shares to the public.

A private company must use 'Private Limited' as last word. *Examples: Competent Automobiles Co. (P) Ltd., Allied Motors Pvt. Ltd.*

(b) Public company

According to According to Section 2 (71) of the Companies Act, 2013, a private company is one which has the following features:

i.   It is not a private company
ii. The minimum paid-up share capital is Rs. 5 lakh
iii. The minimum number of members is seven
iv. The maximum number of members is unlimited
v.   There is no restriction on the right of members to transfer their shares
vi. The company is free to invite the general public to subscribe to its shares and debentures.

Such a company must use 'Limited' as the last word. *Examples: Reliance Industries Ltd., Bajaj Auto Ltd.*

Table 1.1 lists the distinctions between private and public companies.

As per **Companies (Amendment) Act, 2015**, the minimum paid-up share capital requirement of INR 100,000 (for private company) and INR 500,000 (for public company) under Companies Act, 2013 has been removed.[4]

Table 1.1 Distinctions between private and public companies

Nature	Private Company	Public Company
1. Meaning	Which by its article restricts: i. Numbers of members to 200 ii. Transfer of shares iii. Invitation of public to subscribe its debenture, shares, etc. iv. Acceptance of deposits from common public	Which is not private i. No limit on maximum number of members ii. No restriction on the right of members to transfer their shares iii. Is free to invite the general public to subscribe to its shares and debentures.
2. Law	Companies Act, 2013 and 1956	Companies Act, 2013 and 1956; SEBI Act, 1992; and allied laws
3. Minimum no. of shareholders (members)	2	7
4. Maximum no. of shareholders (members)	200	No limit
5. Minimum paid-up capital	Rs. 1,00,000	Rs. 5,00,000
6. Minimum no. of directors	2	3
7. Transferability of shares	Restricted	No restriction, if company is listed in stock exchange
8. Whole time director (WTD)/ Managing director (MD) appointment	Appointment not compulsory (Optional) and No restriction on appointment	Compulsory for (a) all listed companies (b) all public companies with paid-up capital $\geq$ Rs. 10 crore
9. Managerial remuneration	No restriction on amount of managerial remuneration	Managerial remuneration is restricted to 11% of Net profit (subject to conditions); or at least Rs. 30 lakh p.a. depending upon paid-up capital

> ## Box 1.1   Holding, subsidiary and associate companies
>
> Holding company = owns 20% or more shares of 'another company'.
> 'Another company' is further classified into:
>
> *(i)* *Subsidiary company* = if 50% shares are owned by holding company.
> *(ii)* *Associate company* = if 20% or more shares are owned by holding company.

6. One person company

The Companies Act, 2013 introduces a new type of entity to the existing list of a public or private limited company, a 'one-person company' (OPC). An OPC means a company with only one person as its member, both minimum and maximum [Section 2 (62) of 2013, Act]. The minimum capital requirement for OPC is of Rs. 1,00,000.

Section 3 classifies OPC as a private company for all legal purposes. All the provisions related to the private company are applicable to an OPC, unless otherwise expressly excluded.

The concept of OPC in the Indian legal system was introduced to encourage the corporatisation of micro businesses and entrepreneurship with a simpler legal regime. The most significant reason for shareholders to incorporate the 'single-person company' is 'the limited liability'. Though the concept of OPC is new in India, it has long been a very successful form of business in the UK and several Western countries.

> ## Box 1.2   Limited Liability Partnership (LLP)
>
> Limited liability partnership (LLP) is a new corporate structure that combines the flexibility of a partnership of organising their internal management on the basis of a mutually arrived agreement, and the advantages of limited liability of a company at a low compliance cost. Unlike the general partnerships in India, an LLP is a body corporate and legal entity separate from its partners, has perpetual succession and any change in the partners of a LLP shall not affect the existence, rights or liabilities of the LLP. LLPs are governed by the provisions of the Limited Liability Partnership Act, 2008.

Types of public sector enterprises

Public sector enterprises may be organised in any of the following types:

1   Departmental undertakings
2   Statutory corporations
3   Government companies.

Departmental undertakings

Departmental undertaking is the oldest and traditional form of organising public sector enterprises. A departmental undertaking is managed by government officials under the supervision of the head of the department concerned. It may be run either by the central government or by a state government. The undertaking is under the overall and ultimate control of a minister who is responsible to parliament. *Examples are Indian railways, post and telegraphs, the broadcasting department, defence establishments, and atomic energy projects.*

Statutory corporations

A statutory corporation or a public corporation is a body set up under a special act of parliament or of the state legislature. It is known as a statutory corporation because it is created by a statute or law. The statute defines its objects, powers and functions. *Examples are Life Insurance Corporation of India (LIC), Industrial Development Bank of India (IDBI), Unit Trust of India (UTI) and Employees' State Insurance Corporation (ESIC).*

Government company

A government company or public sector undertaking (PSU) is a company in which not less than 51% of the paid-up share capital is held by the central government or by one or more state governments or jointly by the central and state governments. It is formed and registered under the Companies Act, 1956. *Examples are Steel Authority of India Limited (SAIL), Gas Authority of India Limited (GAIL) and Bharat Heavy Electricals Limited (BHEL).*

Points to remember

- A business organisation is one which is engaged in some business or commercial activity. It can be a private sector enterprise or public sector enterprise or joint sector enterprise.
- Private sector enterprises can be in the form of *sole proprietorship, joint Hindu family business, partnership, cooperative organisation* or a *joint stock company.*
- Joint stock company is an association of persons having a separate legal existence, perpetual succession and common seal and incorporated under the Companies Act, 1956.
- Private company is one which cannot invite the general public to invest into it.
- Public company is free to invite the general public to invest into it.
- A one-person company (OPC) means a company with only one person as its member under the Companies Act, 2013.
- Limited liability partnership (LLP) is a body corporate and legal entity separate from its partners, registered under the Limited Liability Partnership Act, 2008.
- Public sector enterprises can be of three types: (i) departmental undertakings, (ii) statutory corporation, or (iii) government company.

Notes

1 Hanson, Albert Henry. 1959. *Public Enterprise and Economic Development.* London: Routledge & Kegan Paul Ltd., p. 115.
2 NDTV Profit, Gujarat State Fertilizers & Chemicals Ltd., http://profit.ndtv.com/stock/gujarat-state-fertilizers-&-chemicals-ltd_gsfc/reports (accessed on 19 May 2017).
3 The Partnership Act, 1932 – Ministry of Corporate Affairs, www.mca.gov.in/Ministry/actsbills/pdf/Partnership_Act_1932.pdf, p. 3 (accessed on 1 July 2016).
4 Narsana Bhavik, et al. 2015. 'India: Companies (Amendment) Act, 2015: Key Highlights,' July 6, Khaitan & Co., http://www.mondaq.com/india/x/410320/Corporate+Commercial+Law/Companies+Amendment+Act+2015+Key+Highlights (accessed on 24 October 2016).

2 Fundamentals of accounting

Accounting is termed as the 'language of the business', as the information about the transactions and events of a business is recorded and presented in the form of reports that are used by various interested persons. This is the most common concept of accounting. It communicates the result of business operations to various stakeholders in the business, namely, the owner(s), investors, managers, creditors, regulators, government and other agencies, and thereby helps them in decision-making.

Meaning of accounting

The term 'accounting' refers to the processes carried out by the accountants of aggregating and shaping information into the financial reports that are meaningful to users of those reports. According to the American Institute of Certified Public Accountant (AICPA 1941), 'Accounting is the art of recording, classifying and summarising in significant manner and in terms of money, transactions and events which are, in part, at least of a financial character and interpreting the results thereof'.

> If accounting is looked at in a narrow perspective of *recording the business transactions only*, it is called 'book keeping'. So, bookkeeping is a part of accounting.

Every user draws on accounting information for various purposes, as follows:

- **Managers** need accounting information to make sound decisions about the day-to-day operations and growth of the business.
- **Owners (shareholders)** require it to find out the well-being of the business for protecting their hard-earned money invested into it.

- **Investors** use it for making profits.
- **Creditors** are always concerned about the entity's ability to repay its obligations.
- **Employees** need the information for evaluating the company's growth for their incentives.
- **Government units** need information for tax and regulation purpose.
- **Analysts** use accounting data to recommend investment strategies.

Accounting process

The accounting process is expressed through following stages (functions) of accounting:

1 **Recording.** This is the basic function of accounting. It is essentially concerned with ensuring that all business transactions of financial character are recorded in an orderly manner. Recording is done in the primary book, called a *'Journal'*.

   The journal book may be further sub-divided into various subsidiary books, such as cash journal (for recording cash transactions), purchases journal (for recording credit purchase of goods), sales journal (for recording credit sales of goods) and so forth. The number of subsidiary books to be maintained varies according to the nature and size of the business.

2 **Classifying.** Classification is concerned with analysing the recorded data, and grouping the transactions or entries of similar nature in one place. The work of classification is done in the book termed '*Ledger*'.

   The ledger book contains on different pages individual account heads under which all financial transactions of similar nature are placed. *For example*, there may be separate account heads for office expenses, sales and so forth. This will help in finding out the total balance under each of those heads.

3 **Summarising.** This involves the presentation of the classified data in a manner which is understandable and useful to the end users of accounting information. This process leads to the preparation of the following statements:

   (i) Trial Balance, (ii) Income Statement, and (iii) Balance Sheet

4 **Analysing and interpreting.** The recorded financial data is analysed and interpreted in a manner that the end users can make a meaningful judgement about the profitability and financial health of the business. *Financial ratios* and other techniques are used for analysis of the financial statements.

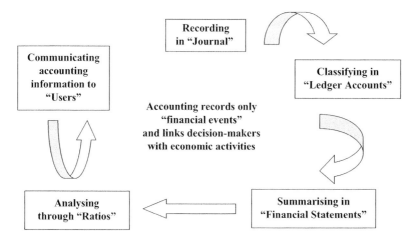

Figure 2.1 Accounting process

5 **Communicating.** The accounting information in the end has to be communicated in a proper form and manner to all the end users. This is done through preparation and distribution of various *accounting reports*.

The 'accounting process' is presented in Figure 2.1.

Branches of accounting

The diversity of interested parties and their diverse needs results in various forms of accounting are depicted in Figure 2.2.

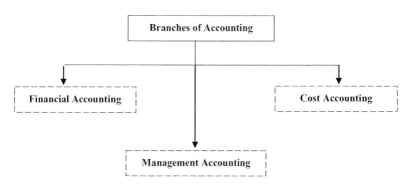

Figure 2.2 Accounting forms

1. Financial accounting

Financial accounting is the original form of accounting. It is mainly concerned with the financial performance of an organisation and involves the preparation of financial statements of profit and loss account and the balance sheet for various stakeholders, like shareholders, debenture holders, creditors, banks, financial institutions. These financial reports are prepared under the relevant accounting principles and standards set by the respective standard-setting bodies. It is external in nature.

2. Cost accounting

Cost accounting is the process of accounting for costs. 'It is the formal mechanism by means of which costs of products or services are ascertained and controlled'. It is a method of accounting in which all costs incurred in carrying out an activity are collected, classified, and recorded. This 'ata is then summarised and analysed to arrive at a selling price, r to exercise cost control and determine where savings are possible.

3. Management accounting

It is the accounting for management, that is accounting which provides necessary information to the management for taking various decisions. Management accounting covers various areas, such as cost accounting, human resource accounting and so forth. Managerial accounting information is intended to serve the specific needs of management, like budgeting, product costing data, human performance and other details that are generally not reported on an external basis.

Objectives of accounting

The following are the main objectives of accounting:

1   **To keep systematic records.** Accounting is done to keep a systematic record of the financial transactions of an organisation. It makes the job of human beings easier.
2   **To ascertain profit or loss.** Accounting helps in ascertaining the net profit earned or loss suffered on account of business operations. This is done by keeping a proper record of revenues and

expenses of a particular period in the form of 'Statement of Profit and Loss'.

3 **To ascertain the financial position of the business.** This objective is served by the 'Balance Sheet' or 'Position Statement'. The balance sheet is a statement of assets and liabilities of the business on a particular date. It serves as barometer for ascertaining the financial health of the business.

4 **To facilitate managerial decision-making.** Accounting records, analyses and reports information at various points of time to the required levels of authority in order to facilitate decision-making.

Limitations of accounting

Accounting is not free from limitations, as follows:

1 **Personal judgement.** Considerable amount of judgement and estimation is involved in maintaining and presenting the accounting information. *For example*, there is discretion involved in sales recognition, that is should sales be record on dispatch of goods or receipt of goods by the buyer? So, in order to present the information in a timely manner, various estimations are made in the preparation of financial reports.

2 **Historical nature.** Accounting is historical in nature. It presents information which has happened in the past. These records do not help for future planning and other managerial decisions.

3 **Cost principle.** Accounting information is recorded on historical cost basis, instead of current or fair value. *For example*, land is typically recorded and carried in the accounting records at the price at which it was purchased. This undermines the value of the business.

4 **No detailed information about cost.** Financial accounting provides information as a whole in terms of income, expenses, assets and liabilities. It does not provide detail of cost involved by departments, processes, products, services or other unit of activity within the organisation.

Accounting elements

The entire accounting cycle is about following elements as depicted in Figure 2.3.

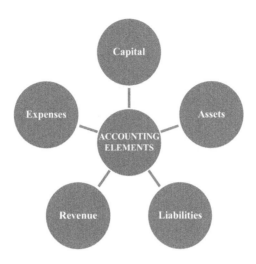

Figure 2.3 Accounting elements

Capital – It is the money contributed by owners. It denotes shareholders' funds in a business.

Assets – These are resources that are owned by a business having a commercial value and which are used for generating return. They can be classified as:

(i) *Non-current assets/fixed assets* – They are long-term resources, more than a year and are used for long-term growth and expansion of a business, *like land and buildings, plant and machinery, furniture and fixtures, motor vehicles and so forth.*

> Fixed assets can be further divided into 'tangible' and 'intangible' fixed assets.
>
> 'Tangible assets' include physical fixed assets, whereas 'intangible assets' include which are not visible, such as goodwill, patents, copyrights and so forth.

(ii) *Current assets* – These are meant for current use, for day-to-day operations and are for less than a year, *like inventory, debtors, cash and bank.*

Liability – It is a debt or outstanding balance owed to another party requiring a future cash flow for payment. It can be grouped as:

(i) *Non-current liability/long-term liability* – These are for more than a year, *like term loans and debentures.*

(ii) *Current liability* – These are for less than a year, *like creditors and bank overdraft.*

Revenue – It is the money that comes in on account of sales of goods or rendering of services. The term 'revenue' is used interchangeable with 'income'. It can be:

(i) *Operating revenue* – It refers to the core income of business, that is *'turnover'* or *'sales and services'.*

(ii) *Non-operating revenue* – It is the income which comes from non-core activities of the business, *like interest on investments and profit on sale of fixed assets.*

Expenses – These are the costs which are incurred to run and maintain a business. These can be:

(i) *Operating expenses* – These are the core expenses of business, *for example salaries, rent, printing and stationery, marketing expenses and so forth.*

(ii) *Non-operating expenses* – These are related to the non-core activities of the business, *such as interest paid on loans.*

Illustration 2.1: Match the following items with their respective accounting categories of capital, asset, liability, revenue and expense.

S. No.	Items	Categories
1.	Machinery	Current Asset
2.	Shares issued by GAIL	Non-current Liability
3.	Sales	Non-operating Income
4.	Borrowings from IDBI	Capital
5.	Cash and Bank Balance	Operating Expense
6.	Accounts Receivable	Non-current Asset
7.	Auditor's Fees	Current Asset
8.	Rent Payable	Operating Expense
9.	Power and Fuel	Current Liability
10.	Dividend Received	Operating Income

Solution

S. No.	Items	Categories
1.	Machinery	Non-current Asset
2.	Shares issued by GAIL	Capital
3.	Sales	Operating Income
4.	Borrowings from IDBI	Non-current Liability
5.	Cash and Bank Balance	Current Asset
6.	Accounts Receivable	Current Asset
7.	Auditor's Fees	Operating Expense
8.	Rent Payable	Current Liability
9.	Power and Fuel	Operating Expense
10.	Dividend Received	Non-operating Income

Double entry system of accounting

In accountancy, *'double entry accounting'* is the basis or the standard system for businesses and other organisations to record financial transactions. The system is called 'double entry' because every transaction is considered to have two effects and is recorded in two accounts. Each transaction results in at least one account being debited and at least one account being credited, so that the total debits of the transaction equal the total credits.

The classification of debit and credit effects is structured in such a way that for each debit there is a corresponding credit and vice versa. Hence, every transaction will have 'dual' effect (i.e. debit effect and credit effect).

Box 2.1   Debit and Credit

Under the 'double entry system', two aspects of transactions are classified under the following types:

1   *Debit*
2   *Credit*

'Debit' is the portion of transaction that accounts for the increase in assets and expenses, and the decrease in liabilities, equity and income.

'Credit' is the portion of transaction that accounts for the increase in income, liabilities and equity, and the decrease in assets and expenses.

Illustration 2.2: Mr. A owns and operates a bookstore. He has identified the following transactions for the month of January 2017 that need to be accounted for in the monthly financial statements:

	Rs.
1. Payment of salary to staff	5,000
2. Sale of books for cash	10,000
3. Sale of books on credit	20,000
4. Purchase of furniture on credit from Smith	25,000
5. Interest paid on loans	1,000

Account the above transactions under double entry system.

Solution

Under double entry system, the transactions will be accounted for as follows:

Account	Effect	Debit	Credit
		Rs.	Rs.
1. Salary expense	*Increase in expense*	5,000	
Cash	*Decrease in assets*		5,000
2. Cash inflow	*Increase in assets*	10,000	
Sales	*Increase in income*		10,000
3. Accounts receivable	*Increase in assets*	20,000	
Sales	*Increase in income*		20,000
4. Furniture	*Increase in assets*	25,000	
Smith	*Increase in liabilities*		25,000
5. Interest paid	*Increase in expense*	1,000	
Cash	*Decrease in assets*		1,000

In a **single entry system**, only one aspect of a transaction is recognised. *For instance*, if a sale is made to a customer, only sales revenue will be recorded. However, the other side of the transaction relating to the receipt of cash or the grant of credit to the customer is not recognised.

The most common expression of double entry system of accounting is the 'accounting equation' which is discussed in Box 2.2.

Box 2.2   The accounting equation

The accounting formula, also called the *balance sheet equation*, represents the relationship between the assets, liabilities, and owner's equity of a business. It shows that the resources owned by a firm (its assets) are always equal to its obligations (its liabilities and capital). This relationship is expressed in the form of an equation:

$$\text{Assets} = \text{Liabilities} + \text{Owner's Capital}$$

This equation balances because everything the firm owns (assets) has to be purchased with something, either a liability or owner's capital. The terms of accounting equation have been defined below.

Assets

Assets, as mentioned above, are the economic resources of the entity, and include items such as cash, stock, land, buildings, and/or intangible assets like patents and copyrights. Assets are used to generate returns for the business.

Liabilities

Liabilities are the amounts owed to outsiders in the form of loans and credit. It is an 'existing' obligation to pay.

Owner's equity

Owner's equity is the owner's 'interest' in the business. In a sole proprietorship, the equity would typically consist of a single owner's capital account. Conversely, in a partnership, equity consists of separate capital accounts for each partner. Finally, in a corporate, the ownership interest is represented by shares (stock). The total owner's equity (i.e. 'stockholders' equity') of a corporate consists of shareholders' initial capital and reserves and surplus.

The following example explains the accounting equation mechanism.

Example

1 Amit and Bros. start a small business of hosiery goods with Rs. 10,000 of capital.

Assets = Liabilities + Capital

Rs. 10,000 = 0 + Rs. 10,000
Note: It increases cash as an asset and also increases owner's equity.

2 Next, they spend Rs. 1,500 on office consumables.
Now, the accounting equation looks like this:

Assets = Liabilities + Capital

Rs. 8,500 = 0 + Rs. 8,500
Note: It will reduce cash as an asset and expenses decrease owner's equity. So, in every case the accounting equation stays balanced.

Basis of accounting

Cash basis of accounting is the more popular method of recording and reporting small business income and expenses. In the cash accounting method, income and expenses are recorded only when funds are received or disbursed.

In the **accrual basis of accounting**, income is recorded when a sale is made, irrespective of the fact whether payment is received or not. Expenses are recorded when they are incurred, without being paid.

Illustration 2.3: During 2014–15, A Ltd. had cash sales of Rs. 1,80,000 and credit sales of Rs. 3,60,000. Their expenses for the year were Rs. 2,40,000 out of which Rs. 80,000 is still to be paid. Commission received in the current year, due of last year of Rs. 5,000. Interest due on investments for the year, Rs. 20,000.

Find out their profit/loss for 2014–15 as per:

1   Cash basis of accounting
2   Accrual basis of accounting.

Solution

1. Profit/loss as per Cash basis:	
Revenue (cash inflow or cash sales)	Rs. 1,80,000
+ Commission received, due of last year	5,000
	1,85,000
Less: Expenses (cash outflow)	1,60,000
(Rs. 2,40,000 – Rs. 80,000)	
Profit	**Rs. 25,000**
2. Profit/loss as per Accrual basis:	
Revenue (total sales)	Rs. 5,40,000
+ Interest due on investments	20,000
	5,60,000
Less: Total expenses for the year	2,40,000
Profit	**Rs. 3,20,000**

Box 2.3   Suitability of accrual basis vs. cash basis of accounting?

One of the accounting rules is that, with few exceptions, reports of the income of a business should be prepared on the *accrual basis*.

Then, what is the rationale of *cash basis accounting*? The answer is that the cash-basis book keeping is very simple, and for small firms, it may be adequate. Therefore, small-scale organisations, professionals like doctors and lawyers, follow cash basis accounting for their tax returns and other purposes.

Points to remember

- Accounting is the art of recording, classifying and summarising the monetary transactions and events and interpreting the results thereof.
- Financial accounting is mainly concerned with the preparation of financial statements of statement of profit and loss and the balance sheet for end users.
- Cost accounting is the formal mechanism by means of which costs of products or services are ascertained and controlled.
- Management accounting is one which provides necessary information to the management for taking various decisions on various areas, such as cost accounting, human resource accounting, etc.
- The entire accounting cycle is about following elements: *capital, assets, liabilities, revenue and expenses.*
- Double entry system of accounting is the premise of accounting. Every transaction is considered to have two effects, i.e. debit and credit.
- In cash basis of accounting, income and expenses are recorded only when funds are received or disbursed.
- In accrual basis of accounting, income and expenses are recorded on occurrence irrespective of realisation or payment.

3   Accounting principles

There are basic accounting principles and guidelines that govern the field of accounting. These are referred to as 'generally accepted accounting principles' (GAAP). They form the groundwork on which legalistic accounting rules are based, commonly called 'accounting standards'. Every country has its own comprehensive set of accounting rules and standards. *For example*, in India the **Accounting Standards Board (ASB)** formulates these standards. In US, the **Financial Accounting Standards Board (FASB)** is responsible for deciding them.

Every company is required to follow generally accepted accounting principles in the preparation of financial statements and reporting to shareholders (stakeholders). GAAP is exceedingly useful because it attempts to standardise and regulate accounting definitions, assumptions, and methods and brings consistency in corporate financial reporting practices. This makes inter-firm comparison meaningful by the users of information for better decision-making.

Box 3.1   IFRS

Now, International Financial Reporting Standards (IFRS) are global standards for the preparation of financial statements by public companies as a part of harmonisation of global reporting. 'On 25 February 2011, the Ministry of Corporate Affairs (MCA), the Government of India, issued 35 Ind ASs (Indian Accounting Standards) equivalent to the International Financial Reporting Standards'.[1]

Basic accounting principles

These principles can be categorised into *accounting concepts* and *accounting conventions* and are presented in Table 3.1.

Table 3.1 Accounting principles

S. No.	Accounting Concepts	S. No.	Accounting Conventions
1.	Business Entity	1.	Materiality
2.	Money Measurement	2.	Full Disclosure
3.	Accounting Period	3.	Consistency
4.	Historical Cost	4.	Conservatism
5.	Going Concern		
6.	Matching		
7.	Revenue Recognition		
8.	Dual Aspect		

Following is the discussion of these accounting principles used by business firms.

A. *Accounting concepts*

These are the basic assumptions or postulates which are required to be followed by business firms in preparing financial statements.

1. *Business entity principle*

It states that all business transactions of the firm should be considered separate from the business owner's personal transactions. For *legal purposes*, the firm and its owner are considered to be one entity, but for *accounting purposes* they are considered to be two separate entities. Therefore, any personal expenses incurred by owners of a business cannot be charged to the business and will not appear in the income statement of the entity. The charging of personal expenses to the business is a concern mostly in sole proprietorship firms, where there is a single owner.

The business entity concept also explains why owner's equity appears on the liability side of a balance sheet (i.e. credit side) as it represents a form of liability of the 'business' that is owed to its owner.

> ### Example
>
> Mohan Traders is a sole proprietorship firm. Mohan paid his house rent from the business bank account. How should this transaction be reflected in the books of Mohan Traders?
> This should be shown as 'drawings' in the books of the firm.

2. Money measurement principle

In accounting books, only those transactions are recorded that can be expressed in money. In India, they are expressed in rupees.

Non-monetary events or activities are not recorded in the books of accounts as they cannot be quantified in terms of money.

> *For example* the loyalty of an employee is not recorded in the financial statements. The skills and competence of employees cannot be monetised and therefore are not recognised as assets in the balance sheet.

However, transactions related to employees that can be measured reliably, such as salary expenses, are recognised in the financial statements.

3. Accounting period principle

Every business organisation must report the results of a business at regular intervals. This time period is of one year, that is 'annual'. But listed companies have to report on quarterly basis. This concept promotes the 'timeliness' principle, that is accounting information should be presented to the users in time to facilitate their decision-making needs.

> *For example*, if a company issues its financial statements to the public after 12 months of the accounting period, it might be too late for the potential investors to decide whether to invest in the company.

Box 3.2   Financial year

In relation to any company or body corporate, it means the period ending on the 31st day of March every year, and where it has been incorporated on or after the 1st day of January of a year, the period ending on the 31st day of March of the following year, in respect whereof financial statement of the company or body corporate is made up[2] (section 2(41) of Companies Act, 2013).

While there are certain exceptions included, this section mandates a uniform accounting year for all companies.

4. *Cost principle*

In accounting, the term 'cost' refers to the amount spent (cash or the cash equivalent) *originally* on the item at the time of acquisition, whether that purchase happened last year or fifty years ago. Therefore, the items are shown in the financial statements at *'historical cost'*. Because of this accounting principle, asset amounts are *not* adjusted upward for inflation. They are shown at 'book value'.

So, a business should only record its assets, liabilities and equity investments at their original purchase costs. This principle is becoming less valid now, on account of the 'fair value' concept.

> **Example**
>
> Innovative Ltd. purchases a land of Rs. 50,000 in the year 2000. Its market value appreciates to Rs. 75,000 in 2002. But the company still has to continue showing the land at the historical cost (original cost).

5. *Going concern principle*

'Going concern' is one of the fundamental assumptions in accounting on the basis of which financial statements are prepared. This accounting principle assumes that a company will continue to exist *'for an indefinite period of life'* to carry out its objectives and commitments and will not liquidate in the near future.

This principle allows the management to make provisions for future contingencies and plan out future growth.

> *For example*, 'provision for bad debts' is made for credit sales to bear the default loss and carry on the operation smoothly.

6. *Matching principle*

This principle is the basis of 'accrual basis of accounting'. The matching principle requires that expenses should be matched with revenues of the same year.

> *For example*, marketing expenses should be reported in the period when the sales were made (and not reported in the period when expense was paid).

Another example is the cost incurred in the manufacture or procurement of inventory is charged to the income statement of the accounting period in which the inventory is sold. Therefore, any inventory remaining unsold at the end of an accounting period is excluded from the computation of the cost of goods sold.

The matching principle therefore results in the presentation of a more balanced and consistent view of the financial performance of an organisation as compared to the cash basis of accounting.

7. Revenue recognition principle

This applies the accrual basis of accounting and states that accounting transactions should be recorded in the accounting period when they actually occur, rather than in the period when they are realised. Revenues are recognised when they occur, that is when the product has been sold or a service has been performed, irrespective of when the money is actually received.

Example

AB Co. Ltd. completes its service at an agreed price of Rs. 10,000. It should recognise Rs. 10,000 of revenue as soon as its work is done – it does not matter whether the payment comes immediately or in 30 days.

8. Dual aspect principle

Dual aspect concept is the underlying basis for double entry accounting system. It states that every transaction has two aspects, 'debit' and 'credit'. The application of the duality principle therefore ensures that all aspects of a transaction are accounted for in the financial statements.

Example

If there is a purchase of machinery in cash, then Machinery A/c will be debited and Cash A/c will be credited.

B. *Accounting conventions*

These are the accounting principles which are pursued by business firms as a part of practice and therefore are included in the financial reporting.

9. *Materiality*

This principle allows accountants to use their discretion in the treatment of an item as 'significant' or 'insignificant' in the books of accounts. Professional judgement is needed to decide whether an amount is insignificant or immaterial. This might lead to violation of another accounting principle.

Example

An MNC purchases a computer worth Rs. 10,000. Because the computer will be used for five years, the *matching* principle directs the accountant to expense the cost over the five-year period. The 'materiality' guideline allows this company to violate the matching principle and to expense the entire cost of Rs. 10,000 in the year it is purchased.

---

10. *Full disclosure principle*

The company must disclose fully and fairly all the information to the stakeholders which they have to report. It is because of this basic accounting principle that 'footnotes' are attached to financial statements.

Example

Let's say a company has a litigation case going in the court of law. At the time of preparation of financial statements, it is not clear whether the company will lose or win the case. The full disclosure principle states the lawsuit will be described in the notes to the financial statements.

---

11. *Consistency*

This principle is based on the assumption that, once you adopt an accounting principle or method, you should continue to use it until a better principle or method is warranted. The accountants are expected to be consistent when applying accounting principles, procedures, and practices. They should not change the methods very often, else it will not lead to a meaningful comparison by the end users.

For example, if a company has a history of using the 'straight line method' of depreciation, it should not change it unless required as the stakeholders would expect that the company is continuing to use the same method. If the company changes this practice and begins using different method of depreciation, that change must be clearly disclosed.

12. Conservatism

Conservatism states that *'Anticipate no profits but provide for possible losses'*. If there is a situation which has two acceptable alternatives for reporting an item, conservatism directs the accountant to choose the alternative that will result in less net income or profit. The management must provide provision for all possible losses to safeguard the business. But gains should not be recorded unless they are realised.

Example

'Expected losses' from lawsuits will be reported in the financial statements, but 'potential gains' will not be reported.

This concept can be taken too far, where a business continuously misstates its results to be worse than actual.

Points to remember

- Accounting principles and guidelines that govern the field of accounting are referred to as 'generally accepted accounting principles' (GAAP).
- International financial reporting standards (IFRS) are global standards for the preparation of financial statements by public companies as a part of harmonisation of global reporting.
- The business entity principle states that all business transactions of the firm should be considered separate from the business owner's personal transactions.

- According to the money measurement principle, accounting records only those transactions that can be expressed in money.
- Every business organisation must report the results of a business at regular intervals as per accounting period concept. This time period is of one year, that is 'annual'.
- The cost principle states all the items are to be shown in the financial statements at *'historical cost'*, that is 'book value'.
- The going concern concept is the fundamental assumption in accounting which assumes that a company will continue to exist *for an indefinite period of life* to carry out its objectives and commitments and will not liquidate in the near future.
- The matching principle is the basis of 'accrual basis of accounting'. It requires that expenses should be matched with revenues of the same year.
- The revenue recognition principle states that accounting transactions should be recorded in the accounting period when they actually occur, rather than in the period when they are realised.
- The dual aspect concept is the underlying basis for double entry accounting system. It states that every transaction has two aspects, 'debit' and 'credit'.
- The materiality principle allows accountants to use their discretion in the treatment of an item as 'significant' or 'insignificant' in the books of accounts.
- The company must disclose fully and fairly all the information to the stakeholders which they have to report as per the full disclosure principle.
- Consistency presumes that, once you adopt an accounting principle or method, you should continue to use it until a better principle or method is warranted.
- Conservatism states that 'Anticipate no profits but provide for possible losses'.

Notes

1 Goel, Sandeep. 2013. 'Impact Analysis of the Proposed Changeover from Indian GAAP to International Financial Reporting Standards', *ASCI Journal of Management*, 43 (1): 86–97.
2 Section 2 – Ministry of Corporate Affairs, www.mca.gov.in/SearchableActs/Section2.htm (accessed on 18 October 2016).

Part II

Financial statements and analysis

4   Financial statements

The corporate organisation needs to provide information about its underlying business performance to various stakeholders at regular intervals. This information is provided by way of published reports in the form of 'financial statements'. These financial statements determine the profitability and financial health of the business. They are drawn on the basis of various rules and guidelines (accounting principles) that govern their form and content. One can gain these financial statements by reviewing corporate websites, filings with the regulators, financial journals and magazines, and other such sources.

Financial statements

Financial statements are *'financial reports in a prescribed format required to be prepared by an entity to meet the information needs of various stakeholders'*. They commonly include the following:

(a)   A *'balance sheet'* as at the end of the period (including statement of changes in equity which is presented as a part of the balance sheet)
(b)   A *'statement of profit and loss'* for the period
(c)   A *'statement of cash flows'* for the period
(d)   Notes, forming a summary of significant accounting policies and other explanatory information.[1]

Box 4.1   Consolidated financial statements

As per Ind AS 110, an entity that is a parent in addition to its stand-alone financial statements, shall also present *'consolidated financial statements'* of a group presented as s single economic entity.

> A parent shall prepare consolidated financial statements using uniform accounting policies for like transactions and other events in similar circumstances.[2]

Statement of profit and loss

A profit and loss statement or income statement is a summary of an entity's **'result of operations'** for a specified period of time. It provides information about the revenues generated and expenses incurred by an organisation during a period. The difference between the revenues and expenses is identified as the *'net profit or net loss'*.

Income statement is flow concept as it reveals the operational performance of a business for the entire period. It relates to the activities of a specified time period (e.g. year, quarter), as clearly noted in the title of the specimen profit and loss statement in Figure 4.1.

The profit and loss statement is based on the **'matching principle'**.*

Example

If there are three shirts of Rs. 2,000 each which are sold by a retail outlet during 2015, the offsetting cost of those sales, that is cost of goods sold (COGS), should be recorded as the cost in 2015 that matches the year 2015 sales.

Thus, the cost (at Rs. 1,000 each) of the three shirts sold in year 2015 (at Rs. 2,000 each) is taken as the 'cost of goods sold', even though the third shirt was not paid for during the year and will be paid next year.

In other words, the matching principle requires the expenses to be deducted from related revenues in the period in which they occur.

* Refer to Chapter 3, 'Accounting Principles', for detailed explanation of the matching principle.

Simply put, the income statement measures all the revenue sources versus business expenses for a given time period.

To explain the income statement and its components in detail, let's take the example of ABC Ltd.

Statement of Profit and Loss of ABC Ltd. for the year ended 31st March, 2015			
			(Rs. in crore)
Particulars	Note No.	2014–15	2013–14
REVENUE			
Turnover		68,000	65,000
Excise Duty		4,500	3,500
Net Turnover		63,500	61,500
Other Income	15	–	4,000
TOTAL REVENUE		63,500	65,500
EXPENSES			
Cost of Materials Consumed	16	6,000	5,000
Changes in Inventories of Finished Goods, WIP and Scrap	17	–	(2,000)
Employee Remuneration	18	30,000	30,000
Finance Costs	19	–	1,000
Depreciation and Amortisation	20	5,800	5,000
Other Expenses	21	14,500	16,000
TOTAL EXPENSES		56,300	55,000
Profit before tax		7,200	10,500
Tax		3,200	4,500
Profit after tax (PAT)		4,000	6,000
Significant Accounting Policies			
Notes to the Financial Statements	1 to 23		

Figure 4.1 Statement of profit and loss

Notes:

1. Rs. 1 crore = Rs. 10 millions.
2. The profit and loss statement is a specimen statement of a company, ABC Ltd. in the manufacturing sector in India, producing yarn.

Turnover/sales

'Sales' refer to what is charged to customers for goods or services. This is the gross revenue generated from the sale of yarn. 'Net sales' are gross sales less returns and allowances in the form of discounts given to customers and after excise duty.

Other income

'Other income' is non-operating income that does not occur during the normal course of business operations. For instance, a yarn manufacturer does not normally earn income from sale of assets or interest on investments, so these income sources are accounted for separately as 'other income'.

Top line: Turnover and other income are added to determine the 'top line' of the company.

For ABC Ltd., the 'top line' for 2014–15 is Rs. 63,500 crores as compared to Rs. 65,500 crores of the previous year. It has declined by 3.05% from previous year, which is a sign of concern for the company.

But, the positive part is that it has declined not on account of sales but due to non-operating income. Sales have rather shown an increasing trend during the period. The gross revenue generated from the sale of yarn for 2014–15 is Rs. 68,000 crores. It has increased by 4.62% from the previous year. Net sales for 2014–15 are Rs. 63,500 crores after excise duty. They have increased by 3.25% from the previous year. So, operating income has shown an increasing trend during the period. This indicates an increase in the core business of the company.

Production expenses and operating expenses

Production expenses. These are manufacturing expenses incurred on manufacturing of the product. These costs include material used, direct labour, freight and other costs associated with operating a plant.

Operating expenses. These include employee-related and other operational expenses that are necessary to run the business. They include:

- *Employee remuneration.* It includes salaries of the staff and all benefits given to them in various forms including provident fund and gratuity.
- *Depreciation.* Depreciation expense is an operating expense because it is incurred on the maintenance and replacement of fixed assets which are used to run the business. It is a non-cash expense in the sense that the cash flows go out only when the asset is purchased, but the cost is taken over period of years depending on the type of asset. ***Its treatment is explained after the 'balance sheet'.***

Finance costs

These are considered as non-operating expense for a non-financing business and include interest on loans, commissions and so forth.

Other expenses

'Other expenses' include those items that are not categorised in the main line of expenses. They range from power and fuel, printing and stationery, insurance and rent to distribution expenses. They are relevant for 'cost control' by the management.

For ABC Ltd., the 'total expenses' have increased from Rs. 55,000 crores in 2013–14 to Rs. 56,300 crores in 2014–15, showing an increase of 2.36%. The increase in expenses reduces the net profit of the company.

Again, the positive part is that 'other expenses' have declined by Rs. 1,500 crores from last year. The increase in total expenses is mainly due to the increase in materials consumed of Rs. 1,000 crores. This indicates operational rise for the company.

Profit before taxes/earnings before taxes (PBT/EBT)

This figure represents the amount of net income earned by the business before paying taxes.

Income taxes

This is the total amount of income taxes paid by the corporate.

Profit after taxes (PAT)

This is arrived at after subtracting taxes paid from net income before taxes.

Bottom line: PAT represents the 'bottom line' of the company, that is the net profit left for distribution to shareholders and reinvestment for future growth.

For ABC Ltd., the 'PAT' has declined from Rs. 6,000 crore in 2013–14 to Rs. 4,000 crores in 2014–15. It is a big blow for the company, as it shows a decline of 33.33% in its net profit. This will affect the company's future growth and shareholder' wealth.

Box 4.2   Comprehensive income[3]

The statement of profit and loss besides the net profit or loss, as discussed above, also includes:

1   *Other comprehensive income*: It includes items of income and expense (including reclassification adjustments) that are not recognised in profit or loss as required or permitted by other Ind ASs.
2   *Total comprehensive income*: It is the change in equity during a period resulting from transactions and other events, other than those changes resulting from transactions with owners in their capacity as owners. Total comprehensive income comprises all components of 'profit or loss' and of 'other comprehensive income'.

Multi-variant profit and loss statement

Financial reporting about net result of the business to its stakeholders in the form of the profit and loss statement is one dimension of communicating information.

But for better decision-making by the management and other users, the statement of profit and loss is evaluated on a 'multi-variant basis'. This information is generally not reported in the external statement. It helps in evaluating the profitability of the company at various levels in terms of margins for gap-analysis and future decision-making.

The above statement of profit and loss of the yarn manufacturer is evaluated on 'multi-variant basis' as follows.

1   **Turnover/sales.** 'Sales' refer to what is charged to customers for goods or services. This is the gross revenue generated from the sale of yarn. 'Net sales' are gross sales less returns and allowances in the form of discounts given to customers and after excise duty.
2   **Cost of goods sold (COGS).** 'COGS' means the cost, to the company, of the merchandise that is sold to customers. This is the direct cost associated with manufacturing of yarn at the plant.
3   **Gross profit.** The gross profit represents the amount of direct profit associated with the actual manufacturing of cloth. It is calculated as:

| Gross profit = Sales *less* cost of goods sold |

4　*Earnings before interest, tax and depreciation and amortisation**
　(EBITDA). This is the amount of profit earned from the core activities of business, excluding finance costs, tax and depreciation provisioning. It is computed as:

> EBITDA = Gross profit *less* operating expenses (office and selling)

EBITDA is a better indicator to analyse and compare the profitability of similar companies and industries because it eliminates the effects of financing and accounting decisions.

5　*Earnings before interest and tax (EBIT)/operating profit.* This represents operating profit earned during the normal course of operations after adjusting non-cash expense of depreciation and amortisation. It is computed as:

> EBIT = EBITDA *less* depreciation and amortisation

An important factor contributing to the widespread use of EBIT is the way in which it nulls the effects of the different capital structures and tax rates used by different companies. By excluding both tax and interest expense, the figure measures the company's ability to earn profit and thus makes for easier cross-company comparisons. EBIT is an extension of EBITDA calculation as it takes the process further by removing non-cash item of depreciation from the equation.

6　*Profit before taxes (PBT/EBT).* This is the amount of profit earned by the business before taxes. It is computed after adjusting non-operating items to the operating profit as follows:

> EBT = EBIT *less* non-operating expenses, like interest paid
> 　　　　*Add* non-operating income, like dividend received

7　*Profit after taxes (PAT).* This is the 'bottom line' (net earnings) of the business. It is computed as:

> PAT = EBT *less* taxes

The above multi-variant profit and loss statement is explained with the help of following case of ABC Ltd.

---

* 'Depreciation' is used for the replacement of tangible assets. 'Amortisation' is used for the replacement of intangible assets.

Example: Following is the multi-variant income statement of ABC Ltd.

Multi-Step Profit and Loss Statement of ABC Ltd. for 2014–15	
	(Rs. in crore)
	2014–15
Sales	68,000.00
Less: Cost of production of goods sold (COGS) / Direct Expenses	10,500.00
Gross Profit - GP	57,500.00
Less: Indirect expenses before depreciation, interest & tax	44,500.00
Earning before Interest,Tax, Dep. &Amort. - EBITDA	13,000.00
Less: Depreciation	5,800.00
Earning before Interest and Tax - EBIT	7,200.00
Less /Add: Non-Operating Expense (Income)	–
Earning before Tax - EBT	7,200.00
Less: Tax	3,200.00
Profit after Tax - PAT	4,000.00

Figure 4.2 Multi-step profit and loss statement
Note: Rs. 1 crore = Rs. 10 millions

The above example shows the evaluation of income statement of ABC Ltd. at various levels as discussed in the preceding section. This is further extended and expressed as margin with respect to sales for managerial decision-making. This is explained in detail in the next chapter on 'Financial Analysis'.

Balance sheet

The balance sheet or position statement is based on the *accounting equation* and depicts the economic resources owned by an entity and the claims against those resources (liabilities and owner's equity). The balance sheet is prepared on a specific date; that is why it is considered as 'stock' concept.

It presents the **'financial position'** of a business in totality, i.e. it presents the information about the business performance from the day of inception to the date of reporting (including *statement of changes in equity*, which is a part of the balance sheet).

Box 4.3   Statement of changes in equity[4]

An entity shall present a statement of changes in equity as a part of the balance sheet. The statement of changes in equity includes the following information:

(a) Total comprehensive income for the period, showing separately the total amounts attributable to owners of the parent and to non-controlling interests
(b) For each component of equity, the effects of retrospective application or retrospective restatement
(c) For each component of equity, a reconciliation between the carrying amount at the beginning and the end of the period.

The specimen balance sheet of ABC Ltd. is given in Figure 4.3.

To explain the balance sheet and its components in detail, let's take the example of ABC Ltd.

Liabilities side of balance sheet

In these liabilities, the following are included:

1. Shareholders' funds

(A) SHARE CAPITAL

The 'share capital' of company represents the funds of a company raised through the issue of shares, either common or preference shares. It consists of authorised capital, issued capital subscribed capital, called-up capital and paid-up capital.

(i) The 'authorised share capital' is the maximum limit of capital which the company is registered with the Registrar of Companies to raise.
(ii) The 'issued share capital' can be equal to or lower than authorised capital and represents that amount actually offered to the public for subscription.

Balance Sheet of ABC Ltd. as at 31st March, 2015

(Rs. In Crore)

Particulars	Note No.	2015	2014
EQUITY AND LIABILITIES			
(1) **Shareholders Funds**			
Share Capital	1	50,000	50,000
Reserves and Surplus	2	4,000	6,000
		54,000	56,000
(2) **Non-Current Liabilities**			
Long-Term Borrowings	3	20,000	20,000
Long-Term Provisions	4	10,000	10,000
		30,000	30,000
(3) **Current Liabilities**			
Short-Term Borrowings	5	4,000	6,000
Trade Payables	6	7,000	5,000
Short-Term Provisions	7	3,700	2,500
		14,700	13,500
TOTAL		98,700	99,500
ASSETS			
(1) **Non Current Assets**			
Fixed Assets			
(i) Tangible Assets, Net	8	54,200	53,000
(ii) Intangible Assets, Net	9	10,000	10,000
(iii) Capital Work-in-Progress	10	4,000	2,000
Non Current Investments		3,000	2,000
Deferred Tax Assets		700	500
		71,900	67,500
(2) **Current Assets**			
Inventories	11	–	2000
Trade Receivables	12	20,000	25,000
Cash and Bank Balances	13	5,800	5,000
Short-Term Loans and Advances	14	1,000	–
		26,800	32,000
TOTAL		98,700	99,500
Significant Accounting Policies			
Notes to the Financial Statements	1 to 23		

Figure 4.3 Balance sheet

Notes:

1. Rs. 1 crore = Rs. 10 millions.
2. The balance sheet is a specimen statement of a company, ABC Ltd. in the manufacturing sector in India, producing yarn.

(iii) The issued share capital can be under-subscribed or over-subscribed, resulting in the 'subscribed share capital'.

(iv) On subscription, the amount called-up by the company is 'called-up share capital'.

(v) On subscription, the actual amount paid up by shareholders is the 'paid-up share capital'.

(B) RESERVES AND SURPLUS

This represents the amount of profit undistributed to the shareholders and kept in the form of 'retained earnings'.

The following reserves are shown in the liabilities side of the balance sheet of a company:

i.   Capital reserve
ii. Share premium account
iii. General reserve
iv. Other reserves
v.   Surplus balance in profit and loss account after providing for dividend.

> 'Net worth': Share capital and reserves and surplus denote the 'net worth' of the company, signifying the shareholders' interest.

> *For ABC Ltd., the 'net worth' for 2015 is Rs. 54,000 crores as compared to Rs. 56,000 crores of previous year, showing a decline of 3.57% from previous year. A decline in net worth denotes erosion of shareholders' wealth. This decline for the company is on account of decline in profits for the current year.*

2. Non-current liabilities

These represent long-term loans taken by the company. They could be:

(A) SECURED LOAN

If any loan is taken by company against security, then it will be shown under the 'secured loan' head. Its details are given below.

i.   Term loans from banks and financial institutions
ii. Debentures issued to the banks and financial institutions
iii. Loan and advances from subsidiaries

iv. Other loans and advances
v.   Interest payable on secured loan.

(B) UNSECURED LOAN
It is a loan is taken by company without any security. Following are
the forms of 'unsecured loan'.

i.   Fixed deposits of public
ii.   Short-term loans and advances
iii. Other loans.

> *Long-term provisions* kept aside for meeting long-term contin-
> gencies are also a part of 'long-term liabilities'.

3. Current liabilities and provisions

All liabilities which are payable within one year will be included under
the 'current liabilities' head.

(A) CURRENT LIABILITIES
i.   Accounts payable
ii.   Acceptance or bill payables
iii. Interest payable other than on loan
iv.   Outstanding expenses.

(B) PROVISIONS
i.   Provision for taxation
ii.   Proposed dividend
iii. Other provisions.

> *For ABC Ltd., the 'non-current liabilities' have remained con-
> stant at Rs. 30,000 crores for the year 2015 from previous year.
> This implies there is no change in the financial risk of the com-
> pany. 'Current liabilities' have increased by 9% in 2015 from
> previous year. There has been an increase in accounts payable
> during the year by Rs. 2,000 crores, but on the other hand
> short-term borrowings have declined by the same amount. This
> indicates the company is using vendor management more for
> short-term financing than bank's borrowings and this verifies the
> confidence of vendors in the company. The short-term provisions
> have increased by Rs. 1,200 crores during the year.*

Assets side of balance sheet

In the assets side, the following are included.

1. *Non-current assets*

These are 'fixed assets' of tangible and intangible nature.

(A) FIXED ASSETS
They are composed of the following 'tangible assets'.

i.   Land
ii. Building
iii. Plant and Machinery
iv. Furniture and Fixtures
v.   Vehicles.

The list also includes 'intangible assets' under the fixed assets head. Following are the main items of intangible assets.

i.   Goodwill
ii. Patents
iii. Trademarks
iv. Copyrights
v.   Licenses.

(B) CAPITAL WORK-IN-PROGRESS (CWIP)
This includes under-construction or under-completion of fixed assets, like a building under construction or machinery in transit.

(C) NON-CURRENT INVESTMENTS
Investment is a financial asset. It is done by the business for getting interest or dividend earning.

Following are the main investments.

i.   Investment in government securities
ii. Investment in shares, debentures or bonds.

Investment will be shown at cost or market value, whichever is less.

(D) DEFERRED TAX ASSETS
These are fictitious assets and arise as a part of accounting differences between the Companies Act and Income Tax Act. These could be 'deferred tax liabilities' as well.

2. Current assets

Current assets are the resources for current usage and consumption. The following components are included here:

(a) Inventory

    i.   Raw material
    ii. Work in progress
    iii. Finished stock
    iv. Stores and spares

(b) Trade receivables (Sundry debtors less provision for doubtful debts)
(c) Cash in hand and bank balances
(d) Short-term loans and advances.

For ABC Ltd., the 'non-current assets' have increased from Rs. 67,500 crores in 2014 to Rs. 71,900 crores in 2015, showing an increase of 6.52% during the period. The increase is on account of tangible assets and capital work-in-progress. The tangible assets have increased by Rs. 1,200 crores and CWIP has increased by Rs. 2,000 crores during the period. This is an indication of growth of the company. Non-current investments have also increased by Rs. 1,000 crores during the period, increasing the financial securities base of the company.

But, 'current assets' have declined from Rs. 32,000 crores in 2014 to Rs. 26,800 crores in 2015. This is mainly of decrease in inventories, receivables and short-term loans and advances, indicating rise in liquidity of the company. Therefore, cash and bank balances of the company have increased from Rs. 5,000 crores in 2014 to Rs. 5,800 crores in 2015.

The above specimen statement of profit and loss and balance sheet of ABC Ltd. are as per Schedule III of Indian Companies Act, 2013.

Refer *Schedule III of Companies Act, 2013* for specific formats of statement of profit and loss and balance sheet and their contents.

Depreciation accounting

'In this world, nothing is certain but decline'. This explains the concept of depreciation. The concept of depreciation is not new and was first used by Vitruvius in architecture, 3,820 years ago. The term depreciation was first used in a book of accounting in 1838.

With the exception of land, all fixed assets have a limited period of useful life. If it is assumed that business enterprises acquire assets essentially to earn profits by buying raw materials, merchandise or services (and converting them into finished products or services) and by selling such products or providing such services at a price higher than the cost of purchase or conversion, it would follow that it would be worthwhile for a business enterprise to continue to use an asset only till such time as economic surpluses accrue.

Depreciation primarily means 'the reduction in or loss of quality or value of a fixed asset through *physical wear and tear in use* or *passage of time or from any other cause*'. It is very important to make it clear that fall in value associated with depreciation is necessarily a fall in 'book value'. Therefore, depreciation refers to a fall in the book value which may or may not be equal to the market value of the asset or cost price except in the first year of the life of the asset.

The Institute of Chartered Accountants of India (ICAI) defines depreciation as follows:

> *Depreciation is a measure of the wearing out, consumption or other loss of value of depreciable asset arising from use, effluxion of time or obsolescence through technology and market changes. Depreciation is allocated so as to charge a fair proportion of the depreciable amount in each accounting period during the expected useful life of the asset.*

'Depreciation accounting' is the process of writing off the fixed asset during its life and providing funds for its replacement when it becomes unproductive.

According to Committee on Terminology of the American Institute of Certified Public Accountants (AICPA), 'Depreciation accounting is a system of accounting which aims to distribute the cost or other basic value of tangible capital assets, less salvage value (if any), over the estimated useful life of the unit (which may be a group of assets) in a systematic and rational manner. It is a process of allocation not of valuation'.

> The term 'depreciation' is used for writing off tangible assets, *such as building, furniture, machinery etc.*
>
> 'Amortisation' is used for writing off and replacing intangible assets, *like patents, copyrights, trademarks, licenses etc.*
>
> 'Depletion' refers to the process of writing off and replacing natural resources, *like coal mines, oil wells etc.*

Depreciation methods

Various methods of depreciation are discussed below.

There are two commonly used methods of depreciation: *the straight line method (SLM) and the written-down-value method (WDV).**

1. Straight Line Method (SLM)

Under the SLM method, the depreciation is charged at fixed amount throughout the life of an asset.

Thus, the amount of depreciation is uniform from year to year.

The amount to be written off every year is arrived at as under:

$$\frac{Cost\ -\ Estimated\ scrap\ value}{Number\ of\ years\ of\ expected\ life}$$

2. Written-Down-Value Method (WDV)

Under WDV method, depreciation is charged at fixed rate on the reducing balance (i.e. cost less depreciation) every year. In other words, depreciation is charged on the net productive value of an asset which reduces with the usage of an asset.

---

* The straight line method (SLM) is also referred to as the 'fixed installment method'.

  The written-down-value method (WDV) is also called the 'diminishing value method' or 'reducing balance method'.

3. Other depreciation methods

Besides the above, the other 'accelerated depreciation methods'*
including WDV which are used for calculating depreciation are:

(a) Double declining balance method

Here, the depreciation expense is computed by multiplying the asset cost
less accumulated depreciation by twice the straight line rate, expressed
as a percentage. No provision is made for the salvage value of the asset.

(b) Sum-of-the-years-digits method

Here, depreciation is calculated by adding up the number of years of
the useful economic life, that is if the asset has five years economic
useful life, the numbers 1, 2, 3, 4 and 5 are added up. The resulting
sum, 15 becomes the denominator while the numerator is the number
of remaining years of the useful economic life of the asset.

The formula to be used to calculate depreciation expense here is:

$$\frac{Remaining\ years\ of\ useful\ life\ of\ the\ asset\ (including\ the\ beginning\ of\ the\ year) \times Original\ cost\ of\ the\ asset}{Sum\ of\ the\ digits\ of\ the\ years\ of\ useful\ life}$$

The following illustration explains the process of depreciation accounting.

Illustration 4.1: Strong Brothers Ltd., a manufacturing firm purchases
machinery for a sum of Rs. 10,000 on 1 January 2011.They incurred
installation charges worth Rs. 1,000 on it. The machinery is depreci-
ated at the rate of 20% per annum and has a useful life of five years.

Compute the necessary depreciation on machinery for five years
according to

1   Straight line method
2   Written-down-value method.

---

* Accelerated depreciation methods are those which charge relatively greater amounts
  of depreciation in the early years in the life of the asset and smaller amounts in the
  later years.

Solution

(a) Effect on Financial Statements – 'SLM'

(In Rs.)

	P/L A/c	B/S	
		Accumulated Depreciation	Net Assets (Net Block)
2011	2,200	2,200	11,000 – 2,200 = 8,800
2012	2,200	4,400	11,000 – 4,400 = 6,600
2013	2,200	6,600	11,000 – 6,600 = 4,400
2014	2,200	8,800	11,000 – 8,800 = 2,200
2015	2,200	11,000	11,000 – 11,000 = 0

It is clear in the above illustration that in SLM the amount of depreciation remains fixed throughout the life of an asset. At the end of the estimated life, the value of an asset becomes zero.

(b) Effect on Financial Statements – 'WDV'

(In Rs.)

	P/L A/c	B/S	
		Accumulated Depreciation	Net Assets (Net Block)
2011	2,200	2,200	11,000 – 2,200 = 8,800
2012	1,760	3,960	11,000 – 3,960 = 7,040
2013	1,408	5,368	11,000 – 5,368 = 5,632
2014	1,126.40	6,494.40	11,000 – 6,494.40 = 4,505.60
2015	901.12	7,395.52	11,000 – 7,395.52 = 3,604.48

It is clear in the above illustration that in WDV the amount of depreciation doses not remain fixed throughout the life of an asset. The depreciation is calculated on the net useful value of the asset.

Cash flow statement

The statement of cash flows describes the enterprise's cash flows position during the time period. It provides the details about how much cash has been generated and expended during a specific period of time from/(on) various sources. It consists of three parts of inflows and outflows resulting from *(a) operating activities, (b) investing activities and (c) financing activities.*

The cash flow statement is a mandatory statement for listed companies. Like the income statement, the cash-flow statement measures the financial activity of a firm 'over a period of time'. The cash-flow statement also tracks the effects of changes in balance sheet accounts. Ind AS 7, 'Statement of Cash Flows' sets out requirements for the presentation of cash flow information.[5]

The specimen cash flow statement of ABC Ltd. is given in Figure 4.4.

Cash Flow Statement of ABC Ltd. for the year ended 31st March 2015		
		(Rs. in crore)
Particulars	2014–15	2013–14
CASH FLOW FROM OPERATING ACTIVITIES		
Net Income before tax	7,200	10,500
Adjustments for:		
Depreciation and Amortisation	5,800	5,000
Interest Income	–	(4,000)
Operating Profit before Working Capital Changes	13,000	11,500
Decrease in Accounts Receivable	5,000	(2,000)
Decrease in Inventories	2,000	4,000
Increase in Accounts Payable	(2,000)	(1,000)
Cash Generated from Operations	18,000	12,500
Taxes Paid	3,000	4,000
Net Cash from Operating Activities	15,000	8,500
CASH FLOW FROM INVESTING ACTIVITIES		
Sale of Equipment	5,000	–
Purchase of Equipment	(2,000)	(5,000)
Interest Income	–	4,000
Net Cash used in Investing Activities	3,000	(1,000)
CASH FLOW FROM FINANCING ACTIVITIES		
Dividends Paid	(4,000)	(5,000)
Interest Paid	–	(1,000)
Net Cash used in Financing Activities	(4,000)	(6,000)
Net Decrease / Increase in cash and cash equivalents	14,000	1,500
Opening Balance of Cash and Cash Equivalents	20,000	18,500
Closing Balance of Cash and Cash Equivalents	34,000	20,000

Figure 4.4 Cash flow statement

Notes:

1. Rs. 1 crore = Rs. 10 millions.
2. The above cash flow statement is a specimen statement of a company, ABC Ltd. in the manufacturing sector in India, producing yarn. The above format of cash flow statement is as per the indirect method under 'Ind AS-7'. It is the most common method of preparing the statement by corporate, being based on the income statement.

To explain the cash flow statement and its components in detail, let's take the example of ABC Ltd.

The cash flow statement is one of the most useful financial management tools for business operations. The cash flow statement is divided into three categories:

1   **Net cash flow from operating activities (CFO).** Operating activities are the core activities of a business that generate cash and also require cash to carry on. They include cash sales, cash collections from customers, cash paid to suppliers and employees, cash paid for operating expenses and taxes paid.
2   **Net cash flow from investing activities (CFI).** Investing activities are discretionary investments made by the management for future. These primarily consist of the purchase (or sale) of equipment, liquidation (or purchase) of deposits and so forth.
3   **Net cash flow from financing activities (CFF).** Financing activities are fund related activities which are either sources or uses of cash and affect cash flow. These include issue of shares, raising of loans, repayments of loans, and dividends paid.

The sum of **CFO, CFI** and **CFF** is the 'net cash flow'. Net cash flow is a very important performance measure as it decides a company's growth plan.

For ABC Ltd., there has been an increase in 'net cash inflow' from Rs. 1,500 crores in 2013–14 to Rs. 14,000 crores in 2014–15, showing an increase of 833.33%. It is phenomenal for the liquidity position for the company. The brightest part of this increase is that cash flow from operating activities (CFO) has increased by 76% during the period.

Cash flow from investing activities (CFI) has resulted in an inflow of Rs. 3,000 crores in 2014–15 due to sale of fixed assets. Generally, negative cash flow related to investing activities are treated as sign of growth, due to purchase of fixed assets.

Cash flow from financing activities (CFF) has shown an outflow of Rs. 4,000 crores on dividend payment.

Cash flow analysis of HCC and L&T

The 'cash flow statements' of leading companies in the Indian construction sector, *Hindustan Construction Company Ltd. (HCC)* and *Larsen and Toubro Ltd. (L&T)* are analysed here for applied learning. **Both these companies are multinationals (MNCs), which makes the analysis relevant at global level.**

Indian construction sector

The Indian construction sector consists of the infrastructure sector and the real estate sector. *Hindustan Construction Company Ltd.* (HCC) is an infrastructure company based in Mumbai, India, and founded in 1926. It specialises in large-scale civil engineering and developing construction technologies–based projects, and has projects that span across such diverse segments as transportation, power, marine projects, oil and gas pipeline constructions, irrigation and water supply, utilities and urban infrastructure.

Larsen and Toubro Ltd. (L&T) is a multinational conglomerate company headquartered in Mumbai, India. It was founded in Mumbai in 1938 by Henning Holck-Larsen and Soren Kristian Toubro. It specialises in implementation of turnkey projects in major core and infrastructure sectors of the Indian industry.

The cash flow analysis of the *Hindustan Construction Company (HCC)* and *Larsen and Toubro (L&T)* is given in Tables 4.1 and 4.2. Their trend is given in Figures 4.5 and 4.6.

Table 4.1 Cash flow analysis of HCC

Industry : Construction – Civil/Turnkey – Large				
	Mar 13	Mar 14	Mar 15	Mar 16
Cash and cash equivalents at beginning of the year	1,588.10	838.50	1,446.70	750.20
Net cash from operating activities	3,415.60	5,030.70	3,832.90	3,709.60
Net cash used in investing activities	257.80	–286.40	–952.10	740.40
Net cash used in financing activities	–4,423.00	–4,136.20	–3,577.30	–4,526.10
Net inc/(dec) in cash and cash equivalents	–749.60	608.10	–696.50	–76.10
Cash and cash equivalents at end of the year	838.50	1,446.70	750.20	674.10

Note: Rs. in millions.

Source: Annual Reports of HCC.

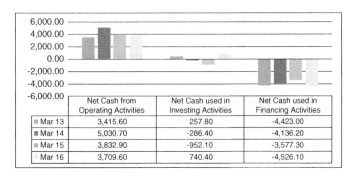

	Net Cash from Operating Activities	Net Cash used in Investing Activities	Net Cash used in Financing Activities
Mar 13	3,415.60	257.80	-4,423.00
Mar 14	5,030.70	-286.40	-4,136.20
Mar 15	3,832.90	-952.10	-3,577.30
Mar 16	3,709.60	740.40	-4,526.10

Figure 4.5 Cash flow trend of HCC

Table 4.2 Cash flow analysis of L&T

Industry : Engineering – Turnkey Services				
	Mar 13	Mar 14	Mar 15	Mar 16
Cash and cash equivalents at beginning of the year	19,060.20	14,963.60	17,941.20	15,914.60
Net cash from operating activities	14,722.40	10,472.40	31,431.30	32,557.20
Net cash used in investing activities	6,567.30	–12,143.20	–19,092.40	–5,220.60
Net cash used in financing activities	–33,162.30	5,040.50	–14,365.50	–25,672.10
Net inc/(dec) in cash and cash equivalent	–11,872.60	3,369.70	–2,026.60	1,664.50
Cash and cash equivalents at end of the year	14,963.60	17,941.20	15,914.60	17,579.10

Note: Rs. in millions.
Source: Annual Reports of L&T.

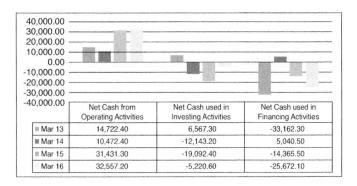

	Net Cash from Operating Activities	Net Cash used in Investing Activities	Net Cash used in Financing Activities
Mar 13	14,722.40	6,567.30	-33,162.30
Mar 14	10,472.40	-12,143.20	5,040.50
Mar 15	31,431.30	-19,092.40	-14,365.50
Mar 16	32,557.20	-5,220.60	-25,672.10

Figure 4.6 Cash flow trend of L&T

Analysis

- HCC has most of its cash inflow from operating activities, but its operational inflows have shown a fluctuating trend during the period. Further, they are not sufficient to support its financing activities. This has resulted in a negative cash flow for the company. Thus, HCC does not have a healthy cash flow.
- For L&T as well, most of the cash is generated from operating activities. The positive part is that it has shown a continuous increasing trend during the period and relatively to HCC, they are adequate to support the outflows from other activities. Cash from operations can take care of the investing activities which will lead future benefits. The major financing is done by the operations, which is a good sign.

Other disclosures in annual report

An annual report, especially of a listed company, is a substantial document. An annual report of a company is not just about financial statements, but it also contains significant information about the company in the form of additional disclosures.

Additional supplemental disclosures provide insight about the related areas of business, as discussed below.

Components of a company's annual report

Chairman's report. This is given by listed companies and some other public interest entities.

Operational and financial review (OFR). This is recommended for listed and some other public interest companies by an Accounting Standards Board (ASB).

Report on corporate governance. This is required for listed companies as per SEBI guidelines.

Directors' report. This is a mandatory requirement, though the contents are not standardised.

Auditors' report. This is an opinion from the auditors as required by the Companies Act.

Statement of accounting policies. In this section of the annual report, the company explains the accounting policies it has used in preparing its accounts.

Notes to the accounts. The notes explain the detailed description of items in the statement of profit and loss, the balance sheet and the cash flow statement. In addition, there are notes dealing with matters such as related party transactions.

Points to remember

- Financial statements are the reports which contain information about the business performance.
- The statement of profit and loss or the income statement is a summary of an entity's 'result of operations' for a specified period of time. It provides information about revenues generated and expenses incurred during a period and net income or net loss thereof.
- The top line of a company represents the total income earned during the period. It includes turnover and other income.
- The bottom line of a company is the net profit for the year, that is 'PAT'.
- The balance sheet presents the 'financial position' of a business, i.e. the economic resources owned by an entity and the claims against those resources (liabilities and owner's equity).
- The net worth of the company indicates the shareholders' interest in the business. It is the sum of share capital and reserves and surplus.
- 'Depreciation accounting' is the process of writing off the fixed asset during its life and providing funds for its replacement when it becomes unproductive.
- 'Depreciation' is used for writing off tangible assets.
- 'Amortisation' is used for writing off and replacing intangible assets.
- 'Depletion' refers to the process of writing off and replacing natural recourses.
- There are two commonly used methods of depreciation: *the straight line method (SLM) and the written-down-value method (WDV)*. Under the SLM method, depreciation is charged at a fixed amount throughout the life of an asset. Under the WDV method, depreciation is charged on the net productive value of an asset which reduces with the usage of an asset.
- Besides WDV, other accelerated methods of depreciation include the *sum-of-the-years-digits method* and *double declining balance method*.
- Cash flow statement describes the enterprise's cash flows generation and spent during a specific period of time. It consists of three parts of inflows and outflows resulting from *(a) operating activities, (b) investing activities and (c) financing*

activities. The cash flow statement is a mandatory statement for listed companies.

- Annual report of a company is not just about financial statements, but it also contains significant information about the company in the form of additional disclosures, *such as chairman's report, report on corporate governance, auditors' report, etc.*

Notes

1 Indian Accounting Standard (Ind AS 1), www.mca.gov.in/Ministry/pdf/Ind_AS1.pdf (accessed on 7 August 2016).
2 Indian Accounting Standard (Ind AS 110), http://mca.gov.in/Ministry/pdf/INDAS110.pdf (accessed on 7 August 2016).
3 Indian Accounting Standard (Ind AS 1), www.mca.gov.in/Ministry/pdf/Ind_AS1.pdf (accessed on 7 August 2016).
4 Indian Accounting Standard (Ind AS 1), www.mca.gov.in/Ministry/pdf/Ind_AS1.pdf (accessed on 7 August 2016).
5 Indian Accounting Standard (Ind AS 7), www.mca.gov.in/Ministry/pdf/Ind_AS7pdf (accessed on 7 August 2016).

5 Financial analysis

Financial statements need to be analysed for meaningful decision-making by various stakeholders, as financial analysis identifies the financial strengths and weaknesses of the firm by establishing relationship between various elements of the financial statements. While appraising a specific company, the financial analyst often focuses on the parameters of profitability, solvency, liquidity, efficiency and market performance. In addition, it involves forecasting the company's future performance for investment decisions. **Various methods that are used in analysing financial statements are discussed here with the help of case companies HCC and L&T and other corporate examples.**

Financial analysis

Financial analysis or financial appraisal is 'the process of analysing the financial statements information at specific level and interpreting the meaning of those numbers with the help of financial tools'. The financial techniques which are generally used to assign meaning to these numbers include comparative analysis, common-size analysis, trend analysis and the most important, 'ratio analysis'. *Ratio analysis* is the most relevant and widely used technique for financial appraisal.

1. Common-size analysis

Common-size analysis is also called 'vertical analysis', as financial statements are analysed on vertical basis to determine the contribution of each item of financial statement in total resources or with regard to a common base.

In case of the *common-size balance sheet*, the contribution of each item is found out in total funds and/or total assets. In case of the *common-size income statement*, the performance of each element is expressed with 'turnover' as common base.

Figures 5.1 and 5.2 present the common-size analysis of balance sheet and income statement.

Rally Industries Ltd.
Common-Size "Balance Sheet" as at 31st March, 2016

(Rs. in Cr.)

Particulars	2015	2016
EQUITY AND LIABILITIES		
Shareholders' Funds		
Share Capital	8,000.00	8,000.00
	(0.55)	(0.53)
Reserves & Surplus	694,985.02	781,413.40
	(47.84)	(51.41)
	702,985.02	789,413.40
	(48.39)	(51.94)
Non-Current Liabilities		
Long-Term Liabilities	694.61	107.57
	(0.05)	(0.01)
Long-Term Provisions	35,618.95	43,328.96
	(2.45)	(2.85)
	36,313.56	43,436.53
	(2.50)	(2.86)
Current Liabilities		
Trade Payables	119,705.91	112,614.00
	(8.24)	(7.41)
Other Current Liabilities	569,393.54	540,167.59
	(39.19)	(35.54)
Short-Term Provisions	24,329.65	34,338.58
	(1.67)	(2.26)
	713,429.10	687,120.17
	(49.11)	(45.20)
TOTAL	1,452,727.68	1,519,970.10
	(100.00)	(100.00)
ASSETS		
Non Current Assets		
Fixed Assets (Incl. of CWIP)	84,780.38	91,087.99
	(5.84)	(5.99)
Non Current Investments	1,198.11	1,911.53
	(0.08)	(0.13)
Deferred Tax Assets	29,949.46	33,779.59
	(2.06)	(2.22)
Long-Term Loans & Advances	15,657.22	15,089.37
	(1.08)	(0.99)
	131,585.17	141,868.48
	(9.06)	(9.33)
Current Assets		
Inventories	329,870.83	336,943.20
	(22.71)	(22.17)
Trade Receivables	412,853.69	378,614.33
	(28.42)	(24.91)
Cash & Bank Balances	456,436.61	588,153.06
	(31.42)	(38.70)
Short-Term Loans and Advances	121,981.38	74,391.03
	(8.40)	(4.89)
	1,321,142.51	1,378,101.62
	(90.94)	(90.66)
TOTAL	1,452,727.68	1,519,970.10
	(100.00)	(100.00)

Figure 5.1 Common-size balance sheet

Notes:

1. Rs. 1 crore = Rs. 10 millions.
2. Figures in parentheses show percentage of each item taking total funds/assets as hundred.

Analysis

(A) FINANCIAL STRUCTURE

It is clear from the above that company's 'net worth' has gone up from 48.39% in 2015 to 51.94% in 2016, an increase of 3.5% during the period under study. It is on account of reserves and surplus which is a good sign for shareholders' interest in the company.

'Loan funds' of the company have decreased from 0.05% in 2015 to 0.01% in 2016. 'Trade payables and other current liabilities' have also shown a decreasing trend during the period. On the whole, the firm's dependence on borrowed capital has decreased. This is a sound affair, particularly from the point of view of long-term stability.

(B) ASSETS STRUCTURE

The share of investment in 'total fixed assets' has increased from 9.06% in 2015 to 9.33% in 2016. The net block and capital work in progress has shown an increasing tend from 5.84% in 2015 to 5.99% in 2016. Similarly the share of long-term investments has also shown an increasing trend during the period. So, the position of investment in fixed assets can be categorised as satisfactory.

The level of 'working capital' has registered almost a stable trend during the period. There is a decline in inventories and trade receivables during the years, resulting in an increase in the cash and bank balances by around 7%. This shows better liquidity of the company.

Rally Industries Ltd.
Common-Size "Profit & Loss" for the year ended 31st March, 2016

(Rs. in Cr.)

Particulars	2014–15	2015–16
REVENUE FROM OPERATIONS		
Turnover		
Sale & Services	617,423.25	669,456.53
Excise Duty	5,195.09	1,902.69
Net Turnover	**612,228.16**	**667,553.84**
	(100.00)	(100.00)
OTHER INCOME	42,847.44	47,795.18
	(7.00)	(7.16)
TOTAL REVENUE	655,075.60	715,349.02
EXPENSES		
Cost of Material Consumed	310,938.06	326,534.05
	(50.79)	(48.92)
Changes in Inventories of Finished Goods,	4,733.28	3,602.18
WIP & Scrap	(0.77)	(0.54)
Employee Benefits Expense	103,042.56	126,345.08
	(16.38)	(18.93)
Finance Costs	339.61	138.38
	(0.05)	(0.02)
Depreciation and Amortisation Expense	14,210.45	15,396.49
	(2.32)	(2.31)
Other Expenses	72,308.59	65,531.99
	(11.81)	(9.82)
TOTAL EXPENSES	505,572.55	537,548.17
	(82.58)	(80.06)
Profit for the period before tax	149,503.05	177,800.85
	(24.42)	(26.63)
Tax Expense	24,311.77	29,944.58
	(3.97)	(4.49)
Profit for the year after tax (PAT)	**125,191.28**	**147,856.27**
	(20.45)	(22.15)

Figure 5.2 Common-size income statement

Notes:
1. Rs. 1 crore = Rs. 10 millions.
2. Figures in parentheses show percentage of each item taking net turnover as hundred.

Analysis

From the analysis of the common-size income statement of Rally Industries, it is evident that at an absolute level the total expenses have shown an increasing figure from Rs. 505,572.55 cr. in 2015 to Rs. 537,548.17 cr. in 2016. But margin-wise, the company has been able to tighten its expenses by over 2%, though not much, during the period. This is mainly on account of reduction in finance costs. Other expenses have also gone down by 2%. This is a positive sign as it has resulted in an increasing profit margin for the company.

2. Trend analysis

It is used to determine the growth pattern of a company. Here, the base year is taken as hundred and the respective years are expressed in percentage to find out the growth trend. In Table 5.1, 2011–12 of Rally Industries Ltd. is taken as the 'base year' to which coming years' financials of income statement and position statement are converted into percentage for studying the trend.

Figure 5.3 shows the graphical presentation of trend analysis of results of the company.

Table 5.1 Rally Industries Ltd. Trend Analysis (2011–12 to 2015–16) (Rs. in Cr.)

	2011–12	2012–13	2013–14	2014–15	2015–16
Results for the Year					
Turnover	73,164	89,124	118,354	139,269	146,328
Index	100	122	162	190	200
Earnings before interest, tax, dep. & amort. (EBITDA)	14,261	14,982	20,525	23,130	19,960
Index	100	105	144	162	140
Profit after tax (PAT)	7,572	9,069	11,943	19,458	15,309
Index	100	120	158	257	202
Dividend payout	1,045	1,393	1,440	1,631	1,898
Index	100	133	138	156	182
Position at the Year End					
Fixed assets*	59,955	91,928	107,061	104,229	149,628
Index	100	153	179	174	250
Net worth	40,403	49,804	63,967	81,449	126,373
Index	100	123	158	202	313

*Fixed assets are inclusive of capital work in progress.

Analysis

It is evident from the above trend analysis that the company has been experiencing an increasing trend in sales during these years; the absolute figures indicate that the company's sales have doubled from Rs. 73,164 cr. in 2012 to Rs. 146,328 cr. in 2016. This indicates a tightening market grip and is a good sign for the long-term growth for the company. A similar trend is evident in its EBITDA figures, except in 2015–16.

Again at an absolute level, the PAT of the company has been showing a continuous increasing trend and doubled up during the period.

But its current year trend is lower than the last year which reflects a declining yearly margin.

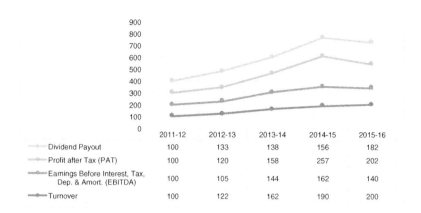

	2011-12	2012-13	2013-14	2014-15	2015-16
Dividend Payout	100	133	138	156	182
Profit after Tax (PAT)	100	120	158	257	202
Earnings Before Interest, Tax, Dep. & Amort. (EBITDA)	100	105	144	162	140
Turnover	100	122	162	190	200

Figure 5.3 Trend graph

3. Ratio analysis

Ratio analysis is the most important tool used in financial analysis. It involves computing *'financial ratios'* and analysing the business performance based on them. A 'financial ratio' is a relationship between two financial elements that indicates information about business activities, such as the ratio between company's current assets and its current liabilities indicate its liquidity position. The basic source of these ratios is the company's financial statements.

These ratios enable to identify the financial strengths and weaknesses of company at an intrinsic level. When assessing ratios, it is important that the results are compared with other companies in the same industry and not to be taken in isolation. What may seem like a poor ratio at first glance may well be normal for that industry, and of course, the reverse applies, in that what may seem a good ratio on its own could be below average for that industry.

The following is the discussion on various types of financial ratios which are used for analysis.

- Profitability ratios
- Operating efficiency ratios
- Liquidity ratios
- Solvency ratios
- Market ratios.

Box 5.1   Financial ratios and their usage

Profitability ratios – the overall performance of the firm and its
   return generation
Efficiency ratios – the efficiency of managing assets
Liquidity ratios – the firm's ability to meet cash needs as
they arise
Solvency ratios – the extent of a firm's financing with debt rela-
   tive to equity and its ability to cover fixed charges
Market ratios – the firm's market standing for shareholders.

A. Profitability ratios

These ratios are used to analyse the profitability of a company in total
and return generated for shareholders. They help in determining the
profit capacity of the firm at different levels. That's why there are several measures to analyse the success of the firm at generating profits.
   These are:

- *sales based ratios*
- *assets/funds based ratios.*

SALES BASED PROFITABILITY RATIOS

1. Gross profit ratio   The gross profit ratio or the gross profit margin
indicates the margin generated out of sales after meeting production
expenses of raw materials, labour and so forth.
   The higher the value of the margin, the better it is for the firm.

$$\text{Gross Profit Ratio} = \frac{\text{Gross Profit}}{\text{Sales}}$$

(*Gross Profit = Sales – COGS**)

Example

Right Ltd. earned Rs. 10,000 from the sale of readymade garments. The production expenses incurred are Rs. 4,000.
   Its gross profit margin would be 60%. It means that for every
rupee earned on sale, it has Rs. 0.60 left for meeting other expenses.

* COGS = Cost of production of goods sold.

2. EBITDA margin EBITDA margin measures the profitability of a concern after meeting other line of operating expenses out of sales, after production expenses. The other operating expenses include office and selling expenses but exclude non-cash expense of depreciation.

$$\text{EBITDA Ratio} = \frac{\text{EBITDA}^{**}}{\text{Sales}}$$

(EBITDA = Gross Profit – Other Operating expenses)

EBITDA margin determines the core strength of the company as it excludes non-operating items and taxes**°. The higher the margin, the better it is.

Example

In the above example, let's assume administrative expenses are Rs. 2,000. Marketing expenses including freight on sales of goods are Rs. 1,000.

The EBITDA amount would be: Rs. 3,000 (Rs. 6,000 – Rs. 3,000). The EBITDA margin is 30%. This implies that 30% is left out for meeting depreciation, interest and tax expenses. From gross margin of 60%, office and selling expenses have consumed another 30% of profit.

---

3. Operating profit ratio/EBIT margin Operating profit margin measures the profitability of a concern after charging non-cash expense of depreciation out of EBITDA.

$$\text{Operating Profit Ratio} = \frac{\text{EBIT}^{***}/\text{Operating Profit}}{\text{Sales}}$$

(Operating Profit = EBITDA – Depreciation)

** EBITDA = Earnings before interest, tax, depreciation and amortisation.
**° For detailed discussion on EBITDA, refer to the section 'Multi-Variant Profitability' in Chapter 4, 'Financial Statements'.
*** EBIT = Earnings before interest and tax.

> 'EBITDA and EBIT': Both EBITDA and Operating profit margin determine the core strength of the company as they exclude non-operating items and taxes.[***σ] The difference between EBITDA and EBIT is of 'depreciation and amortisation'.

The higher the operating profit margin, the better it is.

> **Example**
>
> Taking the above example further, if the depreciation amount is Rs. 1,000, the operating profit would be Rs. 2,000 (Rs. 3,000 – Rs. 1,000).
>
> The operating profit margin is 20%. This signifies that depreciation has consumed 10% of profit from EBITDA margin of 30% and remaining 20% will be used for meeting interest and tax.

4. Net profit ratio/PAT margin   The net profit margin measures the net margin of profitability on sales. It indicates how much of each rupee earned by the company is finally translated into profits. Therefore, this is the net indicator for measuring the efficiency of operations, and a very good indicator of the business's ability to face various pressures. A higher net profit margin is always desirable.

$$\text{Net Profit Ratio} = \frac{\text{PAT}}{\text{Sales}}$$

5. Operating ratio   The operating ratio analyses the profitability of the firm with regard to coverage of expenses. 'Unlike the above profitability

---

[***σ] For detailed discussion on Operating Profit, refer to the section 'Multi-Variant Profitability' in Chapter 4, 'Financial Statements'.

ratios, this ratio should be as low as possible'. The lower the ratio, the greater is the organisation's ability to generate profits if revenues decrease.

$$\text{Operating Ratio} = \frac{\text{Total Operating Expenses}}{\text{Sales}}$$

ASSETS/FUNDS BASED PROFITABILITY RATIOS

1. Return on capital employed*   Return on capital employed (ROCE) measures whether or not a company is generating adequate profits in relation to the funds invested in it and is a key indicator of investment performance. In 'manufacturing sector', figures are expected in excess of 10% rising to over 25% at the top end. In 'retail sector', lower figures would be experienced, ranging between 5% and 15%. 'Construction sector' figures show an average of about 7% increasing to over 35% for the top performers.

$$\text{Return on Capital Employed (ROCE)} = \frac{\text{EBIT}}{\text{Capital Employed}}$$

(Capital Employed = Net worth + Preference Share Capital + Long-term Loans)

2. Return on equity   Return on Equity or Return on Net Worth (ROE/RONW) is a very important ratio for equity shareholders as it indicates whether or not a company is generating enough return for them. ROE is an indicator of how effectively a company's management uses owner's money. It calculates the amount of net income returned as a percentage of equity shareholders.

Higher return on equity is always favourable as it indicates the efficiency of a company in converting the shareholders' capital to profits.

---

* ROCE is often used interchangeably with ROI (Return on Investment).

Return on Equity (ROE)

$$= \frac{\text{PAT} - \text{Preference dividend} - \text{Dividend Distribution Tax}}{\text{Net Worth}}$$

(Net Worth = Equity Share Capital + Reserves and Surplus)

3. Earnings per share   Earnings per share (EPS) is defined as the portion of company's profit allocated to each outstanding share of a common stock. Higher EPS signifies better profitability from a shareholder's point of view.

Earnings per Share (EPS)

$$= \frac{\text{PAT} - \text{Preference Dividend} - \text{Dividend distribution Tax}}{\text{Number of Equity Shares}}$$

Example

A company earned net profit of Rs. 50,000 for 2015. It has 1,000 outstanding equity shares. There are no preference shares.

So, EPS = 50,000 / 1,000
        = Rs. 50

4. Dividend per share   Dividend per share (DPS) is defined as the portion of company's profit distributed to each common shareholder. Higher DPS indicates that company is cash-rich and looks after the equity shareholders well.

Dividend per Share (DPS)

$$= \frac{\text{Dividend paid to Equity Shareholders}}{\text{Number of Equity Shares}}$$

Example

Taking the above example, the company paid dividend of Rs. 10,000 from the net profit of Rs. 50,000 for 2015. It has 1,000 outstanding equity shares.

So, DPS = 10,000 / 1,000
= Rs. 10

5. *Dividend pay-out ratio* The dividend pay-out ratio (D/P ratio) refers to the amount of dividend paid per share with respect to the earnings per share. It denotes the percentage of earnings distributed as dividend to the common shareholders.

$$\text{Dividend Pay-out Ratio (D/P Ratio)} = \frac{\text{DPS}}{\text{EPS}}$$

In the above example,
D/P ratio will be: 10/50 = 20%

Profitability ratios: All profitability ratios, except EPS and DPS, are expressed as a percentage. EPS and DPS are expressed in rupees per share.

Box 5.2   DuPont analysis: shareholders' wealth maximisation (SWM)

The ultimate objective of a company is to 'maximise shareholders' value'. ROE shows the rate of return that the firm earns on stockholder's equity. DuPont analysis is used to find out the factors responsible for performance of shareholders' value in terms of 'ROE'. In short, it is used to analyse the shareholders' wealth maximisation (SWM). If ROE is unsatisfactory, the DuPont analysis helps to locate the part of the business that is underperforming.

DuPont analysis is a method of performance analysis started by the DuPont Corporation in the US in the 1920s. It evaluates the ROE effect on three variables:

1   Profitability, measured by the 'net profit margin'
2   Assets' efficiency, measured by the 'total assets turnover'
3   Financial leverage, measured by the 'equity multiplier'.

ROE = PAT/Shareholders' equity

ROE is further sub-divided into the following ratios for studying in-depth the focus areas for performance of shareholders' value:

ROE = PAT Margin × Total Assets Turnover × Equity Multiplier
ROE = PAT/Sales × Sales/Total Assets × Total Assets/ Shareholders' equity

Profitability analysis of HCC and L&T*

The profitability analysis on sales-based parameters of the companies under study in the Indian construction sector is given in Table 5.6. The financials of balance sheets and profit and loss statements of companies which are used and computed from for the said analysis are given in Tables 5.2 to 5.5.

Table 5.2 Balance sheets of HCC from 2013 to 2016

				(Rs. in Millions)
	Mar 13	*Mar 14*	*Mar 15*	*Mar 16*
EQUITY AND LIABILITIES:				
Share Capital	606.70	606.70	645.90	779.20
Reserves and Surplus	11,021.10	12,027.30	13,228.60	17,849.10
Total Shareholders' Funds	**11,627.80**	**12,634.00**	**13,874.50**	**18,628.30**

---

* The profiles of HCC and L&T have already been discussed in Chapter 4, 'Financial Statements'.

	Mar 13	Mar 14	Mar 15	Mar 16
				(Rs. in Millions)

	Mar 13	Mar 14	Mar 15	Mar 16
Non-current Liabilities				
Long-Term Borrowings	32,570.30	30,051.80	26,276.30	24,822.60
Deferred Tax Liabilities	142.90	237.10	680.70	1,161.70
Other Long-Term Liabilities and Provisions	1,265.40	1,357.40	386.20	379.70
	33,978.60	31,646.30	27,343.20	26,364.00
Current Liabilities and Provisions				
Short-Term Borrowings	13,178.50	15,374.80	19,546.90	20,481.50
Trade Payables	9,600.10	9,511.60	15,378.00	14,087.30
Other Current Liabilities and Provisions	16,905.70	16,792.00	20,243.80	19,938.60
	39,684.30	41,678.40	55,168.70	54,507.40
TOTAL	85,290.70	85,958.70	96,386.40	99,499.70
ASSETS:				
Non-current Assets				
Fixed Assets				
Tangible Assets	10,063.50	9,130.90	7,838.10	6,675.90
Intangible Assets	40.40	23.10	9.30	14.90
Capital Work in Progress	105.50	32.50	45.30	16.80
Intangible Assets under Development	17.20	17.20	17.20	0.00
Non-current Investments	6,012.20	6,899.50	5,972.90	5,147.20
Long-Term Loans and Advances	12,133.10	12,117.60	13,430.00	18,692.90
Other Non-current Assets	6,669.80	10,871.10	14,942.80	23,405.30
	35,041.70	39,091.90	42,255.60	53,953.00
Current Assets				
Current Investments	0.00	0.00	956.00	777.20
Inventories	36,721.80	32,935.60	35,677.60	36,204.90
Trade Receivables	5,701.90	5,273.30	9,227.40	5,073.60
Cash and Bank Balances	991.40	1,469.70	978.40	908.30
Short-Term Loans and Advances	6,745.30	7,125.80	1,498.20	1,271.80
Other Current Assets	88.60	62.40	5,793.20	1,310.90
	50,249.00	46,866.80	54,130.80	45,546.70
TOTAL	85,290.70	85,958.70	96,386.40	99,499.70

Source: Annual Reports of HCC

Table 5.3 Profit and loss statements of HCC from 2013 to 2016

				(Rs. in Millions)
	Mar 13	*Mar 14*	*Mar 15*	*Mar 16*
INCOME:				
Revenue from Operations	38,336.50	40,425.20	41,348.00	40,524.20
Less: Excise Duty	13.60	0.00	0.00	0.00
Net Revenue from Operations	38,322.90	40,425.20	41,348.00	40,524.20
Other Income	1,343.40	2,135.90	1,469.80	1,877.60
Total Income	**39,666.30**	**42,561.10**	**42,817.80**	**42,401.80**
EXPENDITURE:				
Raw Materials	796.00	720.80	110.50	9,520.40
Subcontracting Expenses	0.00	0.00	0.00	13,153.70
Construction Expenses	28,701.80	28,193.00	28,692.40	4,893.80
Employee Benefits Expenses	4,020.30	3,884.60	3,611.10	3,703.50
Finance Costs	5,441.00	6,079.40	6,511.30	6,898.80
Depreciation and Amortisation Expense	1,634.00	1,446.10	1,503.00	1,358.50
Other Expenses	1,164.80	1,327.70	1,116.30	1,277.60
Total Expenses	41,757.90	41,651.60	41,544.60	40,806.30
Profit/(Loss) Before Exceptional Items & Tax	–2,091.60	909.50	1,273.20	1,595.50
Exceptional Items	155.80	0.00	0.00	264.80
Profit/(Loss) Before Tax	–1,935.80	909.50	1,273.20	1,330.70
Tax Expense	559.40	103.10	456.70	481.00
Profit/(Loss) After Tax	**–1,376.40**	**806.40**	**816.50**	**849.70**
EBITDA	3,640.00	6,299.10	7,817.70	7,975.20
EBIT/Operating Profit	2,006.00	4,853.00	6,314.70	6,616.70

Source: Annual Reports of HCC

Notes:

1. EBITDA (Sales – Exp. excld. Int. & Dep.)
2. EBIT/Operating Profit (EBITDA – Dep.)

Table 5.4 Balance sheets of L&T from 2013 to 2016

				(Rs. in Millions)
	Mar 13	Mar 14	Mar 15	Mar 16
EQUITY AND LIABILITIES:				
Share Capital	1,230.80	1,853.80	1,859.10	1,863.00
Reserves and Surplus	2,90,196.40	3,34,764.50	3,68,986.70	4,05,320.30
Total Shareholders' Funds	**2,91,427.20**	**3,36,618.30**	**3,70,845.80**	**4,07,183.30**
Non-current Liabilities				
Long-Term Borrowings	72,710.30	54,781.40	85,086.00	83,392.70
Deferred Tax Liabilities	2,422.20	4,099.20	3,629.90	2,033.60
Other Long-Term Liabilities and Provisions	7,879.50	3,931.80	4,700.70	5,227.70
	83,012.00	**62,812.40**	**93,416.60**	**90,654.00**
Current Liabilities and Provisions				
Short-Term Borrowings	7,345.30	38,760.40	37,910.80	38,818.70
Trade Payables	1,69,326.50	1,63,454.50	1,88,447.70	2,21,188.00
Other Current Liabilities and Provisions	1,73,129.30	1,81,400.20	1,78,416.70	2,12,853.10
	3,49,801.10	**3,83,615.10**	**4,04,775.20**	**4,72,859.80**
TOTAL	**7,24,240.30**	**7,83,045.80**	**8,69,037.60**	**9,70,697.10**
ASSETS:				
Non-current Assets				
Fixed Assets				
Tangible Assets	82,187.50	75,608.10	74,022.00	71,205.90
Intangible Assets	863.90	1,139.90	851.60	1,384.00
Capital Work in Progress	4,910.50	4,118.60	3,045.40	2,506.90
Intangible Assets Under Development	1,057.90	1,505.50	1,895.00	1,589.10
Non-current Investments	1,05,227.00	1,51,684.10	1,76,728.20	1,98,979.40
Long-Term Loans and Advances	36,690.70	37,215.70	27,208.30	30,317.30
Other Non-current Assets	823.20	627.80	1,278.60	1,878.90
	2,31,760.70	**2,71,899.70**	**2,85,029.10**	**3,07,861.50**

(*Continued*)

Table 5.4 (Continued)

			(Rs. in Millions)
	Mar 13	Mar 14	Mar 15	Mar 16
Current Assets				
Current Investments	55,806.90	40,462.30	53,800.80	46,709.80
Inventories	20,641.80	19,825.30	22,077.90	18,880.00
Trade Receivables	2,26,130.10	2,15,387.60	2,30,511.10	2,63,091.90
Cash and Bank Balances	14,556.60	17,828.60	15,158.00	16,809.10
Short-Term Loans and Advances	57,437.60	63,456.50	78,123.50	1,02,051.50
Other Current Assets	1,17,906.60	1,54,185.80	1,84,337.20	2,15,293.30
	4,92,479.60	5,11,146.10	5,84,008.50	6,62,835.60
TOTAL	7,24,240.30	7,83,045.80	8,69,037.60	9,70,697.10

Source: Annual Reports of L&T

Table 5.5 Profit and loss statements of L&T from 2013 to 2016

			(Rs. in Millions)
	Mar 13	Mar 14	Mar 15	Mar 16
INCOME:				
Revenue from Operations	5,21,957.00	5,71,638.50	5,75,580.70	6,04,150.00
Less: Excise Duty	5,847.40	5,649.30	5,406.60	6,353.90
Net Revenue from Operations	5,16,109.60	5,65,989.20	5,70,174.10	5,97,796.10
Other Income	18,872.90	18,808.90	22,833.70	24,059.70
Total Income	5,34,982.50	5,84,798.10	5,93,007.80	6,21,855.80
EXPENDITURE:				
Manufacturing, Construction & Operating Expenses	4,02,048.30	4,33,464.50	4,43,965.50	4,66,290.90
Employee Benefits Expenses	38,609.30	46,623.70	41,508.40	44,802.00
Sales, Administration & Other Expenses	20,856.60	19,320.30	19,971.10	25,050.70
Finance Costs	9,547.50	10,760.80	14,190.30	14,490.40

				(Rs. in Millions)
	Mar 13	*Mar 14*	*Mar 15*	*Mar 16*
Depreciation, Amortisation & Obsolescence	7,277.40	7,924.20	10,081.50	9,988.80
Total Expenses	4,78,203.10	5,18,004.00	5,29,567.20	5,60,567.50
Profit Before Exceptional & Extraordinary Items & Tax	56,779.40	66,794.10	63,440.60	61,288.30
Exceptional and Extraordinary Items	2,543.50	5,885.00	3,571.60	5,602.80
Profit Before Tax	59,322.90	72,679.10	67,012.20	66,891.10
Tax Expense	15,478.00	17,747.80	16,450.40	13,776.50
Profit After Tax	**43,844.90**	**54,931.30**	**50,561.80**	**53,114.60**
EBITDA	54,731.40	66,670.20	64,878.70	61,707.80
EBIT/Operating Profit	47,454.00	58,746.00	54,797.20	51,719.00

Source: Annual Reports of L&T

Notes

1. EBITDA (Sales – Exp. excld. Int. & Dep.)
2. EBIT/Operating Profit (EBITDA – Dep.)

Table 5.6 Sales-based profitability

	Mar '13	*Mar '14*	*Mar '15*	*Mar '16*
(i) EBITDA Margin (%)				
HCC	9.50	15.58	18.91	19.68
L&T	10.60	11.78	11.38	10.32
Industry	15.14	15.34	14.23	10.69
(ii) EBIT Margin (%)				
HCC	5.23	12.00	15.27	16.33
L&T	9.19	10.38	9.61	8.65
Industry	12.73	12.75	10.60	7.18
(iii) Net Profit Margin (%)				
HCC	–3.59	1.99	1.97	2.10
L&T	8.50	9.71	8.87	8.89

Note: Industry figures are taken from the Capitaline database (www.capitaline.com).

Analysis

- The operating profit margin and net profit margin for HCC have shown an increasing trend during the period under study.
- Both EBITDA and EBIT margins of HCC, except in the year 2013, are not only higher than L&T but also to the peers in the Indian construction industry. This is a positive sign for the company.
- L&T wins over HCC in terms of PAT margin. It is much higher for L&T, which indicates that HCC must be losing out on account of non-operating expenses and other items. Thus, L&T is a greater profit-making company as compared to HCC in the ultimate, but its core efficiency is lower than HCC.

'Return generation' of the units is discussed Table 5.7. ROE efficiency is indicated in Table 5.8. This is further discussed with the help of the DuPont analysis as given in Tables 5.9 and 5.10. The graphical representation of the DuPont analysis is given in Figures 5.4 and 5.5. The earnings potential of the units is given in Table 5.11.

Table 5.7 Return on investment – ROI (%)

	Mar '13	Mar '14	Mar '15	Mar '16
HCC	4.40	10.96	15.32	14.71
L&T	12.67	14.71	11.80	10.39
Industry	8.44	7.39	4.72	0.00

Note: Industry figures are taken from the Capitaline database (www.capitaline.com).

Table 5.8 Return on equity – ROE/RONW (%)

	Mar '13	Mar '14	Mar '15	Mar '16
HCC	–11.84	6.38	5.88	4.56
L&T	15.04	16.32	13.63	13.04
Industry	3.75	0.73	6.36	0.00

Analysis

- In the initial years of 2013 and 2014, L&T generates greater return on the funds employed as compared to HCC but in later years of 2015 and 2016, the roles are reversed. This can be attributed to the increasing core efficiency of HCC over the years, as discussed above.
- The positive part is that both the companies have outperformed the industry in terms of return on investment.
- In general, a detailed insight into efficiency of operations, demand for products and utilisation of resources is required to improve the return generation on the resources employed.

Table 5.9 DuPont analysis of HCC

	Mar '13	Mar '14	Mar '15	Mar '16
(1) PAT/Sales (%) – 'Net Profit Margin'	–3.59	1.99	1.97	2.10
(2) Sales/Total Assets (times) – 'Assets Turnover Ratio'	0.45	0.47	0.43	0.41
(3) Total Assets/Shareholders' equity (times) – 'Assets to Equity Ratio'	7.34	6.80	6.95	5.34
1 × 2 × 3 = ROE (%)	–11.84	6.38	5.88	4.56

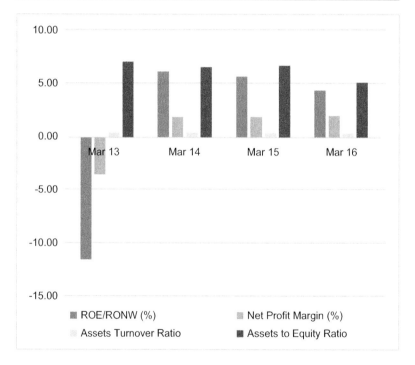

Figure 5.4 DuPont trend of HCC

Analysis

- The return on equity for HCC has been on the decreasing trend during these years with the exception of year 2014 where it showed tremendous performance by turning negative return on equity shareholders positive.
- The decreasing ROE conveys a negative signal to the equity shareholders and affects their outlook towards the company.

- The in optimal use of financial leverage by HCC is the main factor for fall in ROE. From 7.34 in 2013, the 'assets to equity ratio' declined to 5.34 in 2016.
- Additionally, the decline in the efficiency of assets utilisation is another main reason for the decline in ROE. From 0.45 in 2013, the 'assets turnover ratio' has decreased to 0.41 in 2016.
- The net profit margin has showed relatively better performance than other variables, but it needs to be pushed further for greater ROE.

Table 5.10 DuPont analysis of L&T

	Mar '13	Mar '14	Mar '15	Mar '16
(1) PAT/Sales (%) – 'Net Profit Margin'	8.50	9.71	8.87	8.89
(2) Sales/Total Assets (times) – 'Assets Turnover Ratio'	0.71	0.72	0.66	0.62
(3) Total Assets/Shareholders' equity (times) – 'Assets to Equity Ratio'	2.49	2.33	2.34	2.38
1 × 2 × 3 = ROE (%)	15.04	16.32	13.63	13.04

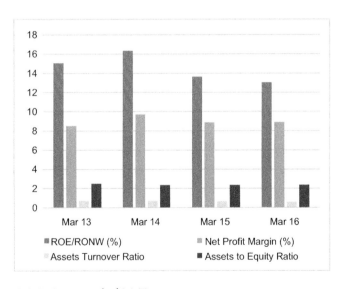

Figure 5.5 DuPont trend of L&T

Analysis

- L&T has also shown a declining ROE trend over the years with marginal increase in 2014. But in spite of this decrease, L&T is much higher return generating company for equity shareholders than HCC.
- The assets utilisation ratio has decreased from 2013 levels of 0.71 to 0.62 in 2016. This can be attributed to factors – decrease in efficiency of operations or reduction in orders due to slump in demand.
- L&T needs to concentrate on both, better efficiency in asset utilisation as well as getting more orders to improve the order to book ratio.
- The leverage ratio is healthy, between 2.30 and 2.50, unlike HCC, which means that debt financing is at acceptable levels. If need arises, it can go for raising further debts though decline in the leverage ratio also attributed to declining ROE.
- The net profit margin has more or less shown an increasing trend over the years and is around 9% in 2016. This is way above the average of HCC of 2.5%. Thus, in terms of net profitability, L&T is sound.

Table 5.11 Earnings per share – EPS (in Rs.)

	Mar '13	Mar '14	Mar '15	Mar '16
HCC	–2.27	1.33	1.27	1.10
L&T	52.55	59.36	54.46	57.07

Analysis

- Earnings per share of L&T is much better as compared to HCC and it has increased in the financial year ending 2016 from 2013, while that of HCC it has reduced significantly in that period which points to some significant problems in terms of profit generation per share.

B. Operating efficiency ratios

Efficiency ratios or 'turnover ratios' are computed to find out the efficiency of the management in utilisation of resources, both long-term and short-term. It is expected, higher turnover leads to greater profits. These ratios are as follows.

1. INVENTORY TURNOVER RATIO (ITR)

This ratio measures the velocity of conversion of inventory in generating sales over a period.

It is an indication of how efficiently inventory is managed by the company.

It is calculated as:

> ITR = Sales or cost of goods sold/average inventory

The higher the ratio, the better it is, as it shows the efficient utilisation of inventory by the firm. When examining this ratio it should be borne in mind that different companies will have varying levels of stock turnover depending on the industry they operate in. Low figures are generally poor as they indicate excessively high or low moving stocks.

2. AVERAGE HOLDING PERIOD (AHP)

It indicates the number of days the company holds its inventory.

It is calculated as:

> AHP = Days in an year/ITR

A lower holding period is desirable as it leads to less obsolescence and deterioration of inventory.

3. DEBTORS TURNOVER RATIO (DTR)

This ratio indicates how quickly the firm is able to sell its products and collect its debts.

It is calculated as:

> DTR = Sales/average debtors

The higher the value, the faster a company is in collecting money from debtors.

4. AVERAGE COLLECTION PERIOD (ACP)

This ratio indicates the number of days taken by the firm in collecting its receivables.

It is calculated as:

$$\boxed{\text{ACP} = \text{Days in an year/DTR}}$$

A shorter collection period is preferable, because it shows higher liquidity. In general terms, the figure indicates the effectiveness of the company's credit control department in collecting the money outstanding.

5. CREDITORS TURNOVER RATIO (CTR)

This ratio is used to measure a company's ability to get trade credit and the speed at which it pays off its suppliers.

It is calculated as:

$$\boxed{\text{CTR} = \text{Purchases/average creditors}}$$

A lower CTR is desirable from a company's perspective because it indicates the higher credibility of firm in the market.

6. AVERAGE PAYMENT PERIOD (APP)

This ratio indicates the average number of days in which the company makes payments to its suppliers.

It is calculated as:

$$\boxed{\text{APP} = \text{Days in an year/CTR}}$$

A longer payment period allows the firm to rotate the credit from the suppliers into the business.

7. WORKING CAPITAL TURNOVER RATIO (WCTR)

This ratio is used to measure the company's ability to utilise its working capital efficiently to generate revenue.

It is calculated as:

> WCTR = Sales/working capital*

The higher the ratio, the better it is, since it implies the company is using its current resources to the fullest.

8. ASSETS TURNOVER RATIO (ATR)

The asset turnover indicates how effectively a company utilises its investment in total assets. It is a measure of how efficient the company has been in generating sales from the assets at its disposal.

It is calculated as:

> ATR = Sales/total assets

The higher the ratio, the better it is, since it implies the company is generating more revenue of its assets. A low figure would suggest either poor trading performance (which can be evaluated by the profit margin, sales per employee figures) or over-investment in costly fixed assets.

Efficiency ratios: All efficiency ratios, including inventory turnover, debtors' turnover, creditors' turnover and assets turnover ratio, are expressed in number of times. Average holding period, collection period, payment period and cash cycle are expressed in number of days.

Operating efficiency analysis of HCC and L&T

The efficiency analysis on the above parameters of the companies under study is given in Tables 5.12 and 5.13. **The financials of balance sheets and profit and loss statements of companies which are used and computed from for the said analysis are given in Tables 5.2 to 5.5.**

---

* Working capital is calculated as 'current assets – current liabilities'.

Table 5.12 Fixed assets utilisation

	Mar '13	Mar '14	Mar '15	Mar '16
(i) Fixed Assets Turnover Ratio (in times)				
HCC	3.75	4.39	5.23	6.04
L&T	5.80	6.87	7.14	7.80
Industry	2.14	1.72	1.33	1.35
(ii) Inventory Turnover Ratio (in times)				
HCC	1.04	1.23	1.16	1.12
L&T	25.00	28.55	25.83	31.66
Industry	2.19	1.90	1.38	1.29
(iii) Average Inventory Holding Period (in days)				
HCC	350	297	315	326
L&T	15	13	14	12
Industry	167	192	264	283

Note: Industry figures are taken from the Capitaline database (www.capitaline.com).

Analysis

- In terms of fixed assets utilisation as well as inventory turnover efficiency, L&T beats HCC and the industry hands down. HCC scores low on both fronts.
- HCC needs to improve its efficiency of utilising its assets to gain maximum productivity out of them. Also, HCC needs to look into its inventory management system and restructure the purchase and utilisation system of inventory. Its inventory holding period is much higher than the industry average of 227 days. This increases the cost of storage and leads to losses due to obsolescence.
- L&T not only has an average holding period of 146 days, which is lower than industry average, but it also has a sufficient margin period to purchase inventory in a scenario of sudden shortage.

Table 5.13 Debtors management

	Mar '13	Mar '14	Mar '15	Mar '16
(i) Debtors Turnover Ratio (in times)				
HCC	6.72	7.67	4.48	7.99
L&T	2.28	2.63	2.47	2.27
Industry	3.78	3.39	2.81	3.05
(ii) Average Collection Period (in days)				
HCC	54	48	81	46
L&T	160	139	148	161
Industry	97	108	130	120

Note: Industry figures are taken from the Capitaline database (www.capitaline.com).

Analysis

- The average collection period for L&T does not stand comparable to HCC due to different sale policies. That is reflected in HCC having an average collection of two months due to higher debtors' turnover ratio.
- L&T, on the other hand, is a very large company which has big customers and massive projects. It does allow its customers leeway to make payments. However, its average collection period is much higher than the industry average, which is a cause for concern. L&T should aggressively work towards faster realisation of payments from customers.
- Thus, as far as collection is concerned, HCC is ahead of L&T. But, this effect largely gets negated by its inefficient use of resources.

C. Liquidity ratios

These ratios are oriented towards evaluating the short-term sustainability of the company. They provide information about a firm's ability to meet its short-term financial obligations. They are of immense use to those extending short-term credit to the firm. These ratios are as follows.

1. CURRENT RATIO
It is calculated as:

> Current assets/current liabilities

It reflects the working capital situation, and indicates the ability of a company to pay its short-term creditors from the realisation of its current assets. *An ideal figure is 2:1,* which indicates that there are sufficient assets available to pay liabilities.

Current assets include inventory, trade receivables and cash and bank balances.

Current liabilities include short-term debts, account payables and so forth.

In the 'retail and manufacturing sectors' the expected figures are between 1.1 to 1.6; in the 'wholesale and construction sectors', it is between 1.1 to 1.5; and in the 'automobile sector', it is around 1.2. Generally where credit terms and large stocks are common to the business, the current ratio will be higher than, for example, a trading business where credit sales are the norm.

2. LIQUID RATIO/ACID-TEST RATIO/QUICK RATIO
It is calculated as:

> Liquid Assets *(Current Assets – Stock- Prepaid Expenses)/* Current Liabilities

It is generally considered to be a more accurate assessment of a company's financial health than the current ratio as it excludes relatively less liquid items like stock and prepaid expenses, thus reducing the risk of relying on a ratio that may include slow moving or redundant stock and items.

An ideal ratio is 1. In the 'manufacturing sector' figures between 0.7 and 1.1 are seen as acceptable and for the 'wholesale sector' it is between 0.7 to 1.0. The 'construction sector' operates between 0.6 and 1.0.

3. SUPER-QUICK RATIO/CASH RATIO
It is calculated as:

> Cash and Bank/Current Liabilities

It is the closest indicator of liquidity of a firm as it focuses only on 'cash and bank balances' availability to meet current liabilities. The IT/ITes sector has the highest cash ratio among all the sectors.

> **Liquidity ratios:** *All liquidity ratios are expressed in number of times.*

Liquidity analysis of HCC and L&T

The liquidity analysis on the above parameters of the companies under study is given in Table 5.14. **The financials of balance sheets and profit and loss statements of companies which are used and computed from for the said analysis are given earlier in Tables 5.2 to 5.5.**

Table 5.14 Liquidity analysis

	Mar 13	Mar 14	Mar 15	Mar 16
(i) Current Ratio (in times)				
HCC	1.27	1.12	0.98	0.84
L&T	1.41	1.33	1.44	1.40
Industry	2.46	2.47	2.56	2.66

Note: Industry figures are taken from the Capitaline database (www.capitaline.com).

Analysis

- L&T shows better liquidity than HCC and the industry. But, both the companies have acceptable liquidity ratios near the industry average.
- HCC's low liquidity ratio is due to the fact that its average collection period is very low as compared to L&T.

D. Solvency ratios

These ratios are used to find out the long-term soundness of the company. They measure how financially sound a company is to meet its long-term obligations and are also known as 'leverage ratios'. They include *debt ratios*, which are based on the balance sheet, and *coverage ratios*, which are based on the income statement.

A high degree of solvency indicates that a company's cash flows are consistent enough to make periodic interest and principal repayments on its debt. These ratios are very significant to banks and financial institutions.

These ratios are discussed as follows.

1. DEBT-EQUITY RATIO (D/E RATIO)
It is calculated as:

Long-term Debt/Equity (Net Worth)

The D/E ratio indicates the relative proportions of debt and equity in financing the assets of a firm and the extent to which the firm depends upon debt capital for its existence. In other words, it reveals whether the firm is 'highly leveraged' or not, that is the benefit of trading on equity is there or not. It also indicates the margin of safety to the creditors, that is the extent to which the creditors face risk in getting their due money back.

This is a measurement of a company's equity-liability relationship and is helpful to investors looking for a quick take on a company's leverage. A high debt/equity ratio generally means that a company has been aggressive in financing its growth with debt. The higher the ratio, the greater will be the risk to the creditors and this indicates too much dependence of firm on debt capital. *The accepted ratio is taken as 2:1.*

The debt to equity ratio also depends on the industry in which the company operates. *For example*, 'Airlines and power sector companies' tend to have a debt/equity ratio above 2:1, while 'Software companies' have a negligible debt to equity ratio.

2. INTEREST COVERAGE RATIO (ICR)

The interest coverage ratio gives an idea about a company's ability to pay interest on its overdue debt.

It is computed as:

> EBIT/Interest on long-term loans

The greater the ratio, the greater the safety of the lender's interest, as it shows the borrower's ability to pay its debt expenses. On the other hand, a lower ratio shows the company in poor light, as it is going to struggle to pay its debt expenses.

3. DEBT SERVICE COVERAGE RATIO (DSCR)

It is the amount of cash flow available to meet annual interest and principal repayments on debt, including sinking fund payments. *This ratio should ideally be over 1.* That would mean there is enough income to pay the debt obligations.

DSCR is calculated as:

> Cash Flow from Operating activities after TAX/
> (Interest Payments + Instalments)

The debt service coverage ratio is an extension of the interest coverage ratio, *but it is a better ratio for solvency than ICR*. It is commonly used by banks and financial institutions for lending.

Box 5.3   DSCR

In calculating *DSCR*:

'Interest' refers to interest on long-term loans. It is easily available in the profit and loss statement.

'Instalments' include the principal repayments and lease repayments of the borrowings which are due upon the company. Instalments cannot be accurately determined from the balance sheet of the firm or from the income statement, as principal and lease repayments are not reflected in the profit and loss statement. The instalments figure is available in the *Cash Flow (from financing activities) Statement of the firm* in which they are shown under the head 'Repayment of Long-Term Borrowings'.

Significance of DSCR:

- DSCR is used by banks and financial institutions giving long-term finance to organisations.
- This ratio is calculated to gauge the capability of the organisation to repay the dues arising as a result of long-term borrowings.
- A high debt service ratio assures the lenders a regular and periodical interest income.
- On the other hand, a low debt service coverage ratio indicates insufficient earning capacity of the organisations to meet the obligations of long-term borrowings.

Solvency ratios: *All solvency ratios are expressed in number of times.*

Solvency analysis of HCC and L&T

The analysis of solvency of the companies under study is given in Table 5.15. The financials of balance sheets and profit and loss statements of companies which are used and computed from for the said analysis are given earlier in Tables 5.2 to 5.5.

Table 5.15 Solvency analysis

	Mar 13	Mar 14	Mar 15	Mar 16
(i) D/E Ratio (in times)				
HCC	2.92	2.50	1.97	1.42
L&T	0.28	0.19	0.25	0.22
Industry	1.72	1.92	1.98	2.19
(ii) Interest Coverage Ratio (in times)				
HCC	0.37	0.80	0.97	0.96
L&T	4.97	5.46	3.86	3.57
Industry	1.34	1.04	0.67	0.42

Note: Industry figures are taken from the Capitaline database (www.capitaline.com).

Analysis

- L&T has a much lower D/E ratio than both HCC and the industry average. However, HCC has a high D/E ratio. The promising side is that it has been decreasing over the years, indicating more reliance on internal financing than debt.
- Both in terms of covering its interests and capital borrowed, L&T beats both HCC and the industry by a large margin. This is due to its higher interest coverage ratio. Thus, for a lending institution, L&T would be a safe bet.

E. Market ratios

Every company strives to maximise the shareholders' value. *Shareholders' value* is directly linked to the market performance of a company, particularly in publicly held companies.

Market ratios are used to determine the market performance of company in the stock market. They indicate the market standing of the company for shareholders' wealth. These are as follows.

1. BOOK VALUE PER SHARE (BV)

It measures the net worth to be enjoyed by the ordinary shareholders of the company after all its debts are paid. In simple terms, it would be the amount of money that a holder of an equity share would get in case of liquidation of a company.

It is defined as:

$$\text{Book value per share} = \text{Net Worth}/\text{Number of Equity shares}$$

2. PRICE TO BOOK RATIO (P/B)

It is a valuation ratio expressed as a multiple (i.e. how many times a company's stock is trading per share as compared to the company's book value per share).

It is computed as:

$$\text{Price to Book value} = \text{Market price per equity share}/\text{Book value per equity share}$$

It is used by the investors to find out what they are paying for each share to the value of the firm.

3. PRICE TO EARNINGS RATIO (P/E)

The price to earnings ratio, often called the P/E ratio or P/E multiple, is a market prospect ratio that calculates the market value of a stock relative to its earnings. It shows what the market is willing to pay for a stock based on its current earnings. This ratio is widely used in valuation of a company for current investments. It is defined as:

> Price to Earnings = Market price per equity share/
> Earnings per equity share

The investors often use this ratio to evaluate what a stock's fair market value should be by predicting future earnings per share. It determines the under-valuation or over-valuation of a company.

4. DIVIDEND YIELD RATIO (D/Y)

Dividend yield ratio (D/Y ratio) refers to the amount of dividend paid per share with respect to the market price per share. It denotes how much cash flow you are getting for each rupee invested in an equity share. It is calculated as following:

> Dividend Yield Ratio (D/Y Ratio) = DPS /MPS

Market ratios: *BV per share is expressed as Rs. per share.*
P/B and P/E are expressed in number of times as they are multiples.
D/Y is expressed in percentage.

Market analysis of HCC and L&T

The market performance of the companies under study is analysed in Tables 5.16–5.18. The financials of balance sheets and profit and loss statements of companies which are used and computed from for the said analysis are given earlier in the Tables 5.2 to 5.5.

Table 5.16 Price/earnings ratio (in times)

	Mar 13	Mar 14	Mar 15	Mar 16
HCC	0.02	0.03	0.01	0.02
L&T	17.32	21.44	31.56	21.31

Table 5.17 Price/book value (in times)

	Mar 13	Mar 14	Mar 15	Mar 16
HCC	0.72	0.81	1.52	0.82
L&T	1.92	3.50	4.31	2.78

Table 5.18 Dividend yield – DY (in %)

	Mar 13	Mar 14	Mar 15	Mar 16
HCC	0.00	0.00	0.00	0.00
L&T	35.20	24.01	29.84	31.98

Analysis

- The price to earnings ratio is very high in case of L&T as compared to HCC throughout the time period. In the year 2015, the valuation of L&T seems to be very high due to dip in the earnings. So, the ratio could be telling the other side of the story as well. For HCC, the ratio has more or less remained constant, which signals less fluctuation in the market performance.
- The price to book value and dividend yield tell another story. HCC seems to be underpriced as compared to L&T. But, the EPS and the P/E show that L&T is a better proposition as investors from a long-term perspective look at growth and not dividends. Also, for short-term investors, the volatility is a deterrent.

Box 5.7 'Golden rules' of financial analysis

1 Analyse a company in totality, not in segments.
2 Compare a firm's performance with the peers, i.e. compare ratios in the industry.
3 Study the trend of ratios for analysing the growth pattern of the firm.
4 Evaluate ratios with benchmarks, if any.
5 Analyse the reasons for performance of ratios.
6 Focus on deviations in ratios.
7 Correlate the numbers with business performance.
8 Look at the management of the company for SWOT and FUTURE OUTLOOK.

Financial forecasting

Financial forecasting is the process adopted by the firms for planning their future financial activities. The forecasting process provides the means for a firm to express its goals to be achieved next year or over the long term and to ensure that they are internally consistent. It also assists the firm in identifying the asset requirements and needs for external financing.

Box 5.8   Sales forecast – 'percentage of sales method'

The principal driver of the forecasting process is generally the 'sales forecast'. Therefore, common forecasting approach used by the firms is the 'percentage of sales method'. It forecasts the balance sheet and income statement by assuming that most accounts maintain a fixed proportion of sales.

$$\text{Forecasted Sales } S1 = S0 \ (1 + g)$$

(i) Since balance sheets and income statements are largely related to sales, the forecasting process can help the firm in assessing the requirement of 'current and fixed assets' needed to support the forecasted sales level.

(ii) Accordingly, the decision about 'capital structure', i.e. how much external financing will be needed, in addition to or above the internal financing, to pay for the forecasted increase in assets can be determined.

Illustration 5.1: E Ltd., an Indian conglomerate, has finalised its results for the year 2014–15. As yearly practice, their finance department is geared up for financial forecasting of the results for 2015–16 in order to plan out their actions better for achieving next year goals. They have used the 'percentage of sales' approach, assuming 19% growth rate in sales based on net profit margin.

The Statement of Profit and Loss and Balance Sheet of E Ltd. for the year 2014–15 are given in Figures 5.6 and 5.7.

Statement of Profit and Loss of E Ltd. for the year ended 2015

(Rs. in million)

Particulars	2014–15
REVENUE	
Turnover	2,500
TOTAL REVENUE	2,500
EXPENSES	
Costs	1,900
TOTAL EXPENSES	1,900
Profit before tax	600
Tax	143
Profit after tax (PAT)	457
Dividends	321
Retained Earnings	136
Other Information:	
Forecasted Growth Rate in Sales (%)	19

Figure 5.6 Statement of profit and loss of E Ltd. for 2015

Balance Sheet of E Ltd. as at 31st March, 2015

(Rs. in million)

Particulars	2015
EQUITY AND LIABILITIES	
Shareholders Funds	
Share Capital	650
Reserves and Surplus	800
	1,450
Non-Current Liabilities	
Long-Term Borrowings	580
Current Liabilities	
Short-Term Borrowings	1,170
Trade Payables	500
	1,670

Figure 5.7 Balance sheet of E Ltd. as of 2015

TOTAL	3,700
ASSETS	
Non Current Assets	
Fixed Assets	
(i) Tangible Assets, Net	1,800
Current Assets	
Inventories	900
Trade Receivables	500
Cash and Bank Balances	500
	1,900
TOTAL	3,700

Other Information:	
External Financing Needed	446

Figure 5.7 (Continued)

Solution

The 'forecasted financial statements' for the year 2016, based on the financial statements of 2015, are given in Figures 5.8 and 5.9.

"Forecasted" Statement of Profit and Loss of E Ltd.		
		(Rs. in million)
Particulars	2014–15	2015–16
REVENUE		
Turnover	2,500	2,975
TOTAL REVENUE	2,500	2,975
EXPENSES		
Costs	1,900	2,261
TOTAL EXPENSES	1,900	2,261
Profit before tax	600	714
Tax	143	170.17
Profit after tax (PAT)	457	543.83
Dividends	321	381.99
Retained Earnings	136	161.84
Other Information:		
Forecasted Growth Rate in Sales (%)	19	

Figure 5.8 Forecasted statement of profit and loss of E Ltd. for 2016

Note: For financial forecasting, as mentioned above, 'percentage of sales' approach is used, assuming 19% growth rate in sales based on net profit margin.

"Forecasted" Balance Sheet of E Ltd.

	(Rs. in million)	
Particulars	2015	2016
EQUITY AND LIABILITIES		
Shareholders Funds		
Share Capital	650	650
Reserves and Surplus	800	962
	1,450	1,612
Non-Current Liabilities		
Long-Term Borrowings	580	580
Current Liabilities		
Short-Term Borrowings	1,170	1,170
Trade Payables	500	595
	1,670	1,765
TOTAL	3,700	3,957
ASSETS		
Non Current Assets		
Fixed Assets		
(i) Tangible Assets, Net	1,800	2,142
Current Assets		
Inventories	900	1,071
Trade Receivables	500	595
Cash and Bank Balances	500	595
	1,900	2,261
TOTAL	3,700	4,403
Other Information:		
External Financing Needed	446.2	

Figure 5.9 Forecasted balance sheet of E Ltd. for 2016

Revised balance sheet for 2016: It is clear in the above fore-casted balance sheet for the year 2016 that there is a shortage of expected funds of Rs. 446 million* to finance the assets requirements for the next year. The company has to decide now whether they will finance it from short-term or long-term financing.

Being short-term funds to be repaid at current intervals; E Ltd. decides to finance it from long-term external borrowing.

This will increase its present long-term borrowings from Rs. 580 million to Rs. 1,026 million. This will provide E Ltd. the necessary funds to finance their assets for next year's sales and growth.

*(Total assets = Rs. 4403 – Total funds = 3957)

The 'revised' forecasted balance sheet for the year 2016, after incorporating the funds requirements for the assets as discussed above, is given in Figure 5.10.

"Forecasted" Balance Sheet of E Ltd. (Revised)		
		(Rs. in million)
Particulars	2015	2016
EQUITY AND LIABILITIES		
Shareholders Funds		
Share Capital	650	650
Reserves and Surplus	800	962
	1,450	1,612
Non-Current Liabilities		
Long-Term Borrowings	580	1,026
Current Liabilities		
Short-Term Borrowings	1,170	1,170
Trade Payables	500	595
	1,670	1,765
TOTAL	3,700	4,403
ASSETS		
Non Current Assets		
Fixed Assets		
(i) Tangible Assets, Net	1,800	2,142
Current Assets		
Inventories	900	1,071
Trade Receivables	500	595
Cash and Bank Balances	500	595
	1,900	2,261
TOTAL	3,700	4,403

Figure 5.10 Revised forecasted balance sheet of E Ltd. for 2016

Points to remember

- Financial analysis is the process of analysing the financial statements and interpreting their numbers with the help of financial tools.
- Common-size analysis is also called 'vertical analysis' as financial statements are analysed on vertical basis to determine the contribution of each item of financial statement in total resources or with regard to a common base.
- Trend analysis is used to see the growth pattern of a company. Here, the base year is taken as hundred and the respective years are expressed in percentage to find out the growth trend.
- Ratio analysis is the most important tool of financial analysis. It involves computing 'financial ratios' and analysing the business performance based on them. A 'financial ratio' is a relationship between two financial elements that indicates information about business activities,
- Profitability ratios are used to analyse the profitability of a company in total and return generated for shareholders. They can be categorised as 'sales based ratios' and 'assets/ funds based ratios'. *Sales based ratios* include gross profit ratio, EBITDA ratio, EBIT ratio and PAT ratio. *Assets based ratios* include ROCE, ROE and EPS.
- DuPont analysis is used to find out the factors responsible for performance of shareholders' value in terms of 'ROE'. It is used to analyse the shareholders' wealth maximisation (SWM).
- Efficiency ratios or 'turnover ratios' are computed to find out the efficiency of the management in utilisation of resources, both long-term and short-term. It is expected that higher turnover leads to greater profits. These ratios are inventory turnover ratio and AHP, debtors' turnover ratio and ACP, creditors turnover ratio and APP, working capital turnover ratio and assets turnover ratio.
- Liquidity ratios are oriented towards evaluating the short-term viability of the company. They include current ratio, liquid ratio and super-quick ratio.
- Solvency ratios are used to find out the long-term soundness of company. These are also known as 'leverage ratios'. They include *debt ratios* which are based on the balance sheet, like

debt-equity ratio and *coverage ratios* based on the income statement, such as interest coverage ratio and debt service coverage ratio.

- Market ratios evaluate the market performance of a company with the help of ratios like book value per share, price to book ratio (P/B), price to earnings ratio (P/E multiple) and dividend-yield ratio (D/Y).
- Financial forecasting is the process adopted by the firms for planning their future financial activities. The common forecasting approach used by the firms is the 'percentage of sales method'. It forecasts the balance sheet and income statement by assuming that most accounts maintain a fixed proportion of sales.

Corporate cases

This section discusses cases from corporate India for further learning into the subject.

First, it discusses the financial analysis of select companies in 'Indian service sector' on comparative basis. Their financial issues and challenges will be different from the manufacturing/construction sector companies, like HCC and L&T as discussed above. Two sectors have been taken here, telecom and banking. **The financials of the companies have been taken from the database Capitaline (www. capitaline.com).**

Second, the 'ROE' performance of top 10 fast-moving consumer goods (FMCG) companies in India is analysed with the help of the DuPont model for shareholders' wealth. **The financials of the companies have been taken from their annual reports.**

The companies analysed here are multinational corporations (MNCs), so their analysis will be useful for the global community.

I Indian telecom sector

The telecommunication industry of India is the world's fastest growing telecom industry. In Indian telecom sector, the financial analysis of Bharti Airtel Ltd. and Idea Cellular Ltd. has been done on comparative basis. Bharti Airtel is the largest cellular provider in India and the world's third largest, single-country mobile operator. Idea Cellular is a leading GSM (Global System for Mobile communication) company in India, part of Aditya Birla group.

1. Profitability

The profitability of these companies is being discussed with the help of various sales based and assets based profitability ratios as given in the following Tables 5.19 to 5.23. Their trends are given in Figures 5.11 to 5.15.

(A) EBITDA RATIO

EBITDA margin for Airtel is much higher than of Idea's, indicating a better operating profit cushion to meet expenses, though the margins of both the companies have shown an increasing trend during the period under study.

Table 5.19 EBITDA ratio of Airtel and Idea (%)

	Mar 13	Mar 14	Mar 15	Mar 16
Airtel	32.93	33.95	38.22	38.38
Idea	23.75	28.72	32.42	33.59

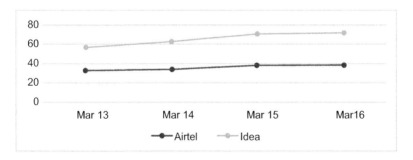

Figure 5.11 EBITDA trend of Airtel and Idea

(B) EBIT RATIO

Airtel is better placed with regard to EBIT margin as well. But, the promising part for Idea is that its margin has almost doubled during the span of four years as compared to Airtel.

Table 5.20 EBIT ratio of Airtel and Idea (%)

	Mar 13	Mar 14	Mar 15	Mar 16
Airtel	17.88	19.46	24.60	22.55
Idea	9.89	13.09	16.90	16.28

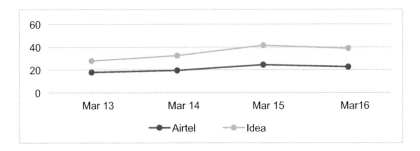

Figure 5.12 EBIT trend of Airtel and Idea

(C) NET PROFIT RATIO

Again, Airtel is better placed than Idea regarding the net profit ratio. It is a good sign for stakeholders, including the company itself for future growth. But there is also a worrying sign for Airtel: its net profit margin has reduced by half in 2016 from 2015.

Table 5.21 Net profit ratio of Airtel and Idea (%)

	Mar 13	Mar 14	Mar 15	Mar 16
Airtel	11.24	13.22	23.79	12.51
Idea	3.71	6.45	8.98	7.31

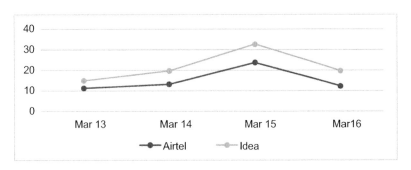

Figure 5.13 Net profit trend of Airtel and Idea

(D) RETURN ON INVESTMENT RATIO

ROI is better for Airtel than Idea. It shows better utilisation of resources and higher return on capital employed by the management as evident in profit margins above.

Table 5.22 ROI of Airtel and Idea (%)

	Mar 13	Mar 14	Mar 15	Mar 16
Airtel	11.66	12.70	14.72	11.38
Idea	8.11	10.62	12.32	9.87

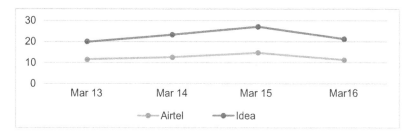

Figure 5.14 ROI trend of Airtel and Idea

(E) RETURN ON EQUITY RATIO

Here, Idea has shown more promise for shareholders' interest in the company, except the year 2013, as compared to Airtel. It is generating more earnings for its investors per rupee of the share capital employed.

Table 5.23 ROE of Airtel and Idea (%)

	Mar 13	Mar 14	Mar 15	Mar 16
Airtel	9.84	10.92	14.47	9.28
Idea	6.07	11.41	15.00	11.33

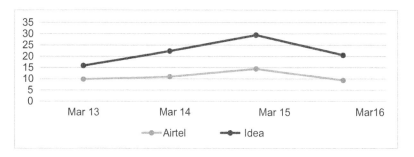

Figure 5.15 ROE trend of Airtel and Idea

Conclusion

Bharti Airtel's outlook is promising in line with the future growth potential of the sector. Its profitability at various levels has been better than Idea's. The business models of telecom operators as a whole are being stress-tested by overcapacity led hyper-competition. With several licensees operating at tariffs lower than cost, the eventual phasing out of this period of overcapacity is inevitable.

II Indian banking sector

The banking system remains the most dominant segment of the financial sector worldwide. Indian banks continue to build on their strengths under the regulator's watchful eye and hence, have emerged stronger. *The Indian banking sector, in addition to being governed by the Companies Act, 1956 and 2013, is also governed by Banking Regulation Act, 1949. Their financial statements and indicators are different from a non-banking sector company. This makes the financial analysis of their performance more challenging.*

The present study analyses the financial performance of *State Bank of India (SBI)* and *ICICI Bank* on a comparative basis, the former being in the public sector and the latter in the private sector. SBI is the largest state-owned banking and financial services company in India. ICICI Bank is a major banking and financial services organisation in India in the private sector.

1. Profitability

Profitability of the banks under study has been discussed with the help of following ratios as given below in Tables 5.24 and 5.25.

Table 5.24 Profitability ratios of SBI

	Mar 13	Mar 14	Mar 15	Mar 16
1. Net Profit Ratio (%)	11.79	7.99	8.60	6.08
2. ROE (%)	15.43	10.03	10.62	7.30
3. EPS (Rs.)	200.71	141.88	16.97	12.39
4. DPS (Rs.)	41.50	30.00	3.50	2.60

Table 5.25 Profitability ratios of ICICI Bank

	Mar 13	Mar 14	Mar 15	Mar 16
1. Net Profit Ratio (%)	20.77	22.21	22.76	18.44
2. ROE (%)	13.10	14.02	14.55	11.62
3. EPS (Rs.)	69.63	82.93	18.81	16.24
4. DPS (Rs.)	20	23	5	5

(A) NET PROFIT RATIO

ICICI Bank has a growing and higher ratio while SBI shows a fluctuating ratio during the period. The reason for the lower net profit margin of SBI is due to the increased expenses incurred by the bank in the last financial year for provisions of contingency and doubtful loans/NPA (non-performing asset). It is an area of concern for future viability, especially if this trend continues for a long period.

(B) ROE

ROE for SBI shows the same trend except the year 2013. The higher ROE of ICICI Bank indicates better returns to the shareholders.

(C) EPS

SBI's EPS in the years 2013 and 2014 was more than three time than of ICICI Bank's. In the later years, for both SBI and ICICI Bank, the EPS has been moving downwards due to reduction in profits and increase in the equity funds.

(D) DPS

Like EPS, the same trend can be observed in DPS of both the banks. But the dividend payment of SBI is better than that of ICICI Bank, hence a larger share of earnings of SBI are distributed as dividends to its shareholders as compared to that of ICICI Bank. This is generally seen as a good trend for investors with preference for current income.

2. Banking performance

As mentioned earlier, *the banking sector company's financial statements and indicators are different from a non-banking sector company.* So, in addition to the profitability ratios discussed above, 'core banking ratios' of the units under study are discussed in Tables 5.26 and 5.27. These ratios are relevant for analysing the performance of banking companies.

Table 5.26 Banking ratios of SBI

	Mar 13	Mar 14	Mar 15	Mar 16
1. Interest Expended/Interest Earned (%)	62.95	63.86	63.90	65.25
2. Credit to Deposit Ratio (%)	85.17	86.84	84.47	83.56
3. CAR (Capital Adequacy Ratio) (%)	11.22	0.00	0.00	0.00
4. Net NPA Ratio (Net Non-Performing Assets/Net Advances) (%)	2.10	2.57	2.12	3.81

Table 5.27 Banking ratios of ICICI Bank

	Mar 13	Mar 14	Mar 15	Mar 16
1. Interest Expended/Interest Earned (%)	65.40	62.71	61.22	59.76
2. Credit to Deposit Ratio (%)	99.25	100.71	104.72	105.08
3. CAR (Capital Adequacy Ratio) (%)	16.90	0.00	0.00	0.00
4. Net NPA Ratio (Net Non-Performing Assets/Net Advances) (%)	0.77	0.97	1.61	2.98

(A) INTEREST EXPENDED/INTEREST EARNED

This ratio indicates the potential of earnings of the banks by way of interests paid or received from the deposits and loans of the bank. A lower ratio of interest expended/interest earned indicates higher efficiency of bank in managing and matching interest expenditure and interest income. The reducing trend of ICICI Bank indicates higher efficiency in managing the interest expenditure and earnings. This would have a strong effect on the bottom line of the company.

(B) CREDIT TO DEPOSIT RATIO

The ratio is indicative of the percentage of funds lent by the bank out of total amount raised through deposits. Higher ratio reflects the ability of the bank to make optimal use of the available resources and hence the possibility of earning higher returns through its resources. It can be seen that a higher and increasing percentage of amount received through deposits is utilised by ICICI Bank as compared to SBI.

(C) CAPITAL ADEQUACY RATIO (CAR)

This is capital to risk weighted assets ratio which signifies the risk exposure of the bank. Its minimum limit prescribed by RBI is 9% for scheduled banks. The higher the ratio, the greater the capacity of the bank to absorb losses. As can be seen, the CAR of ICICI Bank is higher than that of SBI in 2013. A bank's capital is the cushion it provides for potential losses to its depositors. Being a private company, ICICI Bank is expected to have a higher CAR.

From 2014 onwards, both banks have shown zero CAR probably on account of two factors: *(i) the Indian banking sector is in the restructuring phase on account of bad loans, and (ii) they will need additional capital to comply with the Basel-III norms.*

(D) NET NPA RATIO

The net non-performing assets to loans (advances) ratio is used as a measure of the overall quality of the bank's loan book. Net NPAs are calculated by reducing cumulative balance of provisions outstanding at a period end from gross NPAs. A higher ratio reflects rising bad quality of loans. Thus in the long run, the bank has high chances of huge losses. ICICI Bank scores better than SBI and it can be inferred that the loans issued by ICICI Bank are quality loans and there is more probability of earning returns from those loans.

Conclusion

ICICI Bank shows higher efficiency over SBI in areas, such as managing interest expenditure, improvement in earnings, and deposits' utilisation. The public sector banks (PSBs), which are the base of the banking sector in India, account for more than 78% of the total banking industry assets. Therefore, they have to really look at cleaning the excessive non-performing assets (NPAs), with private sector banks for future stability of the banking sector in India.

III Indian fast-moving consumer goods (FMCG) sector

According to the Assocham-TechSci Research report, the fast moving consumer goods (FMCG) is the fourth largest sector in the Indian economy with a total market size of USD 49 billion in 2016. The sector is projected to grow at a CAGR of 20.6% to reach USD 103.7 billion by 2020. The FMCG industry in India, has grown rapidly over the last decade, predominantly on account of increasing income levels and changing lifestyle of Indian consumers.[1]

In the Indian FMCG sector, 'ROE' performance of top 10 companies is analysed with the help of the DuPont model for finding out whether these companies contribute to shareholders' wealth or not. These companies are chosen based on their market capitalisation as of 10 June 2013.

ITC Ltd. is an Indian diversified conglomerate with operations in five segments, namely fast moving consumer goods (FMCG), agribusiness, paperboards, paper and packaging, and hotels. Although primarily known for its vast cigarette and tobacco business, some of its major brands include Mangaldeep, Goldflake, Sunfeast and Vivel, among others. *Hindustan Unilever Ltd. (HUL)* is more than 100 years old in the sector in India with brands like Dove, Lux, Lipton and Lifebuoy, among others. *Nestle India Ltd.* is again a prominent company in the sector with a product line of soups, chocolates, baby milk powder, Maggi and so forth. *Dabur India Ltd.'s* product line includes health and beauty products like Dabur Amla hair oil, personal care and packaged foods.

Godrej Consumer Products Ltd. (GCPL) operates in three major segments – home care, personal wash and hair care. The company is into oleo chemicals which are used in a variety of applications including personal care (hair care, skin care, oral care, cosmetics), home care (laundry detergents) and pharmaceuticals. *Colgate-Palmolive India Ltd.* is active mainly in the oral and dental care category. *GlaxoSmithKline Consumer Healthcare Ltd.'s* portfolio includes Horlicks, Boost, Viva and others. *P&G Hygiene and Health Care Ltd'.s* core business is manufacturing, marketing and distribution of healthcare and feminine hygiene products, such as Vicks, the healthcare brand and Whisper, feminine hygiene brand. *Marico Ltd.'s* brands include Parachute, Saffola, Nihar and others. *Emami Ltd.'s* core business is health care and beauty products, like the Zandu range of products.

DuPont analysis of these companies is given in Table 5.28.

Table 5.28 Competitive DuPont analysis of FMCG companies for 2012

Rank	Name	Market capitalisation (Rs. in crores)	Total assets turnover	Net profit margin (%)	Equity multiplier	ROE (%)
1	ITC	1,51,078	0.69	24	2.01	33
2	HUL	67,858	2.12	12	3.12	79
3	Nestle India	39,819	1.62	13	2.87	60
4	Dabur India	18,632	1.32	12	2.18	35
5	GCPL	13,335	0.87	19	1.42	23
6	CP*	12,764	2.42	16	2.59	100
7	GSKCH**	9,842	1.05	16	1.88	32
8	P&G	9,778	1.49	14	1.26	26
9	Marico	9,078	1.52	8	2.29	29
10	Emami	6,836	1.26	18	1.66	38

Source: Companies' Annual Reports

Note: 1 crore = 10 million

* Colgate-Palmolive
** Glaxo SmithKline

Ranking and weight based on the DuPont scores

The companies were ranked on each of the four scores and a weight was assigned to them based on their ranking. The lowest weight indicates the highest rank.

Rank as per Market Cap	Company	Ranking as per Total Asset Turnover	Ranking as per Net Profit Margin	Ranking as per Equity Multiplier	Ranking as per ROE	Total Score	Final Ranking
1	ITC	10	1	6	6	23	5
2	HUL	2	9	1	1	14	2
3	Nestle	3	7	2	2	15	3
4	Dabur	6	8	5	5	24	6
5	GCPL	9	2	9	9	30	9
6	CP	1	5	3	3	10	1
7	GSKCH	8	4	7	7	26	7
8	P&G	5	6	10	10	30	10
9	Marico	4	10	4	4	26	8
10	Emami	7	3	8	8	22	4

Analysis

- It can be inferred that Colgate-Palmolive, although sixth in the ranking as per market capitalisation, ranks the highest in terms of 'shareholders wealth maximisation'. It is an ideal investment for shareholders even during weak market conditions.

Conclusion

It is clear that FMCG companies are usually zero/low debt companies with high reserves and surplus. They are growth companies and hence are stable companies. Therefore, they are considered ideal for long-term investment by shareholders.

Note

1 Assocham & TechSci Research, Indian FMCG Market 2020, www. techsciresearch.com/admin/gall_content/2016/11/2016_11$thumbimg1 02_Nov_2016_004628313.pdf (accessed on 1 June 2017).

Part III

Cost accounting and management

6 Cost concepts and classification

'Financial accounting', discussed in the last section, is external in nature and primarily aims at financial reporting and analysis of financial statements. '**Cost accounting**' is internal in nature and involves the appraisal of the cost structure of a business. It collects information about the costs incurred by various activities, assigns them to products and services (the cost objects), evaluates the efficiency of cost usage, and leads to cost control. Cost accounting is mostly concerned with providing the details of where a company earns and loses money, and thereby rationalising the resources for future viability. It supplements and supports financial accounting by providing the necessary cost information.

Cost accounting

Cost accounting is the 'process of accounting for costs'. It is a 'rational procedure followed by accountants for accumulating cost and assigning such costs to specific products or services for their pricing and effective management action'. *For example*, cost accounting is used to compute the unit cost of a manufacturer's product in order to report the cost of inventory on its 'balance sheet' and the cost of goods sold on its 'income statement'.

It assists the management by providing cost information about products or services or departments and helps in the policy formulation for day-to-day operations of an undertaking.

> Cost accounting is a management information system that analyses the past, present and future data to provide the basis for managerial decision-making. Therefore, it is used interchangeably with *'management accounting'*.

It involves the application of techniques and methods of standard costing, budgetary control, marginal costing, and variance analysis by the management for planning various business activities. The subject matter of cost accounting is the 'cost' and 'price' data.

Significance of cost accounting

Cost accounting plays a significant role in the following areas:

Product and service costing	:	Measures the costs of resources used to manufacture a product or service, and market and deliver the product to customer.
Operational control	:	Provides feedback about the efficiency and the quality of the tasks performed.
Management control	:	Provides information about the performance of managers and operating units.
Strategic control	:	Provides information about the enterprise's long run competitive performance, market scenario, customer preferences, and technological innovations.

Cost

Cost means 'the amount of expenditure (actual or notional) incurred on, or attributable to, a given thing'. In business, cost is usually a monetary valuation of (1) material, (2) labour, (3) resources, (4) efforts, and (5) opportunity forgone in the production and delivery of a good or service.

Cost not only includes cash expenses but non-cash expenses as well. All expenses are costs, but not all costs (such as those incurred in acquisition of an income-generating asset) are expenses.

> **Cost:** 'Actual expenditure + Notional expenditure'

Elements of cost

There are three key elements of cost: **(i) material, (ii) labour** and **(iii) expenses,** which are used in determining the cost of a product or service. They can be further divided into 'direct' and 'indirect' according to the contribution to the main product.

(i) Direct material is one which forms an integral part of the product, like raw material. *Indirect material* would be the additional material used for product, such as lubricants.

> **Examples**
>
> Cotton in textiles industry, steel used to make automobiles or primary packing material like wrapper, card boxes are 'direct material'. Oil and lubricants, printing and stationery material used for the final delivery of product are 'indirect material'.

(ii) Direct labour takes an active part in the production process of goods and services, whereas *indirect labour* is the supporting staff which carry out tasks incidental to providing goods and services.

> **Examples**
>
> Engineers in the plant, teachers in the school, a branch manager in a bank and a CEO of the company are 'direct labour'. Wages of storekeepers and commission paid to salesmen come under 'indirect labour'.

(iii) Direct expenses are 'chargeable expenses' to the product, other than the direct material and direct labour which are directly incurred on a specific product or job. *Indirect expenses* are 'overheads'. They could be further categorised into *manufacturing overheads*, *office overheads* or/and *selling overheads*.

> **Examples**
>
> Cost of hiring special machinery for a job, cost of transport to the job site are 'direct expenses'. All expenses other than direct at any level of organisation are classified as 'overheads'.

Illustration 6.1: A company manufactures and retails clothing. Group the costs listed below into the following classification:

    (a) Direct material
    (b) Direct labour
    (c) Direct expenses
    (d) Indirect production costs
    (e) Selling and distribution costs
    (f) Administration costs.

Solution

1. Telephone rental plus metered calls	Administration costs
2. Wages of security guards for factory	Indirect production costs
3. Parcels sent to customers	Selling and distribution costs
4. Wages of operatives in cutting department	Direct labour
5. Wages of storekeepers in materials store	Indirect production costs
6. Chief accountant's salary	Administration costs
7. Cost of advertising on television	Selling and distribution costs
8. Lubricants for sewing machines	Indirect production costs
9. Floppy disks for general office computer	Administration costs
10. Market research undertaken	Selling and distribution costs
11. Carriage on purchase of raw materials	Direct expenses

Table 6.1 Industry-wise classification of cost units

S. No.	Industry	Cost units
1.	Furniture, ship building, automobile	Number of items
2.	Electricity companies	Kwh/kWh (Kilowatt hour)
3.	Transport companies	per passenger-km
4.	Steel and cement	per tonne of steel made per tonne of cement produced

Cost unit

A cost unit is the 'quantitative unit' of a product or service, in relation to which cost is ascertained. It refers to the unit of output in relation to which costs are incurred by a cost centre. It is a useful measurement of costs for comparative purposes.

Different industries used different units of cost for measurement. The examples of cost units used in various industries are given in Table 6.1.

Cost centres

Cost centres refer to the 'segments of activity' or 'area of responsibility' for which costs are accumulated. It can be a person, location or item of equipment for which cost may be ascertained and used for the purpose of cost control. In simple words, a cost centre is any unit of the organisation to which costs can be separately attributed.

From a *functional point of view*, cost centres are categorised into:

(a) Production cost centres (where the production or the actual job is carried on)
(b) Service cost centres (the support staff of an organisation).

Examples:

Production cost centres: Production department, factory, site a machine or group of machines with in a department or a work group etc.

   Service cost centres: Office place, human staff, transport department, commissioning agents, etc.

Box 6.1   Cost centres and 'cost control'

Cost centres are used for 'cost control'. Cost control is ensured by making cost centres responsible for their activities and processes. Different persons are allotted different cost centres and each person is held responsible for the control of cost of that centre under him. These centres are called 'responsibility centres' and the process is called 'responsibility accounting'.

Process of costing

Costing is a three-stage process, whereby *first* costs about the product or service are collected from various sources and assigned based on the specification to the cost object for price-determination.

Second, if there is over- or under-costing, then gap analysis is required. The control mechanism is sought to take the necessary corrective actions for future. *Third*, if the business is planning something new, either diversification or innovation, it identifies the relevant cost for decision-making. The time and efforts involved in the process depends on various factors, such as type of industry, the business model, scale of transactions, volume of turnover and so forth. These three stages are expressed in the following box.

Box 6.2   Process of costing

(a) Score Keeping ————————▶ Cost Ascertainment
(b) Attention Directing ————————▶ Cost Control
(c) Problem Solving ————————▶ Cost for Decision-making

Cost classification

The cost is classified on the basis of factors, like nature, traceability of direct/indirect, controllability, managerial decisions and so forth. The different types of costs are discussed below.

1. On the basis of traceability

(a) *Direct cost:* It is a cost that can be specifically identified with a cost object. This includes direct material, direct labour and direct expenses.

(b) *Indirect cost:* It is a cost which cannot be directly identified with a single product or service. It is incurred for several products. These are the 'common cost' of support centres. It includes all indirect material, indirect labour and indirect expenses incurred at various levels. They are commonly referred to as 'overheads'.

Conversion cost: It is the cost of transforming direct materials into the finished products exclusive of direct material cost.
  It is calculated as:

  Cost of Direct labour +
  Direct expenses +
  Factory overheads

---

2. On the basis of association

(a) *Product cost:* It is a cost which is associated with unit of output. It is 'absorbed by' the units produced. It consists of direct materials, direct labour and factory overheads. It is regarded as a part of inventory. It is shown in the Balance Sheet.

(b) *Period cost:* It is a cost which is associated with time period rather than the unit of output or manufacturing activity. These are called 'period costs' because they are charged as expense in the period in which they are incurred. They are divided into two categories: *administrative costs* and *selling costs*. They are shown in the income statement.

3. On the basis of nature

(a) **Fixed cost:** This cost remains constant at different levels of output. It is independent of any changes in the volume of activity. *For example*, employees' salaries on monthly basis, insurance charges, depreciation on straight line method and so forth. Fixed cost can be further sub-categorised into:

   (i) *Committed fixed cost* – It is unavoidable in the short run if the organisation has to function, like depreciation, rent, pay and allowances of staff and so forth.
   (ii) *Discretionary fixed cost* – It is the cost which is set at a fixed amount for specific time periods by management in the budgeting process, like research and development costs, advertising expenses.

(b) **Variable cost:** This cost changes with the changes in the volume of output. It changes in direct proportion to changes in volume of activity. *For example*, electricity and power expenses, raw material used.

(c) **Semi-variable cost:** It refers to the cost which is partly fixed and partly variable. *For example*, depreciation charged initially on the straight-line method (SLM) is fixed cost, whereas depreciation charged in later years on the written-down value method (WDV) is variable cost. *Another example* could be salary inclusive of fixed component and incentive-based variable component.

4. On the basis of controllability

(a) **Controllable cost:** This cost can be influenced by the action of a manager of a cost centre and is dependent on his activity.

(b) **Uncontrollable cost:** It is a cost that is beyond the control of a manager.

The *distinction between controllable and uncontrollable cost* is not very clear. That's why it is usually left to individual judgement. Some expenditure which may be uncontrollable in the short term may not be so in the long term. Therefore, a careful analysis is required to be done before classifying cost on the basis of controllability for managerial decision-making.

5. On the basis of decision-making

(a) *Out-of-pocket cost:* It is cost that will result in a necessary outflow of cash. This cost is relevant in specific decision-making situations, *like* 'make or buy' decision.

(b) **Shut down cost:** It is the cost of an idle plant. *Example:* fixed costs, such as rent and insurance of non-functional plant will have to be incurred for the stated term.

(c) **Sunk cost:** Sunk costs are historical or past costs. *Example:* investment in plant and machinery before operations is a prime example of such costs. Since sunk costs cannot be altered by later decisions, they are irrelevant for capital investment decision-making.

(d) **Opportunity cost:** It refers to the advantage, in measurable terms, which has been forgone on account of not using the available resources. It is the return that can be earned by investing funds in assets similar to those which are owned by the firm. In simple words, it is the cost of next best alternative (return) sacrificed in decision-making. *For example*, if a company owns a vacant premise with a market value of Rs. 1 million and they use it for the office, Rs. 1 million is considered an opportunity cost associated with the decision to use the said premise for the business.

Components of total cost

Total cost of a product is computed as given below.

1. Prime cost

Prime cost is the direct cost, which is also known as basic or flat cost.

> Direct material + direct labour + direct expenses

2. Factory cost

Factory overheads are added to prime cost to get 'factory cost'. Factory overheads include *cost of indirect material, indirect labour,* and *indirect expenses of the factory.* The cost is also known as works cost, production or manufacturing cost.

> Prime cost + Works or factory overheads

3. Office cost or cost of production

Office overheads are added to factory cost to get 'office cost'. Office overheads include *cost of indirect material, indirect labour*, and *indirect expenses incurred at the office*.

> Factory cost + Office and administrative overheads

4. Total cost/cost of sales

Finally, selling and distribution overheads are added to office cost to get 'Cost of sales'. Selling and distribution overheads include *cost of indirect material, indirect labour*, and *indirect expenses of selling and distribution divisions*.

> Office cost + Selling and distribution overheads

Cost sheet

The cost sheet is the 'cost statement' which is prepared internally to show the cost structure of the total output produced during the period.

It provides the detailed cost in respect of cost centres and cost units after collecting data from various sources. Thus, it facilitates the price determination of products.

A specimen of a cost sheet is given in Figure 6.1.

COST SHEET
for the year ended 31 March 20XX

Direct material +	
Direct labour +	
Direct expenses	
Prime Cost / Direct Cost	
Add: Factory overheads	
Factory Cost	
Add: Office overheads	
Office Cost	
Add: Selling and distribution overheads	
Cost of Sales / Total Cost	

Figure 6.1 Cost sheet

Illustration 6.2: Sweet and Nuts Ltd. is a chocolate making company. It supplies the following information for the year ended 31–03–2015. Prepare a Cost Statement.

	Rs.
Cocoa and other materials used	40,000
Factory wages	35,000
Freight inwards	12,500
Factory rent and taxes	7,250
Plant manager's salary	20,000
Power expenses	9,500
Office staff salaries	30,000
Other office expenses	20,500
Promotional expenses	15,000

Solution

COST SHEET
for the year ended 31–03–2015

	Rs.	
Materials used	40,000	
Factory wages	35,000	
Freight inwards	12,500	
Prime Cost		87,500
Add: *Factory overheads*		
Plant manager's salary	20,000	
Factory rent and taxes	7,250	
Power expenses	9,500	
Factory Cost	36,750	1,24,250
Add: *Office overheads*		
Office staff salaries	30,000	
Other office expenses	20,500	
Cost of Production	50,500	1,74,750
Add: *Selling and distribution overheads*		
Promotional expenses	15,000	
Cost of Sales/Total Cost		1,89,750

Methods of costing

The methods used for the ascertainment of cost of production primarily depend on the manufacturing process and the nature of industry. Basically, there are two methods of costing: **job costing and process costing.**

1. Job costing

Job costing is a form of specific order costing which is used in those business concerns where production is carried out as per specific order and customer specifications, that is where production is not highly repetitive and each order is of comparatively short duration.

This method of costing is very popular in enterprises engaged in *house building, machinery production* and *repair.*

In all these cases, an account is opened for each job and all appropriate expenditure is charged thereto.

Job costing is further extended to *batch costing* **and** *contract costing.*

Box 6.3   Batch costing and contract costing

Batch costing

It is an extension of job costing. 'A quantity of identical articles when produced as a single job is termed as a batch'. It is suitable in the following situations:

(i)   When customer's annual requirement is to be supplied in uniform quantities over the year.

(ii) When certain physical characteristics, like size, colour, taste, quality, etc. are required uniformly over a collection of units, for example garments of the same colour or size, sports goods of same measurement. In industries where batch costing is employed, an important decision is the determination of the 'optimum quantity of batch'.

Contract Costing

Contract costing does not differ in principle from job costing. 'A contract is a big job while a job is a small contract'. Each customer order is of long-term duration.

It is mainly applied in *civil construction, engineering*, and *ship building*. This method of contract costing is used in contracts for which substantial time is taken to complete the contract and the project extends into different accounting periods.

2. Process costing

This method is used in those industries where a product passes through different stages of production and each stage is distinct and well-defined. It helps in ascertaining the cost of production at each stage by opening separate account for each process.

This system of costing is suitable for the extractive industries: chemical manufacture, paints, oil, gas, paper, soap making and so forth.

Techniques of costing

In its functioning, cost accounting uses several tools and techniques such as:

1. Budgetary control

'Budgetary control' is used as a tool for planning and control. Through this, the management is able to assess the performance of each and every individual/unit/department in the organisation.

2. Standard costing

Standard costing is one of the important techniques of cost control. It is a system under which the cost of the product is determined in advance on certain predetermined standards. It helps in enhancing the efficiency of operations and taking corrective actions for future by 'variance analysis'.

3. Marginal costing

Marginal costing is a technique of costing which is concerned with changes in costs resulting from changes in the volume of production. Here, those expenses are allocated to production which arise as a result of production, that is *direct material, direct labour, direct variable expenses* and *variable overheads*.

This technique is commonly used in 'manufacturing industries with varying levels of output'. It does not recognise fixed overheads, as their inclusion may give misleading results where production varies. The managerial decision-making for utilisation of resources is assessed with the help of marginal costing.

4. Absorption costing

Absorption costing is the practice of 'charging all costs' – both variable and fixed to operations, products or processes. It is not restricted to any specific industry.

Points to remember

- Cost accounting is the 'process of accounting for costs'. It is a rational procedure followed by accountants for accumulating cost and assigning such costs to specific products or services for their pricing and effective management decision.
- Cost accounting is a management information system that analyses past, present and future data to provide the basis for managerial decision-making. Therefore, it is used interchangeably with 'management accounting'.
- Cost means 'the amount of expenditure (actual or notional) incurred on, or attributable to, a given thing'. Cost does not include only cash expenses but non-cash expenses as well.
- There are three key elements of cost: *material, labour* and *expenses*, which are used in determining the cost of a product or service. They can be further divided into 'direct' and 'indirect' according to the contribution to the main product.
- Cost unit is the 'quantitative unit' of a product or service, in relation to which cost is ascertained.
- Cost centres refer to the segments of activity or area of responsibility for which costs are ascertained and used for the purpose of cost control. From a functional point of view, cost centres are categorised into *production cost centres* and *service cost centres*.
- *Direct cost* can be specifically identified with a cost object and indirect cost cannot be directly identified with a single product or service. They are the common cost of support centres.

- *Product cost* is associated with unit of output. It is regarded as a part of inventory. *Period cost* is associated with time period rather than the unit of output or manufacturing activity. They are administrative costs and selling costs.
- *Fixed cost* remains constant at different levels of output. *Variable cost* changes with the changes in the volume of output.
- *Controllable cost* can be influenced by the action of a manager of a cost centre, but *uncontrollable cost* is beyond the control of a manager.
- Other costs include (1) *out-of-pocket cost* that will result in a necessary outflow of cash, (2) *shut down cost* which is the cost of an idle plant, (3) *sunk cost* that is historical or past cost and (4) *opportunity cost* which refers to the cost of next best alternative sacrificed.
- Total cost of a product consists of *prime cost, factory cost, office cost* and *cost of sales.*
- 'Job costing' is a form of specific order costing, such as house building or machinery production. 'Batch costing' is an extension of job costing. 'Contract costing' does not differ in principle from job costing. *A contract is a big job while a job is a small contract.*
- 'Process costing' is used in those industries where a product passes through different stages of production and each stage is distinct and well-defined, for example chemical manufacture and paints.
- In its functioning, cost accounting uses several tools and techniques such as budgetary control, standard costing, marginal costing and absorption costing.

7 Budgeting

Budgeting is used by the business organisations not only for planning the activities and forecasting but also as a financial control tool. Budgets are prepared by different departments to monitor their activities and to review the performance for ensuring that it meets the targets. Budgets cover a specific period of time: a year, quarter and/or month. Though budgeting uses historical information, its objective is to plan the activities in future.

Budgeting

Budgeting is the process followed by the management in performing its functions of planning, organising, and controlling the operations effectively with the help of ' budgets'. Budgeting is the act of building budgets and with their help coordinates the various departments of the firm.

Budget

A budget is 'a plan expressed in numerical or financial terms'. It is prepared in advance for a future period. Budget is a formal statement of the financial resources set aside for achieving specific objectives in a given period of time. Examples are an advertising budget, sales budget and purchase budget.

> A plan quantified in monetary terms prepared and approved prior to a define period of time usually showing planned income to be generated and/or expenditure to be incurred during the period and the capital to be employed to attain a given objective.
> —Chartered Institute of Management Accountants (CIMA), England

Budgetary control

Budgetary control is a tool used by the management to allocate responsibility and authority in planning for future and to develop a basis of measurement to evaluate the efficiency of operations. It helps the management to control the activities of an organisation by continuous comparison of actual performance with the budgeted performance. Basically, budgetary control is used for 'business planning and control'.

Process of budgetary control

The process of budgetary control involves assigning responsibility to various centres or departments headed by the chief officer. These assume the role of 'responsibility centres' with the required authority whose performance is evaluated at the end of the period by budgeting.

Box 7.1 Responsibility centre

A *responsibility centre* is a functional unit headed by a manager who is responsible for the activities of that unit. There are four types of responsibility centres:

a) *Revenue centres.* These are the organisational units whose performance is evaluated by the amount of revenue (output in monetary terms) generated by them. Example: sales unit.
b) *Expense centres/Cost centres.* These units are measured in terms of resources (inputs in monetary terms) spent by them. Example: accounts department, repairs and maintenance department.
c) *Profit centres.* The performance of these units is measured by the difference between revenues (outputs) and expenditure (inputs). Inter-departmental sales are often made using 'transfer prices'.
d) *Investment centres.* These units are evaluated by comparing their outputs with the assets employed in producing them, that is ROI concept is used here.

The 'process' of organising and administering a budget system consists of the following steps:

a) *Budget centres*: The units for which budgets are required need to be identified.

b) *Budget period*: The period for which a budget is prepared is defined. The budget period depends upon the nature of the business and the control techniques. For example, a seasonal industry will budget for each season, while a construction industry requiring long periods to complete project will budget for four, five or even larger number of years.

c) *Key factor*: It is the most important factor for the success of an organisation. It is also called 'limiting factor'. The extent of influence of this factor must first be evaluated in order to ensure that the budget targets are met. For example, in the petroleum refining industry, the key factor would be 'supply of crude oil'. Similarly, in the automobile industry, the sales demand would be the most important factor.

d) *Budget committee*: A committee is to be constituted consisting of various functional heads of the organisation (Production, Sales, Finance, Personnel, etc.), with the managing director as chairman. The committee will coordinate the preparation of budgets and ensure the timely completion of the process. Every part and function of the organisation should be represented on the committee for a meaningful result.

e) *Budget controller*: Though the Chief Executive is ultimately responsible for the budget programme, some other senior executive can also be designated as the budget controller or director.

f) *Budget manual*: The document which lists all the details about the budget process including the chart of the organisation is prepared and communicated to all.

g) *Comparison of results*: The actual performance is analysed and compared with the budgeted figures for gap analysis.

h) *Remedial measures*: The necessary corrective actions are taken to correct the deviations and improve the performance in future.

Budgets are the individual activities or objectives of a department whereas **budgeting** is the formulation of budgets. **Budgetary control** is the process of the establishment of various budgets for the enterprise for the future period and then comparing the actual results with the budgeted figures for finding out the deviations and taking necessary corrective actions.

So, a budget is a 'mean' and budgetary control is the 'end result'.

Types of budgets

Budgets can be categorised in various ways according to time, function and so forth. These are discussed as follows.

A. On the basis of time

1. Long-term budgets

These budgets are oriented towards long-term growth and expansion of the business. They range from a period of five to ten years.

> *Examples*: capital expenditure budget, research and development budget, etc.

2. Short-term budgets

These are meant for planning working capital requirements and are generally for one or two years.

> *Example*: operative expenses budget come under this category.

3. Current budgets

These budgets require immediate focus. The period for these budgets is usually of months and weeks.

> *Example*: Budgeting for tackling an immediate labour problem is a part of current budgeting.

B. On the basis of functions

1. Functional budgets

They relate to various function of the firm, such as sales, production, cash and so forth. Following budgets are prepared under functional budgets:

- Sales budget
- Production budget
- Material budget
- Labour budget

- Administrative cost budget
- Cash budget.

Box 7.2   The chain of budget preparation

The flow in which various functional budgets are prepared by the management is depicted in Figure 7.1 and explained below.

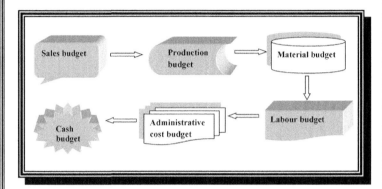

Figure 7.1 Budget flow

First, the *sales budget* is prepared to forecast a realistic sales for the next period. This is prepared in units of each product and also in sales value.

Next, the *production budget* is set in quantitative terms according to the sales budget.

Third, the *material purchases budget* is designed, geared to the production target.

Fourth, the *labour budget* is expressed both in quantitative and financial terms according to the production requirement of man-hours.

Fifth, the *administrative cost budget* is then prepared, keeping in view the estimate of total overheads on the complete operations.

Last, the **cash budget** is set summarising the receipts and payments for the period and highlighting surpluses and deficits of actual cash.

The cash budget is the most important 'financial budget' as it determines the liquidity of a firm. It is prepared to calculate budgeted cash flows (inflows and outflows) during a specific period of time.

Cash budget is useful in determining the 'optimum level of cash' to avoid excessive cash or shortage of cash in future and thereby helps in maintaining a desired level of cash in all conditions.

Being a part of master budget, the following activities are included in a cash budget:

(i)   Cash receipts
(ii) Cash payments
(iii) Administrative and selling expenses

2. Master budget

This budget is very important for the top management of the company because it is the budget for the whole organisation. It covers the complete information of an organisation in a summarised manner. It presents the 'comprehensive picture' of the plans of organisation and sets the course of action of how the plans will be accomplished.

C. On the basis of flexibility

1. Fixed budget

The fixed budget is a rigid budget, as it does not change with the change in the output or any activity. There is no change in the budget level of a fixed budget. It is also called a 'static budget'.

2. Flexible budget

This budget is flexible enough to adapt the changes which occur due to change in the output or any other factor. In a competitive environment, flexible budget is the 'need of the hour'. It is also suitable in following cases:

- New or growing organisations
- Firms with seasonal nature of demand
- Industries based on change of fashion
- Firms which are on an expansion or diversification spree.

Example: Following is an example of 'factory overheads budget' under fixed and flexible conditions.

Factory Overheads Budget 'FIXED'	Rs.	Factory Overheads Budget 'FLEXIBLE'	Rs.
Production: 1,20,000 units		Production: 1,50,000 units	
Variable overheads: Indirect Material @ Rs. 2 per unit	2,40,000	*Variable overheads:* Indirect Material @ Rs. 2.2 per unit (20 paise extra as premium for shortage of material)	3,30,000
Indirect Labour @ Re 1 per unit	1,20,000		
Fixed overheads: Maintenance Supervision Engineering Services	10,000 80,000 50,000	Indirect Labour @ Rs. 1.1 per unit (10 paise extra for additional shift)	1,65,000
Total Factory Overheads	5,00,000	*Fixed overheads:* Maintenance Supervision Engineering Services	10,000 80,000 50,000
		Total Factory Overheads	6,35,000

Note: In this example, 'fixed budget' is for fixed level of current production of 1,20,000 units. It does not consider any change in the demand or conditions. But 'flexible budget' will change with the additional demand of 30,000 units and consider all the changes, like when there is an additional demand of 30,000 units, it impacts both the material and labour cost for various reasons. Thus, the budgeted figure goes up under dynamic conditions.

The fixed budget and flexible budget are differentiated in Table 7.1.

Table 7.1 Distinction between fixed budget and flexible budget

	Fixed Budget	*Flexible Budget*
Nature	It is prepared for a fixed level of activity	It is redrafted as per the changed circumstances
Rigidity	Remains same irrespective of change in activity	Changes with the change in activity
Cost classification	Costs are generally not classified	Costs are studied as per their nature, i.e. fixed, variable, semi – variable
Cost control	It is used as an effective tool to control costs	Due to its limitations, it is not used as cost control tool
Forecasting	Forecasting of accurate results is difficult	Forecasting is accurate

Box 7.3   Zero Based Budgeting (ZBB)

ZBB is not based on the incremental approach of traditional costing. It is the process of starting from 'scratch'.

The normal technique of budgeting is to use previous year's cost levels as a base for preparing this year's budget. Here, every year is taken as a new year and the previous year is not taken as a base. The budget for this year has to be justified according to the present situation. 'Zero' is taken as a base and likely future activities are decided according to the present situation.

It involves a detailed cost-benefit analysis for each centre. ZBB is particularly done for responsibility centres in which there is relatively high proportion of discretionary costs. ZBB is a planning, resource allocation and control tool.

The Indian scene

ZBB has been adopted by the departments of the central government from 1 April 1987. PSUs use it in revenue budgets. The budget is prepared annually but ZBB is done once in five years.

Essentials of good budgeting

Following are some of the best practices that can transform budgeting into a value-added activity:

1   **Strategic linkage.** Budgeting must be linked to strategic planning since strategic decisions have financial implications.
2   **Complete process.** Budgeting procedures should be followed in total. Their assessments should include historical trends, competitive analysis and other procedures that might affect the budgeting process.
3   **Time allocation.** The budgeting process should minimise the time spent in collecting and gathering the data and spend more time generating information for strategic decision-making.
4   **Management by objectives (MBO).** All the departments should agree upon the common organisation objectives before you spend time preparing detailed budgets. They all should lead to achieving these objectives.
5   **Automation.** Automate the collection and consolidation of budgets within the entire organisation. The budgeting system should be easily accessible to all for the necessary updating.

6 **Continued activity.** Budgeting should be a continuous process in order to accept changes quickly and easily.
7 **Involvement of all.** The budgeting process should have the active participation of all in the organisation. It should invite lower level managers as well and provide some form of fiscal control to them over what is going on.
8 **Data warehouse.** There should be a proper data warehouse for financial systems that can be used for both financial reporting and budgeting.

Case lets of different budgets

1. Manufacturing overhead budget

From the following average figures of previous quarters, prepare a manufacturing overhead budget for the quarter ending 31 March 2015. The budgeted output during this quarter is 2,000 units.

	Rs.
Fixed overhead	20,000
Variable overheads	10,000 (varying @ Rs. 5 per unit)
Semi-variable overheads	10,000 (40% fixed and 60% varying @ Rs. 3 per unit)

Solution

Manufacturing overheads budget for the quarter ending 31 March 2015

		Rs.
Fixed overheads		20,000
Variable overheads (2,000 × Rs. 5)		10,000
Semi-variable overheads		
Fixed	4,000	
Variable (2,000 × Rs. 3)	6,000	
		10,000
Total Overhead Costs		40,000

2. Sales overhead budget

Prepare a sales overhead budget from the estimates given below.

	Rs.
Advertisement	2,500
Salaries of the Field Sales department	5,000
Expenses of Desk Sales department	1,500
Desk Salesmen's Salaries	7,000

Commission to desk salesmen is 1% on their sales.

Field salesmen's commission is 10% on their sales and expenses are 5% on their sales.

The sales during the period (October–December, 2015) were estimated as follows.

Desk sales	Field sales
50,000	10,000
80,000	20,000
1,00,000	40,000

Solution

Sales overhead budget for the period ending October–December 2015

	Estimated Sales		
	Rs. 60,000	Rs. 1,00,000	Rs. 1,40,000
Fixed Overheads:			
Advertisement	2,500	2,500	2,500
Salaries of Field Sales Department	5,000	5,000	5,000
Expenses of Desk Sales Department	1,500	1,500	1,500
Desk Salesmen's Salaries	7,000	7,000	7,000
	16,000	16,000	16,000
Variable Overheads:			
Desk Salesmen's Commission @ 1% on sales	500	800	1,000
Field Salesmen's Commission @ 10%	1,000	2,000	4,000
Expenses 5%	500	1,000	2,000
	2,000	3,800	7,000
Total Sales Overheads	18,000	19,800	23,000

3. Cash budget

Prepare a cash budget for the months of October, November and December 2016 on the basis of the following information.

1   Income and expenditure forecasts:

Month	Credit Sales Rs.	Credit Purchases Rs.	Wages Rs.	Production Expenses Rs.	Office Expenses Rs.	Selling Expenses Rs.
August	60,000	30,000	10,000	4,000	2,000	4,000
September	65,000	35,000	8,000	2,000	1,000	5,000
October	70,000	32,000	10,000	5,000	2,500	4,500
November	58,000	35,000	8,000	3,000	2,000	3,000
December	62,000	40,000	9,000	4,000	1,000	4,000

2   Cash balance on 1 October 2016 = Rs. 10,000.
3   Machine of Rs. 20,000 is due for delivery in December, payable 20% on delivery and the balance after two months.
4   Advance tax of Rs. 8,000 each is payable in April, July and October.
5   Period of credit (i) allowed by suppliers – two months and (ii) to customers – one month.
6   Credit in payment of office and selling expenses – one month.

Solution

Cash budget for the period ending October–December 2016

Particulars	October 2016	November 2016	December 2016
	Rs.	Rs.	Rs.
Opening Balance	10,000	16,000	33,000
Estimated Cash Receipts:			
Debtors (Credit Sales)	65,000	70,000	58,000
	75,000	86,000	91,000
Estimated Cash Payments:			
Credit – (Credit purchases)	30,000	35,000	32,000
Wages	10,000	8,000	9,000

(Continued)

(*Continued*)

Particulars	October 2016	November 2016	December 2016
	Rs.	Rs.	Rs.
Production Expenses	5,000	3,000	4,000
Office expenses	1,000	2,500	2,000
Selling expenses	5,000	4,500	3,000
Machine – payment on delivery			4,000
Advance Tax	8,000		
Total	59,000	53,000	54,000
Closing Balance	**16,000**	**33,000**	**37,000**

Points to remember

- Budgeting is the act of building budgets and with their help coordinates the various departments of the firm.
- A budget is 'a plan expressed in numerical or financial terms'. It is prepared in advance for a future period.
- 'Budgetary control' is a tool for the management to allocate responsibility and authority in planning for future and to develop a basis of measurement to evaluate the efficiency of operations. It is used for 'business planning and control'.
- A responsibility centre is a functional unit headed by a manager who is responsible for the activities of that unit. There are four types of responsibility centres: revenue centre, cost centre, profit centre and investment centre.
- The process of budgetary controls consists of following steps: (i) budget centres, (ii) budget period, (iii) key factor, (iv) budget committee, (v) budget controller, (vi) budget manual, (vii) comparison of results and (viii) remedial measures.
- *Long-term budgets* range from a period of five to ten years, such as capital expenditure budget and R&D budget. *Short-term budgets* are for one or two years. *Current budgets* are for months and weeks.
- *Functional budgets* relate to functions of the firm, such as sales, production, cash, etc. The *master budget* is very

important for the top management of the company because it is the budget for the whole organisation.

- First, the *sales budget* is prepared, followed by *the production budget*. Then, the *material purchases budget* and *labour budget* are designed. Afterwards, the *administrative cost budget* is prepared, and finally the *cash budget* summarises the cash position.
- A *fixed budget* is a rigid budget and it does not change with the change in the output or any activity. A *flexible budget* changes due to change in the output or any other factor. In a competitive environment, flexible budget is the 'need of the hour'.
- *Zero based budgeting (ZBB)* is not based on the incremental approach of traditional costing. It is starting from 'scratch'. It involves a detailed cost-benefit analysis for each centre. ZBB is particularly done for responsibility centres in which there is relatively high proportion of discretionary costs. ZBB is a planning, resource allocation and control tool.
- Good budgeting must have practices, like linkage to strategic planning, complete process, efficient time allocation, consensus on common goals, automation of process, continuous activity, involvement of all and data warehouse.

8 Marginal costing and managerial decision-making

In managerial decision-making, the nature of cost plays a very important role. The cost that varies with the decision should be included in decision-analysis by the management. For many decisions that involve relatively small variations from existing practice and/or are for relatively limited periods of time, fixed cost is not relevant to the decision. The reason is that fixed cost cannot be changed in the short run. The variable cost assumes significance in this situation and 'Marginal costing' is applied here to know the impact of variable cost on the volume of production or output and arrive at suitable managerial decision-making.

Marginal cost

Marginal cost is the change in the total cost with the change in the quantity produced, that is it is the cost of producing an additional unit of product.

Example

A factory produces 500 chairs per annum. The cost sheet of 500 chairs is as follows:

	Rs.
Variable cost (500 × Rs. 100)	50,000
Fixed cost	10,000
Total cost	60,000

If production is increased by one unit, that is if 501 chairs are produced per annum, the cost sheet will then appear as follows:

	Rs.
Variable cost	50,100
Fixed cost	10,000
Total cost	60,100

Marginal cost per unit is, therefore, Rs. 100.

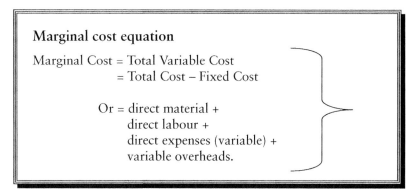

Marginal cost equation

Marginal Cost = Total Variable Cost
= Total Cost – Fixed Cost

Or = direct material +
direct labour +
direct expenses (variable) +
variable overheads.

Marginal costing

The marginal costing technique is one which makes a clear distinction between 'variable cost' and 'fixed cost'. It is used to analyse the effect of variable cost on the level of production.

Following are the key features of marginal costing:

1   **Variable cost focus:** Here, the production and sales policies are designed by the firm on the basis of variable cost.
2   **Inventory valuation:** Under marginal costing, inventory/stock for profit measurement is valued at 'marginal cost' unlike at total unit cost under absorption costing method.
3   **Contribution factor:** Marginal costing technique makes use of 'contribution' for marking various decisions. 'Contribution' is the difference between sales and marginal cost. This becomes the deciding factor for determining profitability of different products or departments.

Box 8.1   Marginal costing vs. absorption costing

Under *absorption costing* or *traditional costing*, total costs are charged to production, that is all fixed and variable costs are recovered from the production, while under *marginal costing*, only variable costs are charged to production. Fixed costs are ignored as for additional output only variable costs are incurred and fixed costs remain constant.

Cost-Volume-Profit analysis (CVP analysis)

'CVP Analysis' is a technique for studying the relationship between cost, volume and profit at different levels of sales or production.

> CVP analysis is the study of the effects on future profits of changes in fixed cost, variable cost, sales price, quantity and mix.
>
> —CIMA, London

In a narrow sense, it means 'break-even analysis' and refers to a technique of determining that level of operation at which there is no profit and no loss, that is where total revenue equals total cost. Break-even analysis is an integral and important part of marginal costing.

CVP analysis is an important tool to the management and used in various areas of decision-making of cost control, profit planning, performance evaluation and so forth. The key assumption under CVP analysis is 'costs are classified into fixed and variable cost'.

Tools of CVP analysis

To apply the CVP analysis and study the relationship between cost, volume and profit, let's understand the following tools which are used under CVP analysis:

(a) Contribution
(b) Contribution/sales (C/S) ratio or profit volume (P/V) ratio
(c) Break-even point
(d) Margin of safety

(a) Contribution

It is the difference between 'sales and variable cost'. It contributes toward fixed cost recovery.

The concept of 'contribution' helps in deciding the break-even point and profitability of products, departments etc. to perform the various activities.

It is expressed as follows:

Basic Equation: Sales = Total Cost + Profit		
Sales	=	*Total Cost + Profit*
Sales	=	*Fixed cost + Variable cost + Profit*
Contribution (i)	=	**Sales – Variable cost**
Fixed cost + Profit	=	*Sales – Variable cost*
Contribution (ii)	=	**Fixed cost + Profit**
Profit	=	**Contribution – Fixed cost**

Example:

Variable Cost	= Rs. 50000
Fixed Cost	= Rs. 30000
Sales	= Rs. 80000
So, Profit	= Sales – Total Cost (Fixed Cost + Variable Cost)
	= Rs. 80,000 – Rs. 80,000
	= 0
Contribution	= Sales – Variable Cost
	= Rs. 80,000 – Rs. 50,000
	= Rs. 30,000

(b) Contribution margin/(P/V) ratio

It is the contribution per rupee of sales. It is calculated as:

$$P/V \text{ Ratio} = \frac{\text{Contribution}}{\text{Sales}} \times 100$$

$$= \frac{\text{Sales } - \text{ Variable Costs}}{\text{Sales}} \times 100$$

A fundamental property of marginal costing system is that P/V ratio remains constant at different levels of activity. The P/V ratio is an extension of the concept of 'contribution' and useful in various managerial decisions of price determination, profit planning and so forth.

Example:

	Rs.
Sales	2,00,000
Variable Costs	80,000
Fixed Costs	40,000

$$\text{P/V Ratio} = \frac{\text{Rs. 2, 00,000 - Rs. 80,000}}{\text{Rs.2, 00,000}}.$$

$$= \quad 0.6 \text{ or } 60\%$$

Note: This ratio would remain constant at different levels of production since variable cost as a proportion to sales remain constant at various levels.

(c) Break-even point

It is the volume of sales or production where there is neither profit nor loss.

Its computation under marginal costing is given as:

$$\frac{\text{Break-even Point}}{\left(\text{of output/number of units}\right)} = \frac{\text{Fixed Cost}}{\text{Contribution per unit}}$$

$$\frac{\text{Break-even Point}}{\left(\text{of sales}\right)} = \frac{\text{Fixed Cost}}{\text{P/V Ratio}}$$

> At the break-even point, profit is zero and contribution (sales-variable cost) is equal to fixed cost, as shown above.

$$\text{Unit for a desired profit} = \frac{\text{Fixed Cost + Desired Profit}}{\text{Contribution per unit}}$$

Desired Profit = Units × Contribution per unit – Fixed Cost

$$\text{Sales for a desired profit} = \frac{\text{Fixed Cost} + \text{Desired Profit}}{\text{P/V Ratio}}$$

$$\text{Desired Profit} = \text{Sales} \times \text{P/V Ratio} - \text{Fixed Cost}$$

> To determine 'units for desired profit or sales for a desired profit', the amount of desired profit should be added to fixed cost. This is expressed above.

Illustration 8.1: From the following data, calculate:

(a) P/ V Ratio
(b) Break- even sales
(c) Sales required to earn profit of Rs. 50,000

Fixed Expenses	= Rs. 8, 000
Variable Cost per unit:	
Direct Material	= Rs. 5
Direct Labour	= Rs. 2
Direct Overheads	= 50% of Direct Labour
Selling price per unit	= Rs. 10

Solution

(a)

$$\text{P/V Ratio} = \frac{\text{Selling Price per unit} - \text{Variable Cost per unit}}{\text{Selling price per unit}} \times 100$$

$$= \frac{10 - 8^*}{10} \times 100$$

$$= \frac{2}{10} \times 100$$

$$= 20\%$$

*[V.C. per unit = 5 + 2 + 1 (50% of Direct Labour)]

(b)

$$\text{Break-even sales} = \frac{\text{Fixed Cost}}{\text{P/ V Ratio}}$$

$$= \frac{8,000}{0.20}$$

$$= \text{Rs. 40,000}$$

(c) Sales required to earn profit of Rs. 50,000

$$\text{Sales} = \frac{\text{Fixed Cost} + \text{Desired Profit}}{\text{P/V Ratio}}$$

$$= \frac{8{,}000 + 50{,}000}{0.20}$$

$$= \frac{58{,}000}{0.20}$$

$$= \text{Rs. } 2{,}90{,}000$$

(d) Margin of safety

The margin of safety implies the 'cushion' over break-even sales.

Every enterprise wants to know how much above they are from the break-even point. This is technically called the 'margin of safety'. It is an indicator of the strength of a business. A large margin of safety indicates the soundness and financial strength of business.

It is computed as:

> Margin of Safety = Total Sales – Break-even sales

Example:

A company produces a single product.
S.P per unit = Rs. 20
V.C. per unit = Rs. 10
Total fixed cost = Rs. 10,000
Actual Sales = 2,000 units

$$\text{Here, Break-even sales (units)} = \frac{10{,}000\,(\text{Fixed Cost})}{10\,(\text{Contribution per unit})}$$

and Break-even unit sales to cover fixed cost = 1,000 units
Thus, Margin of safety = 2,000 – 1,000 = 1,000
  or 1,000/2,000 × 100 = 50%.

Implications

- If a company sells more than 1,000 units, it will earn profit as fixed cost remains constant. But, if it sells less than 1,000, there will be a loss.

- A high margin will indicate that profit will be made even if there is a substantial fall in sales or production by, say 30%, the company will still make profits. But, if margin is small, a little drop in sales or production will also be a serious matter.

Managerial decision-making

Marginal costing is applied with the help of 'cost-volume-profit analysis' and tools of *Contribution, P/V ratio, Break-even point* and so forth by the management for decision-making in various situations as discussed below.

1. Pricing decisions

CVP analysis plays a very important role in the 'fixation of price' of a product under different market conditions. The management has to decide on the price which is not only reasonable for the customers but also competitive enough to yield profit for the business.

Case: Foreign Ventures Ltd. (FVL)

FVL is planning to set up a subsidiary company in India to produce 'red coloured pens'.

Based on the estimated annual sales of 50,000 pens, following are the cost details for the Indian subsidiary.

	Total Annual Cost Rs.	Per Cent of Total Annual Cost that is Variable
Material	2,10,000	100%
Labour	80,000	50%
Overhead	70,000	40%
Administration	20,000	20%

The company has tied up with Indian traders for selling the product at a commission of 5% of the sale price.

i.   Compute the sale price per pen to enable management to realise estimated 10% profit on sale proceeds in India.
ii. Calculate the break-even point in rupee sales for Indian subsidiary on the assumption that the sale price is Rs. 8 per pen.

Solution

Assuming the selling price per unit is x.

Total Sales = 50,000x (50,000 * x)
Total Commission = 2,500x (5/100 * 50,000x)
Total Profit = 5,000x (10/100 * 50,000x)

Total Sales = Total Cost + Profit

So, 50,000x = 2,10,000 + 80,000 + 70,000 + 20,000 + 2,500x + 5,000x
50,000x = 3,80,000 + 7,500x
42,500x = 3,80,000
x = Rs. 8.94

Thus, S.P. = Rs. 8.94

$$\text{Break-even Point (in sales)} = \frac{\text{Fixed Cost}}{\text{P/ V Ratio}}$$

$$= \frac{98,000\#}{0.245\#^*}$$

$$= \text{Rs. } 4,00,000$$

 # Fixed cost

Labour = Rs. 40,000 (50/100 × 80,000)
            [100 – 50% V.C. = Fixed Cost]
Overhead = Rs. 42,000 (60/100 × 70,000)
            [100 – 40% V.C. = Fixed Cost]
Administration = Rs. 16,000 (80/100 × 20,000)
            [100 – 20% V.C. = Fixed Cost]
            = Rs. 98,000

$$\#^*\text{P/ V Ratio} = \frac{\text{Contribution}}{\text{Sales}} \times 100$$

$$= \frac{\text{Sales} - \text{Variable Cost}}{\text{Sales}} \times 100$$

$$= \frac{(50,000 * 8) - 3,02,000}{(50,000 * 8)} \times 100$$

$$= \frac{4,00,000 - 3,02,000}{4,00,000} \times 100$$

$$= \frac{98,000}{4,00,000} \times 100$$

$$= 24.5 \%$$

Variable Cost	Rs.
Material	2,10,000
Labour	40,000 (50/100 × 80,000)
Overhead	28,000 (40/100 × 70,000)
Administration	4,000 (20/100 × 20,000)
Sales Commission	20,000 (5/100 × 4,00,000)
	3,02,000

2. Key factor

'Key factor' is the most important factor for taking decision about the profitability of a product. It is not the maximisation of total contribution that matters, but the contribution in terms of key factor is important for relative profitability. Thus, it is the limiting factor or the governing factor for relative profit decision-making.

The managers in their decision-making process often come across certain limiting factors that play a pivotal role in arriving at an optimal solution or deciding the profitability.

Key factor can be labour, finance, material, machine usage and so forth.

Example:

- If labour is a problem, labour is regarded as the key factor.
- If raw material is in short supply, contribution has to be expressed in relation to per unit of raw material required.

In case of key factor, the profitability is measured by the following formula:

Profitability = Contribution/Key factor

Case: Aspirations Ltd

Aspirations Ltd. is a labour-intensive company in the handicraft segment. Comment on the relative profitability of the following products with regard to working hours.

	Product A Rs.	Product B Rs.
Material	500	700
Wages	200	300
Fixed Overhead	450	200
Variable Overhead	250	100
Profit	600	700
	2,000	2,000
Labour hours per week	200 hrs.	150 hrs.

Solution

Comparative statement of profitability

	Product A Rs.	Product B Rs.
Sales Price per unit (Sale = Cost + Profit)	2,000	2,000
Less: Variable cost per unit (Materials + Wages + Variable Overhead)	950	1,100
Contribution per unit	1,050	900
Less: Fixed cost per unit	450	200
Profit per unit	600	700
P/V Ratio	52.5%	45%
Contribution per hr. (Contribution/hrs.)	5.25	6

Contribution per unit and P/V Ratio are higher in case of product A.

If 'labour hours' are the limiting factor, product B is more profitable, otherwise product A would be more profitable.

3. Profit planning

The management has to forecast future sales and plan out for maintaining a desired level of profit. They are generally confronted with problem of analysing the effect of changes in sales price or cost on the profitability of the concern and determining the units to be sold thereto. The desired sales to be done and the potential effect of changes in selling price and various costs on profits can be easily analysed with the help of CVP analysis.

The following formula is used for profit planning.

$$\text{Desired Sales} = \frac{\text{Fixed Cost} + \text{Desired Profit}}{\text{P/V Ratio}}$$

Case: Star Battery Company

The price structure of a battery manufactured by the company is as follows.

	Per Battery Rs.
Material	80
Labour	40
Variable Overheads	30
	150
Fixed Overheads	50
Profit	50
Selling Price	250

The estimated production of batteries per annum is 50,000.

The company expects that due to competition they will have to reduce the selling price, but they want to keep the total profits intact.

What level of production they will have to reach, i.e. how many batteries will have to be produced to get the same amount of profit if:

(a) The selling price is reduced by 5%.

Solution

$$\text{Desired Units} = \frac{\text{Fixed Cost} + \text{Desired Profit}}{\text{Contribution per unit}}$$

(a) If the selling price is reduced by 5%:
New selling price per unit: Rs. 237.5 (250 – 12.5)

$$\text{Desired Units} = \frac{25,00,000^* + 25,00,000^*}{(237.5 - 150)}$$

$$= \frac{50,00,000}{87.5}$$

$$= 57,143 \text{ batteries}$$

*Fixed Cost:	*Present Profit:
= Fixed Overheads per unit * Units	= Profit per unit * Units
= 50 × 50,000	= 50 × 50,000
= Rs. 25,00,000	= Rs. 25,00,000

4. Make or buy

There is often a situation where the management has to decide is it viable to make the component in-house or buy from outside, especially if it does not require huge set up or it has a major effect on the production process.

To make or buy decision depends on:

i. Variable cost of manufacturing the component
ii. Purchase price (market price) of that component.

Decision

If M.P. > V.C. ⟶ Manufacture it
If V.C. > M.P. ⟶ Buy it

Case: In-house or dilemma?

Young Blood Co. Ltd. is a two-year-old company. They are into manufacturing ready-made garments for youth in the urban market. They get an export order to be delivered within one month. But, in order to meet that order they need to upgrade the existing plant line for which they require a special component.

They can make the component in their own workshop at Rs. 7 each and the same is available in the market at Rs. 7.50. Should they make or buy this component?

The supplier is ready to reduce the price from Rs. 7.50 to Rs. 6.50 on bulk order. What is your view in case the supplier reduces the price?

The cost data is as follows:

	Rs.
Material	4
Direct Labour	2
Other Variable Expenses	1
Depreciation and Other Fixed Expenses	1
	8

Solution

Fixed costs will be incurred whether they manufacture this component or not. The decision depends upon the 'marginal cost' of making the component.

Marginal Cost of Component (per unit)

	Rs.
Material	4
Direct Labour	2
Other Variable Expenses	1
	7

OPTION 1:

Here, Marginal Cost is Rs. 7 and the purchase price is Rs. 7.50.

So, it is advisable to make the component, as 'marginal cost' of making the component is Rs. 7. It is lower than the 'purchase price' from outside, that is Rs. 7.50.

It should be produced in the own workshop because every component manufactured will give a contribution of 50 paise (7.50 – 7).

OPTION 2:

If the purchase price is reduced to Rs. 6.50, then the purchase price becomes lower than the marginal cost.

In this case the company should not manufacture the component and rather buy it from outside.

5. Continue or discontinue

There can be a situation where the product seems loss-making financially but there are various other benefits attached to the product. In such case, the management has to decide should they discontinue the product or continue with the plan of its revival and wait for the results. This problem is usually faced by firms in their initial years.

Case: Indian Engineers Ltd. (IEL)

The price structure of a spare part made by IEL is as follows.

	Per Spare part *Rs.*
Material	80
Labour	10
Variable Overheads	10
	100
Fixed Overheads	70
Profit	30
Selling Price	200

The company's present operating capacity is 2,00,000 spare parts per annum.

They are facing stiff competition in metros. Due to this, they will have to reduce the selling price by 18%. Advise them whether they should they continue in such a situation.

Solution

$$\text{Contribution per unit} = \text{Selling Price} - \text{Variable Cost}$$
$$= 164^* - 100 = \text{Rs. } 64 \, ^*[200 - 36]$$

Profit = Selling Price – Total Cost
          = 164 – 170 = Rs. – 6

If the management goes by the 'profit factor', the product is unviable and should be discontinued.

But, the 'contribution factor' indicates that the product can be continued as it still gives a positive contribution of Rs. 64. If it is discontinued, the company will be deprived of the contribution. The better strategy can be to continue it for the time being and pass on its fixed overheads to other products or departments.

6. Selection of best method of production

Many a times, the management has to choose the best method among the alternative methods of production. For example, the same product may be produced either by Machine A or Machine B. In such circumstances, CVP analysis is applied and the method providing the highest contribution is adopted.

Case: Strong Brothers Ltd

The company has two machines, both of which can produce the product no. 1. It can be manufactured either by machine A or machine B. Machine A can produce 50 units of A per hour and machine B, 120 units per hour.

Total machine hours available are 2,500 hours per annum.

Taking into account the following cost data, determine the most profitable method of manufacturing:

	Product no. 1 (per unit)	
	Machine A Rs.	Machine B Rs.
Direct Material	7	9
Direct Wages	12	13
Variable Overhead	4	5
Fixed Overhead	5	5
Total Cost	28	32
Selling Price	30	30

Solution

	Profitability Statement	
	Machine A Rs.	Machine B Rs.
Selling price per unit	30	30
Less: Variable cost		
- Direct material	7	9
- Direct wages	12	13
- Variable overhead	4	5
	23	27
Contribution per unit	7	3
Output per hour	50 units	120 units
Contribution per hour	Rs. 350	Rs. 360
Total machine hours (per annum)	2,500	2,500
Total contribution	Rs. 8,75,000	Rs. 9,00,000

Hence, Production of Machine B is more profitable.

Points to remember

- 'Marginal costing' helps in knowing the impact of variable cost on the volume of production or output and arrive at suitable managerial decision-making.
- Marginal cost is the change in the total cost with the change in the quantity produced, that is it is the cost of producing additional unit of product.
- Under *absorption costing* or *traditional costing*, total costs are charged to production, while under *marginal costing*, only variable costs are charged to production.
- Cost-volume-profit Analysis (CVP analysis) is technique for studying the relationship between cost, volume and profit at different levels of sales or production. It is useful to the management in various areas of decision-making of cost control, profit planning, performance evaluation and so forth.
- Tools of CVP analysis include contribution, profit volume (P/V) ratio, break-even point and margin of safety.
- Contribution is the difference between sales and variable cost. It contributes toward fixed cost.
- Contribution margin/(P/V) ratio is the contribution per rupee of sales. It is calculated as the ratio of contribution divided by sales and expressed in percentage.

- Break-even point is the volume of sales or production where there is neither profit nor loss.
- Margin of safety implies the 'cushion' over break-even sales. It is an indicator of the strength of a business.
- Marginal costing is applied with the help of CVP analysis by the management for decision-making in various situations, such as pricing decisions, key factor, profit planning, make or buy and so forth.

Part IV
Financial system

9   Financial markets

The financial system is the most important functional vehicle for economic growth of an economy. It is a set of inter-related financial constituents of various markets, institutions, instruments, services and mechanisms, and facilitates the process of capital formation through mobilisation of savings and channelisation of investments into different sectors. The Indian financial system in the post-independence period has undergone a developmental change and made an enormous growth in diverse fields. There has been a quantitative expansion as well as diversification of economic activities in the post-liberalisation era (post-1991).

Financial markets

The financial market is a place where buyers and sellers come together and participate in the trade of securities, such as equities, bonds and derivatives. They provide the necessary linkage between the savers and investors, and help them in the exchange of their assets.

The classification of financial markets is discussed below.

1. Based on the nature of securities

(a) *Money market*: It refers to the market for short-term funds, that is funds up to one year.
(b) *Capital/stock market*: It refers to the market for long-term funds, that is funds more than one year.

2. Based on the timing of issue

(a) *Primary market*: It is a market which refers to the first time issue of securities, that is 'Initial Public Offering (IPO)'.

(b) *Secondary market*: It is a market which refers to the trading of existing securities.

The following chart presents the financial markets and their constituents.

Regulatory institutions

The financial system in India is regulated by the Government of India at the central level in the field of banking, insurance, capital market, commodities market and pension funds. These government regulatory bodies are responsible for governing the financial system through policy-making, supervision, monitoring and controlling the activities of the financial markets.

The key regulatory institutions for the Indian financial markets are:

- Banking Sector – *Reserve Bank of India (RBI)*
- Stock Market – *Securities and Exchange Board of India (SEBI)*

Other regulatory institutions in the Indian financial system are given below.

- Insurance Sector – *Insurance Regulatory and Development Authority (IRDA)*
- Commodities Market – *Forward Markets Commission (FMC)*
- Pension Funds – *Pension Fund Regulatory and Development Authority (PFRDA)*

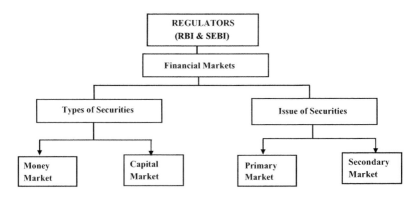

Figure 9.1 Indian financial markets

1. *Reserve Bank of India (RBI)*

The Reserve Bank of India is the Central Bank of India with head office at Mumbai. It was established on 1 April 1935 in accordance with the provisions of the Reserve Bank of India Act, 1934. It is responsible for regulating the banking system of the country. It plays a major role in regulating and controlling the India money market. The intervention of RBI is varied – curbing crisis situation by reducing the cash reserve ratio (CRR) or infusing more money into the economy.

Box 9.1   Tools of monetary control

RBI uses its 'monetary policy' for balancing the economy by using one or more of the following key tools of monetary control:

(i)   Bank Rate – It is the rate of interest charged by the central bank on the loans and advances to a commercial bank.

(ii) *Repo Rate* – It is the rate at which banks can acquire funds from RBI by selling the securities and at the same time agreeing to repurchase them at a later date at a predetermined price. This is a short term measure used for regulating the position of money in a bank.
[So, borrowing against securities is categorised under 'repo rate', and simple borrowing is categorised under 'bank rate'.]

(iii) *Reverse Repo Rate* – It is the rate paid by RBI to the banks on deposit of funds with RBI.

(iv) *Cash Reserve Ratio (CRR)* – It refers to the cash that banks are required to maintain with RBI as a certain percentage of their demand and time liabilities (DTL). It is a type of regulatory cash reserve with RBI.

(v)   *Statutory Liquidity Ratio (SLR)* – It refers to the liquid reserve which is required to be maintained by the banks in form of cash and cash deposits.

- • Bank Rate = 6.50%
- • Repo Rate = 6.25%
- • Reverse Repo Rate = 6.00%
- • CRR = 4%
- • SLR = 20.5%

Source: RBI – As of 2 June 2017.[1]

2. Securities and Exchange Board of India (SEBI)

SEBI is the regulatory body which regulates securities markets in India. It was set up under SEBI Act, 1992. It is entrusted with the responsibility of protecting the interests of investors in securities. Its functions extend to the issuance of capital and transfer of securities, in addition to controlling the activities of all intermediaries and persons associated with securities market. It has full autonomy and authority to regulate and develop an orderly securities market.

A. Markets based on types of securities

Financial markets, as mentioned above, based on 'the nature of securities' are classified into *money market* and *capital market*.

I. Money market

A money market is a market where short-term debt instruments (maturity of less than one year) are traded. It refers to that segment of the financial market which enables the exchange of short-term funds and earning returns. It plays an important role in banks' liquidity management and the transmission of monetary policy. The major participants in the money market in India are the Reserve Bank of India (RBI) and commercial banks. India money market has seen exponential growth since globalisation in 1992.

Following are the 'money market instruments'.

1. Call money

Call money is the money lent by a bank which is repayable on demand. Therefore, the 'call market' is the most liquid market. The loans made in this market are of the shortest term: overnight. If it exceeds one day and extends up to 14 days, it is called 'notice money'. It is basically an inter-bank market, where banks facing short-term cash crunch borrow funds from the cash surplus banks for maintaining their CRR and making the payments.

2. Treasury bills (T-bills)

Treasury bills are short-term government securities issued by RBI on the behalf of the central government. They are risk-free instruments and hence yield low returns. They are traded in both the primary and secondary market. There are three types of treasury bills issued through auctions, namely, 91-day, 182-day and 364-day.

They are issued at a discounted price, that is less than their face value and redeemed at full. So, the difference between the purchase price and the maturity value is the interest earned by the buyer of the instrument.

3. Commercial paper (CP)

Commercial paper is the short-term unsecured debt instrument issued by corporate and financial institutions at a discounted price, like T-bills. These are issued at a discount and redeemed at face value. The rate of interest is market driven and depends on the current liquidity position and the creditworthiness of the issuing company. They have a fixed maturity period ranging from seven days to one year.

4. Certificates of deposit (COD)

A certificate of deposit is a short-term bank deposit, wherein a certificate is issued by a bank which entitles the bearer to receive interest. The certificate bears the maturity date, fixed rate of interest and the value. These deposits by the banks range from seven days to one year. The returns on certificate of deposits are higher than T-bills because they carry a higher level of risk.

5. Discounted bills

Bills of exchange are a short term, negotiable, and liquidating instrument with low risk. They are issued by the seller (drawer) on the buyer (drawee) for the value of the goods delivered which can be encased with the bank for a fee. The maturity period of the bills varies from 30 days to 90 days or longer, depending on the credit extended in the industry.

6. Inter-corporate deposit (ICD)

ICDs are usually unsecured inter-corporate loans. The corporate with surplus funds lends to other companies. Since the cost of funds for a corporate is much higher than for a bank, the rates of such deposits are higher than other markets.

The following table presents the comparative picture of these instruments.

Table 9.1 Money market instruments

Instruments	Maturity	Major participants
1. Call money	Overnight	Banks
2. Notice money	2 to 14 days	
3. Treasury bills	91, 182 and 364 days	Banks, foreign institutional investors, insurance companies & other non-bank entities
4. Commercial paper	Minimum 7 days	Corporate & all India financial institutions
5. Certificate of deposit	Minimum 7 days	Banks
6. Bills discounting	Need based	Banks, insurance companies & mutual funds
7. Inter-corporate deposit	Flexible	Corporate

II. Capital market

The capital market is a market for long-term financial instruments. These long-term instruments include company shares, government bonds and corporate bonds. It is the major source of financing fixed investments in contrast to the money market, which is the institutional source of working capital finance. The main participants in the capital market are corporate, foreign institutional investors, mutual funds, insurance organisations and retail investors.

The capital market in India has come a long way in the past decade and a half in terms of economic reforms, making India one of the world's largest equity markets. With over 9,000 companies listed on the stock exchanges and 20 million shareholders, India has emerged with a large investor base in the world after countries, like the USA and Japan.

The 'capital market instruments' are discussed below.

1. Owned instruments

1. EQUITY SHARES

Equity shares are those shares which do not carry any special or preferential rights in the payment of annual dividend or repayment of capital.

They do not have a fixed rate of dividend, and their dividend is paid out of the residual profits left after paying interest on debentures and dividend on preference shares. Similarly, equity shareholders are paid at the time of winding up of the company, after all debts and preference shareholders have been paid off. Therefore, equity shareholders are called the 'real risk-takers'. But, they enjoy full voting rights in the management affairs of the company.

2. PREFERENCE SHARES

Preference shares are those shares which carry certain special or preferential rights in the payment of dividend and repayment of capital as compared to equity shareholders.

They are paid a fixed rate of dividend, but they do not carry voting rights. Unlike equity shares, they have a fixed maturity date.

> *Preference shares* are called 'hybrid security' because they are a mix of debt and equity. Like equity, they get dividends, and like debt, they get a fixed rate of dividend and have fixed maturity.

Preference shares can be further classified into varied types:

(a) **According to redemption**

   (i) **Redeemable preference shares:** They are refundable during the lifetime of the company.
   (ii) **Irredeemable preference shares:** They are issued for perpetuity.

(b) **According to convertibility**

   (i) **Convertible preference shares:** They are convertible into equity shares after a specified period of time.
   (ii) **Non-convertible preference shares:** They are not convertible into equity shares.

(c) **According to dividend payment**

   (i) **Cumulative preference shares:** Here dividend gets accumulated and paid in total if not paid in a specific year.
   (ii) **Non-cumulative preference shares:** They do not have a cumulative advantage of dividend.

3. DEPOSITORY RECEIPTS (DRS)

These are owned securities of domestic companies issued in a foreign country in its currency. Depositary receipts commonly represent a foreign equity, but can also be issued to represent ownership of preferred stock, debt or warrants. They are:

(a) **American Depositary Receipts (ADRs)**
These depositary receipts are issued by the non-US companies to raise capital in the US equity market from US investors. These investors can invest in international stocks without having to purchase ordinary shares.

(b) **Global Depositary Receipts (GDRs)**
GDRs are similar to ADRs, the only difference is ADRs represent depository receipts issued in the US, whereas GDRs are depository receipts issued outside the US.

2. Borrowed instruments

1. GOVERNMENT SECURITIES (G-SECS)
They refer to government and semi-government debt securities issued by the Reserve Bank of India (RBI) and are also known as the gilt-edged securities. These are risk-free securities, therefore they offer the most suitable investment opportunity from the safety point of view.

A *government security* is a debt obligation of the Indian government to fund its fiscal deficit. These instruments are tradable and are issued either by the central or the state government. These securities are offered for short term as well as long term.

The 'short-term instruments' with a maturity of less than one year are called *treasury bills*, discussed above, whereas 'long-term instruments' are called *government bonds* or *dated securities* with a maturity of one year or more.

---

2. DEBENTURES/BONDS
Debentures or bonds are known as creditorship securities because debenture holders are the creditors of a company. A debenture is a document or certificate issued by a company under its seal as an acknowledgement of its debt for a fixed term.

They carry a fixed rate of interest which is payable every year irrespective of profits. Debenture holders do not have any voting rights.

Debentures can be further classified into following types:

(a) **According to security**

   (i) **Secured debentures:** These are secured against the assets of the company.
   (ii) **Unsecured debentures:** These are simple debentures and have no security.

(b) **According to maturity**

   (i) **Redeemable debentures:** These are repaid within the lifetime of the company.
   (ii) **Irredeemable debentures:** These are issued for perpetuity. Nonetheless if the company has to wind up, then they have to repay these debenture holders.

(c) **According to convertibility**

   (i) **Convertible debentures:** These are convertible into shares after a specified period of time.
   (ii) **Non-convertible debentures:** These are not convertible into equity shares.

Box 9.2   Zero coupon bonds

Zero coupon bonds do not have a specified interest rate. They are issued at substantial discount but redeemed at full. The interest is the difference in face value and issue price. Therefore, they are also called 'deep discount bonds'.

---

3. PUBLIC DEPOSITS

Public deposits refer to the deposits received by a company from the public as loan or debt. The companies prefer public deposits because these deposits are cheaper than bank loans. The investors invest in them as the interest on these deposits is more than interest which is given by banks and post offices.

Public deposits can be further classified into following categories:

(i) **Cumulative fixed deposits:** Here the interest accumulates with principal so as to earn higher returns when compared to non-cumulative plan. They pay interest on maturity.
(ii) **Non-cumulative fixed deposits:** They pay off the interest earned on investment on regular basis (half yearly basis or annual basis).

Table 9.2 Distinction between equity shares, preference shares and debentures

S. No.	Basis	Equity Share	Preference Share	Debenture/ Loan
1.	Type	Ownership	Ownership	Borrowing
2.	Rate of Return	Variable	Fixed	Fixed
3.	Repayment	Last	Second	First
4.	Voting Right	Yes	No	No
5.	Dilution of Control for Company	Yes	No	No
6.	Maturity	Perpetual	Fixed	Fixed
7.	Tax Deductible	No	No	Yes

4. TERM LOANS

Term loans are long-term loans provided by the central and state level financial institutions to the business firms. Some of the prominent financial institutions are IFCI, Small Industries Development Bank of India (SIDBI) and State Finance Corporations (SFCs).

Table 9.2 differentiates between various instruments of finance.

B. Markets based on issue of securities

Financial markets based on 'the timing of issue of securities' are classified into primary market and secondary market.

I Primary market

A primary market is one in which new issues of a security, both debt and equity, are sold to initial buyers. It is also called the 'new issue market (NIM)'.

The process of capital formation occurs in the NIM as it supplies additional funds to the corporate directly. It does not have any physical setup like a stock market and is recognised by the services rendered by various institutions to the buyers and sellers of securities.

In the *primary market*, when securities are exclusively offered to the existing shareholders it is called 'right issue', and when it is issued to selected institutional investors as opposed to general public it is called 'private placement issue'.

II Secondary market

The secondary market, or 'stock market' as it is commonly called, is a market for old securities. It has a physical existence and is located in a particular geographical area in the form of 'stock exchanges'.

Box 9.3   Stock exchanges

Stock exchanges are marketplaces where buyers and sellers come together to trade in a firm's shares and other securities. The buying and selling on an exchange is only open to its affiliates and brokers.

The two leading stock exchanges in India are BSE and NSE, along with regional stock exchanges and others.

The Bombay Stock Exchange (BSE) is the oldest stock exchange in Asia (established in 1875) and the first in the country to be granted permanent recognition under the Securities Contract Regulation Act, 1956. It has played a pioneering role in the development of the Indian securities market. Its Sensitive Index (SENSEX) is the benchmark equity index that reflects the health of the Indian economy.

The National Stock Exchange of India Limited (NSE) was set up by financial institutions to provide access to investors from all across the country on an equal footing at the behest of the Government of India in November 1992 as a tax-paying company unlike other stock exchanges in the country. On its recognition as a stock exchange under the Securities Contracts (Regulation) Act, 1956 in April 1993, NSE commenced operations in the Wholesale Debt Market (WDM) segment in June 1994. The Capital Market (Equities) segment commenced operations in November 1994 and operations in Derivatives segment commenced in June 2000. NIFTY is its pioneer equity index.

C. Other markets

Besides above, a new financial market has come up during the last two decades in India, that is the *derivatives market*.

Derivatives market

Derivatives were introduced in India in 2000. They can be used both for hedging (protecting oneself against financial risks) as well as for speculation.

'Derivatives' are instruments whose value is derived from the price of some underlying asset like securities, commodities, bullion, currency, interest level, stock market index and so forth. For example, a derivative of Tata Motors share will derive its value from the share price (current value) of some other company.

The common types of derivatives are as follows.

1. FORWARDS

A forward contract is a contract between two parties, where settlement takes place on a specific date in future at today's pre-agreed price. Forwards represent the obligation to make a transaction at a set point in time in the future. They have a limitation of being informal in nature.

2. FUTURES

A future is a contract between two parties to buy or sell an asset in future at a specific price. A future contract is a 'formal forward contract'. They are traded in an exchange.

Example

Amit sells the futures contract of Reliance Industries Ltd. stock to Mohit. The agreed price is Rs. 900, quantity is 100 shares, and the expiry date is after one month. After a month, the price goes up to Rs. 950 then irrespective of the market price of the stock, Amit would make the delivery to B at Rs. 900.

---

3. OPTIONS

An option gives the contract holder the right to buy or sell on a specified date in the future – but they are under no obligation. The pre-decided price for the exchange of asset here is called the 'strike price'.

There are of two types of options: call and put.

(a) **Call option:** It gives the buyer the right but not the obligation to buy a certain quantity of the underlying asset, at a given price on or before the specified date in future.

(b) **Put option:** It gives the buyer the right but not the obligation to sell a certain quantity of the underlying asset at a given price on or before the specified date.

Example

In the above example, 'the call option' gives Mohit the *right*, but not the *obligation*, to purchase shares of Reliance at Rs. 900 at any point in the next month. The 'put option' is the opposite of the call option.

A **futures contract** gives the buyer the obligation to purchase a specific asset, and the seller to sell and deliver that asset at a specific future date, whereas an *option contract* gives the buyer the right, but not the obligation to buy (or sell) a certain asset at a specific price at any time during the life of the contract.

Points to remember

- The financial system is a set of inter-related financial constituents which includes various markets, the institutions, instruments, services and mechanisms and facilitate the process of capital formation.
- Financial market is a marketplace where buyers and sellers come together and take part in the trade of assets, such as equities, bonds and derivatives.
- The *money market* is a market for short-term funds, that is funds up to one year. The *capital/stock market* is a market for long-term funds, that is funds more than one year.
- The *primary market* is a market which refers to first time issue of securities, that is 'Initial Public Offering (IPO)'. The *secondary market* is a market which refers to the trading of existing securities.
- The key regulatory institutions of the Indian financial markets are: (a) banking sector – *Reserve Bank of India (RBI)* and (b) stock market – *Securities and Exchange Board of India (SEBI)*.
- Money market instruments are call money, treasury bills, commercial papers, certificate of deposits, discounted bills and inter-corporate deposits.
- The owned instruments of the 'capital market' are equity shares, preference shares and depository receipts.
- The borrowed instruments of the 'capital market' are government securities, debentures, public deposits, and term loans.

- The two leading stock exchanges in India are BSE and NSE, along with regional stock exchanges and others. SENSEX is the benchmark equity index of BSE, and NIFTY is the pioneer equity index of NSE.
- The derivatives market was introduced in India in 2000. They can be used both for hedging (protecting oneself against financial risks) as well as for speculation.
- 'Derivatives' are instruments whose value is derived from the price of some underlying asset like securities, commodities, bullion, currency, interest level, stock market index, etc. The common types of derivatives are forwards, futures and options.

Note

1 Reserve Bank of India, www.rbi.org.in/ (accessed on 2 June 2017).

10 Mutual funds

The last two decades have witnessed a phenomenal expansion in the scope and coverage of the Indian financial system. The mutual fund industry too has come out leaps and bounds to occupy an important place, particularly for retail investors on account of enjoying market returns with low risk unlike with direct investment in securities market. Mutual funds render a large bouquet of services that are not available to investors who invest in securities directly. There are large number of asset management companies (AMCs) which have set up their operations since the liberalisation of the Indian economy in 1991. These comprise the public sector companies including Unit Trust of India (UTI), private sector companies, joint ventures (including those with foreign entities) and bank-sponsored.

What are mutual funds?

A **mutual fund** is a pool of money mobilised from numerous investors and invested on their behalf in securities market. The returns from such investments, both in terms of dividends and capital appreciation, the net of incidental expenses, accrue to the investors.

Each unit of a mutual fund represents the unit holder's proportionate ownership in the fund's total holdings. The investors of mutual funds are known as *unit holders*. The companies that operate the mutual funds are known as *asset management companies (AMCs)*. The mutual fund process is depicted in Figure 10.1.

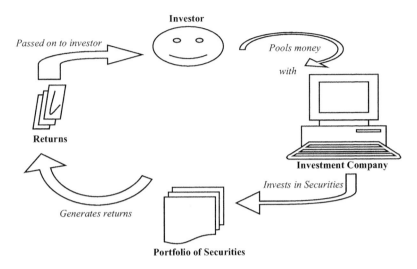

Figure 10.1 Mechanism of mutual funds

Growth of mutual funds

Mutual funds in India began in 1963 with the setting of the public sector undertaking, Unit Trust of India (UTI). UTI was set up with the twin objective of mobilising household savings and investing the funds in the capital market for industrial growth. UTI monopolised the mutual funds industry in India for more than two decades.

During 1987–1993, some other public sector organisations entered into the Indian mutual funds industry, such as *SBI (1987), Canara Bank (1987), LIC (1989), Punjab National Bank (1989), Indian Bank (1989), GIC (1990) and Bank of India (1990).*

After liberalisation in 1992, the government allowed the setting up of asset management companies by private enterprises. That led to the establishment of asset management companies in the private sector by Indian corporate, foreign and joint venture companies as well.

Presently, there are 42 asset management companies as per the list of Association of Mutual Funds in India (AMFI).[1]

Types of mutual funds

The categorisation of mutual funds is depicted in Figure 10.2 and explained thereafter.

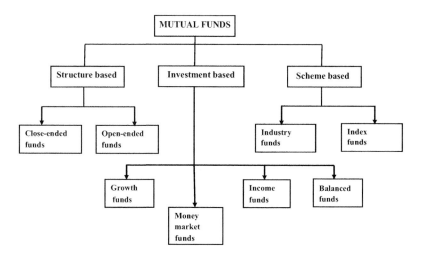

Figure 10.2 Classification of mutual funds

1. Based on structure

Based on the structure, mutual funds can be classified as 'close-ended' or 'open ended'.

(a) **Close-ended funds:** These funds are with a pre-specified life, and are redeemable at the end. These are listed in the stock exchanges and traded like stocks. So, if an investor wishes to sell the holdings or buy into such a fund before the maturity it can be done in the stock exchange where the units are listed. *Reliance Equity Fund is an example of a well-known close-ended mutual fund.*

(b) **Open-ended funds:** These funds are irredeemable and open for investment and redemption throughout the year. Unlike close-ended funds, they are traded at 'net asset value' (NAV) of the fund held by AMC. That's why, in an open ended scheme, the number of outstanding units varies on a daily basis. *Examples: UTI Dividend Yield and Axis Short Term Fund.*

Box 10.1   Net Asset Value (NAV)

The NAV of a fund is the total of the market value of the assets (securities) that comprise its portfolio, net of any liabilities at that time.

NAV of a unit $=$

$$\frac{\text{Market value of funds (total assets)} - \text{Market value of total liabilities}}{\text{Number of units outstanding}}$$

Example: Innovative mutual fund held Rs. 10,00,000 worth of securities, Rs. 2,00,000 of cash, and Rs. 5,00,000 of liabilities on the closing day. The units outstanding were 1,00,000. What is the NAV?

Solution: NAV = (Rs. 10,00,000 + 2,00,000 – 5,00,000)/1,00,000
= Rs. 7

2. Based on investment objective

Mutual funds based on investment objective may be classified as follows:

(a) **Growth funds:** These funds predominantly invest in equities. They aim to grow faster than other funds, so there is usually a higher risk. They focus more on growing the value of the fund by re-investing rather than on paying out dividends.

(b) **Income funds:** These funds are primarily a debt fund. They invest in securities that pay a fixed rate of return like government bonds and corporate bonds. They aim to provide return on a regular basis, mostly through interest that the fund earns.

(c) **Balanced funds:** These funds invest in a mix of equities and fixed income securities.

Therefore, they are more risky than fixed income funds, but less risky than pure equity. A typical balanced fund might have a weight age of 60% equity and 40% fixed income. *Example: Balanced HDFC Children's Gift-Inv Fund.*

(d) **Money market funds:** These funds invest in short-term fixed income securities, such as treasury bills, commercial papers and certificates of deposits. They are relatively a safer investment, but have lower return than other mutual funds. They are basically meant for liquidity.

3. Based on special schemes

Mutual funds based on other factors or special schemes are as follows:

(a) **Industry specific funds:** These funds are industry specific. It could be fast-moving consumer goods (FMCG), pharmaceuticals, or banking. It can extend to even geographic sectors. For example, an MNC fund invests in multinational or transnational companies.

(b) **Index funds:** These funds invest in a specific set of stocks of an index like BSE Sensex or NSE Nifty. *For example*, let us assume that a sample index consists of three Stocks, Stock A, Stock B and Stock C in the proportion of 50%, 30% and 20%. An index fund with a corups of say Rs. 100,000 will invest Rs. 50,000 in Stock A, Rs. 30,000 in Stock B and Rs. 20,000 in Stock C.

The value of the mutual fund will go up or down as the index goes up or down. Index funds typically have lower costs than actively managed mutual funds because the research put in by portfolio managers is less as in other investment decisions.

Box 10.2   Equity Linked Saving Schemes (ELSS)

An ELSS is an equity mutual fund which is qualified for tax exemption under Section 80C of the Income Tax Act, 1961. It offers the twin advantage of capital appreciation and tax benefits. It comes with a lock-in period of three years.

ELSS funds not only save tax under Section 80C but also give the opportunity of earning high returns from the equity market. Moreover, compared to other tax saving options, ELSS has the shortest lock-in period of three years. *Example: Axis Long Term Equity Fund (G).*

Importance of mutual funds

Mutual funds provide the benefits of a diversified portfolio and expert management to a large number of investors, particularly small investors. They offer following advantages:

1 **Small investment:** Mutual funds are a boon for small investors as it is less expensive to invest in a mutual fund. The investment amount in mutual fund units can be as low as Rs. 500.

2   **Diversification of risk:** The risk is diversified in mutual fund investments as it is not an investment in one stock but a bundle of stocks. It automatically brings diversification to the investor's portfolio with a wide variety of securities.

3   **Professional management:** Mutual funds are managed by professionals who have a better knowledge of market behaviour. So with mutual funds, the investors get the added advantage of experienced professional management of the portfolio.

4   **Low cost:** The cost of managing mutual funds by the companies is very low. Mutual funds usually hold numerous securities, therefore the actual level of fees can vary. But the expense ratio of mutual funds investment is relatively low.

5   **Liquidity:** Mutual funds are liquid investments that can be sold anytime. Investors can plan out their cash requirement with these investments. The price per unit at which you can redeem units is known as the fund's net asset value (NAV).

6   **Convenience:** The investor can purchase or sell fund shares directly from a fund or through a broker, by any medium, physically or electronically.

7   **Tax relief:** The mutual funds also provide a tax advantage to investors. ELSS mutual funds provide tax relief under Section 80C of the Income Tax Act, 1961. Like shares, long-term capital gain is zero and dividend is tax-free in the hands of recipient.

Box 10.3   Systematic Investment Plan (SIP)

A SIP involves investing a fixed amount in a mutual fund at regular intervals, monthly or quarterly over a period of time, thereby averaging out the cost of investing and yielding the benefit from power of compounding. It is similar to investment in a recurring deposit account in a bank.

In SIP, the investors do not have to worry about the market timing as it is governed by the principle of 'rupee cost averaging' (RCA).

Points to remember

- A 'mutual fund' is a pool of money mobilised from various investors and invested on their behalf in several securities in the market. The investors of mutual funds are known as *unit holders*. The companies that operate the mutual funds are known as *asset management companies (AMCs)*.

- Mutual funds in India began in 1963 with the setting of the public sector undertaking, Unit Trust of India (UTI). During 1987–1993, some other public sector organisations entered into the Indian mutual funds industry. After liberalisation in 1992, the government allowed setting up of asset management companies by private enterprises. Presently, there are 42 asset management companies.
- *Close-ended funds* are funds with a pre-specified life, and are redeemable at the end. These are listed in the stock exchanges and traded like stocks. *Open-ended funds* are irredeemable and open for investment and redemption throughout the year. Unlike close-ended funds, they are traded at *net asset value (NAV)* of the fund held by AMC.
- The *NAV of a unit* is the total of the market value of the assets (securities) that make up its portfolio, net of any liabilities at that time, divided by the units outstanding.
- *Growth funds* predominantly invest in equities. *Income funds* are primarily debt funds. *Balanced funds* invest in a mix of equities and fixed income securities. *Money market funds* invest in short-term fixed income securities, such as treasury bills, commercial paper and certificates of deposit.
- *Industry specific fund* focus upon specific industries. *Index funds* invest in a specific set of stocks of an index like BSE Sensex or NSE Nifty.
- An *Equity Linked Saving Scheme (ELSS)* is an equity mutual fund which is qualified for tax exemption under Section 80C of the Income Tax Act, 1961.
- Mutual funds offer multiple benefits, such as small investment, risk diversification, professional management, low cost, liquidity and tax benefit.
- A *Systematic Investment Plan (SIP)* involves investing a fixed amount in a mutual fund at regular intervals, monthly or quarterly over a period of time, thereby averaging out the cost of investing.

Note

1 Association of Mutual Funds in India, www.amfiindia.com/amfi-members-details (accessed on 2 June 2017).

11 Forex market

The international financial system provides the framework within which foreign exchange rates are determined, international trade and capital flows are accommodated, and balance of payments (BoP) adjustments are made. The forex market is an integral part of the international financial system. The increase in world trade and the reduction in capital controls have led to tremendous growth in the foreign exchange market over the years. The Indian forex market has seen a tremendous growth since liberalisation in 1991. The four-decade-old, fixed exchange rate system replete with severe import and foreign exchange controls was replaced with a less regulated, 'market driven' arrangement.

Forex market

The forex market or 'foreign exchange market' is the market which brings the participants across the globe together to buy, sell, exchange and speculate on currencies. It comprises banks, financial companies, central banks, investment management firms, hedge funds and retail forex brokers and investors. The currency market is considered to be the largest financial market in the world, processing trillions of dollars' worth of transactions each day.

Features

1 *OTC market*: The forex market is an 'over-the-counter market' (OTC market). This means that there is no single market or physical stock exchange but an electronic market where trading takes place. The traders sit in the offices (foreign exchange dealing rooms) of major commercial banks around the world and communicate with each other through telephones, telexes, a satellite communication network, SWIFT and other electronic means of communication. All transactions happen here via phone or electronic network.

SWIFT is an acronym for 'Society for Worldwide Interbank Financial Telecommunications'.

It is a cooperative society owned by about 250 banks in Europe and North America and registered as a cooperative society in Brussels, Belgium. It is a communications network for international financial market transactions which links effectively more than 25,000 financial institutions throughout the world who have been allotted bank-identified codes.

2 *24-hour market*: It is a market that operates 24 hours a day at global level. It spans all the time zones of the world and enables a trader to offset a position created in one market using another market. The major market centres are London, New York and Tokyo.

3 *Participants*: The major participants of the forex market are central banks, commercial banks, financial companies, and retail investors. The central banks are the biggest players in the forex market which are involved in massive buying and selling of currency to fix exchange rates through their open market activities, not for mere profit reasons, but rather for policy matters.

Box 11.1   Structure of forex market

The market for foreign exchange can be divided into 'retail market' and 'wholesale market'.

In the *retail market*, tourists and travellers exchange one currency in the form of currency notes or travellers' checks for meeting their foreign exchange requirements. The average transaction size is very small. The retailers buy or sell foreign currency from banks and other institutions which are authorised to deal in foreign exchange.

The *wholesale market* is often called the *interbank market*. The participants in this market are commercial banks, investment banks, corporate houses and central banks. The average transaction size is very large (deals may be in millions of US dollars or other currency).

4   *Risk*: The participants in this market trade in currencies of various countries and generate profits for their organisations. In this process, these organisations get exposed to 'foreign exchange risk'.

5   *Process*: In a 'forex trade', you buy one currency while simultaneously selling another, that is you are exchanging the sold currency for the one you are buying. Currencies are traded in pairs, like the euro-US dollar (EUR/USD) or US dollar/Japanese yen (USD/JPY).

The global foreign exchange turnover is given in Table 11.1.

Table 11.1 Global foreign exchange market turnover

OTC foreign exchange turnover
Net-net basis,[1] daily averages in April, in billions of US dollars

Instrument	2001	2004	2007	2010	2013	2016
Foreign exchange instruments	1,239	1,934	3,324	3,973	5,357	5,067
Spot transactions	386	631	1,005	1,489	2,047	1,652
Outright forwards	130	209	362	475	679	700
Foreign exchange swaps	656	954	1,714	1,759	2,240	2,378
Currency swaps	7	21	31	43	54	82
Options and other products[2]	60	119	212	207	337	254
Memo:						
Turnover at April 2016 exchange rates[3]	*1,381*	*1,884*	*3,123*	*3,667*	*4,917*	*5,067*
Exchange-traded derivatives[4]	*12*	*25*	*77*	*145*	*145*	*115*

1 Adjusted for local and cross-border inter-dealer double-counting (i.e. 'net-net' basis).

2 The category 'other FX products' covers highly leveraged transactions and/or trades whose notional amount is variable and where a decomposition into individual plain vanilla components was impractical or impossible.

3 Non-US dollar legs of foreign currency transactions were converted into original currency amounts at average exchange rates for April of each survey year and then reconverted into US dollar amounts at average April 2016 exchange rates.

4 Sources: Euromoney Tradedata; Futures Industry Association; The Options Clearing Corporation; BIS derivatives statistics. Foreign exchange futures and options traded worldwide.

Source: Triennial Central Bank Survey of foreign exchange and OTC derivatives markets in 2016

Bank for International Settlements (BIS)- Triennial Central Bank Survey.[1]

Foreign exchange market in India

The forex market in India can be discussed with regard to its growth, structure, process and role of CCIL under following heads:

1. Growth

The growth of forex market in India is discussed as follows.

(a) *Before 1991*: Traditionally the Indian forex market was highly regulated. Till liberalisation in 1991, the government exercised absolute control on the exchange rate, export-import policy and FDI (foreign direct investment) policy. The Foreign Exchange Regulation Act (FERA), 1973, strictly controlled all foreign exchange related activities. Under the Act, all forex earnings by companies and residents had to reported and surrendered (immediately after receiving) to RBI (Reserve Bank of India) at a rate decided by RBI.

(b) *After 1991*: The new Foreign Investment Policy announced in July 1991 declared automatic approval for Foreign Exchange in India for 34 industries. These industries were designated with high priority, up to an equivalent limit of 51%. The foreign exchange market in India is regulated by the Reserve Bank of India through the Exchange Control Department.[2]

Post-liberalisation, the Government of India liberalised the foreign exchange policy in the form of Foreign Exchange Management Act (FEMA) 1999. FEMA expanded the list of activities in which a person/company can undertake forex transactions. Through FEMA, government liberalised the export-import policy, limits of FDI (foreign direct investment) and FII (foreign institutional investors) investments, cross-border M&A and fund-raising activities.

> The Foreign Exchange Management Act, 1999 regulates the whole foreign exchange market in India. The Reserve Bank of India (RBI) regulates the Indian foreign exchange market through the Exchange Control Department.

2. Structure

The foreign exchange market in India consists of three interdependent segments or tiers.

(a) *RBI and authorised dealers (ADs)*: The first is an apex segment consisting of transactions between RBI and authorised dealers. ADs are usually commercial banks authorised by the RBI to deal in foreign exchange. The exchange rates are set by RBI. It facilitates exchange rate movements in tune with international developments as residual partner rather than as an active market participant.

(b) *Interbank market*: This is the major segment of the forex market in which the ADs deal with each other. More than 70% of the trading in foreign exchange takes place in the inter-bank market. The big commercial banks are the 'market makers' in this market as they are willing to buy or sell foreign currencies at the rates quoted by them up to any extent.

The trading is regulated by the Foreign Exchange Dealers' Association of India (FEDAI), a self-regulatory association of authorised dealers. The market consists of 101 ADs (mostly banks and others include financial institutions and others) as of June 2017.[3]

> The foreign exchange reserves of India as of 26 May 2017 were USD 378,763.5 million.[4]

(c) *Retail market*: In this segment, ADs deal with their corporate clients and other retail customers. The retail market deals in currency notes and travellers' checks to tourists. It also consists of moneychangers and foreign exchange brokers.

3. Centres

The leading foreign exchange market in India is Mumbai. Other forex centres include Kolkata, Chennai and Delhi. As a result of RBI's efforts to decentralise exchanges operations and develop broader based exchange markets, new centres of forex market have come out, like Cochin, Bangalore, Ahmadabad and Goa.

4. CCIL – role in clearing process

The Clearing Corporation of India Ltd. (CCIL) was set up in April 2001 to provide guaranteed clearing and settlement functions for transactions in money, government securities, foreign exchange and derivative markets.[5] It was set up on the initiative by RBI to mitigate risks in the Indian financial markets. Since 2001, as India's first centralised clearing and settlement house for the financial sector, it facilitates settlement of both debt and forex transactions.

Types of foreign exchange markets

Depending upon the time elapsed between the transaction date and the settlement date, foreign exchange transactions can be categorised into the following.

1. Spot market

'Spot market' is the market where transactions for the exchange (purchase and sale) of currencies take place two days after the date of the contact.

For instance, if the contract is made on Monday, the delivery should take place on Wednesday. If Wednesday is a holiday, the delivery will take place on the next day, that is Thursday. The rupee payment is also made on the same day the foreign currency is received.

Similarly, if the contract is made on Wednesday, then the delivery should take place on Friday. If Friday is a holiday, the delivery will take place on Tuesday of the following week if Saturday and Sunday are bank holidays, as they are at most of the financial centres.

The exchange rate for spot delivery is called *spot exchange rate* and is denoted by $S(\ )$. *For example,* $S(Rs/USD) =$ Rs. 65.10/USD is the relationship between rupees and dollars, which says that one dollar is equivalent to Rs. 65.10.

2. Forward market

The 'forward market' is the place where the transactions for the exchange of currencies take place at a specified future after the spot date. The forward transaction can be for delivery one month, two months, three months and so forth.

This may be done to secure against adverse movements in currencies (a *hedging transaction*) or to trade a currency (a *speculative transaction*).

3. Swap market

It is a combination of a spot and a forward transaction. The term 'swap' implies a temporary exchange of one currency for another with an obligation to reverse it at a specific future date. Swaps are two-way deals, one deal involving a buy and the other involving a sell, at different times, but one has to cancel the other.

Following are the categories of swaps:

(i)   *Spot-forward swap*: In this swap, one deal is done in the spot market and another in the forward market, that is one buys in the spot and sells in the forward or vice versa. If the buy is in spot and sell in the forward it is called a 'swap-in'.

> For example, if an exporter expects to receive USD 5,000 two months hence but needs money at present, he goes to a bank and asks for a swap. He buys USD 5,000 in the present and sells them in the forward at the agreed price. Conversely, if sell is in the spot and buy is in the forward, it is called a 'swap-out'.

(ii)   *Forward-forward swap*: Here, both the deals are in the forward, that is one buys two months forward and sells three months forward, each deal cancelling the other or vice versa.

> For example, an exporter expects a receipt of USD 2,000 after three months and has to pay to the suppliers after two months. So the exporter contacts a bank for a swap. The bank agrees to the swap and sells USD 2,000 two months forward to the exporter and buys USD 2,000 three months forward from him at the agreed rates.

Foreign exchange quotations

A 'quotation' is the amount of currency that is exchanged for a unit of another currency. When a currency is quoted, it is done in relation to another currency, so that the value of one is reflected through the value of another.

Following are the types of forex quotations.

I *Two-way quotations*

Typically, the quotation in the interbank market is a two-way quotation. It means the rate quoted by the bank will indicate two prices, *one* at which it is willing to buy the foreign currency, and *the other* at which it is willing to sell the foreign currency. 'A two-way quote includes both bid and offer rate'.

The buying rate is also known as the 'bid rate' and selling rate as the 'offer rate'.

The difference between these rates is the gross profit for the bank and is known as 'the spread'.

For example, a Delhi bank may quote its rate for US dollar as: USD 1 = Rs. 68.10/15. More often, the rate would be quoted as 10/15, since the players in the market are expected to know the 'big number', that is Rs. 68. In the given quotation, there are two rates, that is the bank is prepared to buy USD at Rs. 68.10 and sell at Rs. 68.15.

II *Direct quotations*

The exchange quotation which gives the price for the foreign currency in terms of the domestic currency is known as 'direct quotation'.

Here, the *unit of foreign currency* is kept constant and its value is expressed in terms of variable domestic currency.

For example: USD 1 = Rs. 68.10
GBP 1 = Rs. 86.50

III *Indirect quotations*

The exchange quotation which gives the quantity of foreign currency per unit of domestic currency is known as 'indirect quotation'.

Here, the *unit of home currency* is kept constant and its value is expressed in terms of foreign currency.

For example: Rs. 100 = USD 1.47
Rs. 100 = GBP 1.15

Points to remember

- The forex market is an 'over-the-counter market' (OTC market) that operates 24 hours a day at the global level. The major participants of the forex market are central banks, commercial banks, financial companies and retail investors.
- The market for foreign exchange can be divided into 'retail market' and 'wholesale market'. In the *retail market*, tourists and travellers exchange one currency in the form of currency notes or travellers' checks for meeting their foreign exchange requirements. The *wholesale market* is often called the *interbank market*.
- Traditionally the Indian forex market was highly regulated. Till liberalisation in 1991, government exercised absolute control on the exchange rate, export-import policy and FDI (foreign direct investment) policy. The Foreign Exchange Regulation Act (FERA), 1973, strictly controlled all foreign exchange related activities. Post-liberalisation, the Government of India liberalised the foreign exchange policy in the form of the Foreign Exchange Management Act (FEMA) 1999.
- The foreign exchange market in India consists of three inter-dependent segments or tiers: RBI and authorised dealers (ADs), the interbank market and the retail market.
- The Clearing Corporation of India Ltd. (CCIL) was set up in April 2001 by RBI as India's first centralised clearing and settlement house for the financial sector. It facilitates settlement of both debt and forex transactions.

- The 'spot market' is the market where transactions for the exchange (purchase and sale) of currencies take place two days after the date of the contact.
- The 'forward market' is the place where the transactions for the exchange of currencies take place at a specified future after the spot date. The forward transaction can be for delivery one month, two months, three months and so forth.
- The 'swap market' is a combination of a spot and a forward transaction. The term 'swap' implies a temporary exchange of one currency for another with an obligation to reverse it at a specific future date. Swaps can be spot-forward swaps and forward-forward swaps.
- A 'two-way forex quotation' includes two prices by the bank, one at which it is willing to buy the foreign currency, and the other at which it is willing to sell the foreign currency. 'A two-way quote includes both bid and offer rate'.
- In 'direct quotations', the *unit of foreign currency* is kept constant and its value is expressed in terms of variable domestic currency.
- In 'indirect quotations', the *unit of home currency* is kept constant and its value is expressed in terms of foreign currency.

Notes

1 Bank for International Settlements, Triennial Central Bank Survey of Foreign Exchange and OTC Derivatives Markets in 2016, www.bis.org/publ/rpfx16.htm (accessed on 2 June 2017).
2 Foreign Exchange Market in India, Indian Economy – Indianetzone, www.indianetzone.com/38/foreign_exchange_market_india.html (accessed on 8 August 2016).
3 Member Banks, www.fedai.org.in (accessed on 2 June 2017).
4 Reserve Bank of India, www.rbi.org.in/Scripts/WSSView.aspx?Id=21429 (accessed on 2 June 2017).
5 The Clearing Corporation of India Ltd., www.ccilindia.com/ABOUTUS/Pages/CompanyProfile.aspx (accessed on 10 August 2016).

Part V

Financial management

12 Nature of financial management

Almost everything in life eventually boils down to the rupee sign. Money, and therefore, finance, is an integral part of life.[1] It is equally applicable to a business organisation. The success of business depends upon the efficient financial management. Therefore, every business enterprise needs to be efficient in managing its finance. They need to ensure that adequate funding is available at the required time and invested into the right projects.

What is financial management?

Financial management is the process of acquisition and disbursement of funds. It includes all the activities relating to planning, organising, directing and controlling the funds of the enterprise.

Elements

1 **Investment decision** – It implies the allocation of funds into various assets of an undertaking. The investment in fixed assets is called *capital budgeting decision* and the investment in current assets is called *working capital decision*.
2 **Financing decision** – It refers to the process of raising funds from various sources depending on factors, like cost of funds, control, liquidity and so forth.
3 **Dividend decision** – This decision involves the distribution of net profit of business. The finance manager decides what percentage of profits would be distributed as dividend to shareholders and how much profits to be kept aside as reserves for future contingencies.

Objectives of financial management

The main objectives of financial management are:

1   **Profit maximisation:** It is the core objective of financial management. Every business enterprise strives to maximise its profits, both in the short term and the long term.
2   **Wealth maximisation:** Shareholders' value maximisation is the key objective of financial management and *is preferred over profit maximisation on account of market interest*. Wealth maximisation is a combination of regular return to shareholders in the form of dividend and appreciating market returns.
3   **Liquidity:** Liquidity maintenance is one of the most important objectives of financial management. The firm must have sound cash position for meeting day-to-day expenses; otherwise there might be a threat to the survival of the firm.
4   **Solvency:** Long-term soundness is another key objective of financial management. The company must be sound enough to pay interest on long-term loans and repay these loans at regular intervals. Lack of solvency can be a big blow to the firm in this competitive scenario.

Functions of financial management

Following are the main functions of financial management:

1   **Forecasting financial requirements:** The financial management has to correctly estimate the financial requirements of business is, keeping in view its current operations and future growth.
2   **Acquisition of funds:** Funds acquisition is another important function of financial management. After estimating the financial requirements, the finance manager has to raise funds from various sources of finance, like equity, debt, bank loans and so forth. The optimum capital mix must be maintained.
3   **Proper allocation of finance:** The next task of finance manager is to efficiently allocate these funds according to the nature of assets. Long-term funds should be invested in fixed assets and short-term funds should be invested in current assets.
4   **Distribution of profits:** The distribution of net profit of business is the most important function of the finance manager as it is oriented towards the shareholders' interest. He has to judiciously plan out about dividend payment and reinvestment of earnings.

5 **Working capital management:** The finance manager must ensure adequate liquidity. He should ensure that enough cash is there for meeting various requirements of the firm, like payment of salaries, bills, meeting current liabilities and so forth.
6 **Financial control:** Sound financial control is the prerequisite for the growth of business. The finance manager must exercise proper control with the help of techniques like budgetary control, cost analysis, financial forecasting and so forth.

Financial management scene in India

Traditionally, a single manager would manage the entire operations of business. With the business becoming globalised, the finance function has become a specialised function. There are finance specialists now to manage your operations.

Since liberalisation in 1991, the Indian corporate has changed tremendously in its form and working, making finance as the most sophisticated function of corporate enterprise. There are specialist group of executives in companies today, managing the finance function, called director-finance, chief finance officer and financial controller.

The finance manager is not merely concerned with maintaining accounts of the business. He has to perform multiple tasks, including fundraising to procurement of assets to distribution of profits, and to ensuring safety of the financial assets of the company. He has to plan out the operations of a business in such a manner so that both continuity and growth of the business are maintained at the same time. He is expected to generate maximum profits for the company and keep shareholders satisfied.

The financial management is continuously progressing. A good finance manager must see all updates, changes in the fields of financial management and implement them accordingly. He should be interested to know what new sources of funds are developed at international level, what new projects are there and what amendments are done by government in various laws. In short, a good finance manager must be aware of what is happening around.

Box 12.1 Controller's and treasurer's functions in the Indian context

The 'controller' and 'treasurer' are essentially American terms. However, this pattern is not being widely followed in India. There are companies in India who have designations of the controller or the financial controller.

The 'controller' or the financial controller in India performs the functions of a chief accountant or management accountant. The officer with the title of 'treasurer' can also be found in a few companies in India. However, in most cases, as mentioned above in case of Indian companies, the terms like general manager (finance) or vice-president (finance) are more popular.

Some of the functions of the controller and the treasurer, such as government reporting, insurance management and so forth are taken care of by the company secretary in India. In the American business, the management of finance is treated as a separate activity and is performed by the treasurer.

Following are the main changes which have tuned the field of financial management in India during last few decades:

Interest rates. The interest rates are controlled by RBI and thus, commercial bank's rates are affected by RBI's action. This has an important bearing on the cost of debt.

Valuation of shares. Value of shares now can be determined at premium or discount freely. One should determine its shares value at optimum level because it directly affects the EPS.

Mergers and acquisitions. As good finance manager should keep his eye on who is taking over which company. To merge with another company may be sometimes more profitable than going alone.

In conclusion, financial management has evolved with the times and become very scientific with the latest principles and practices of management.

Financial management problems

Various problems relating to the financial management faced by corporate enterprises are discussed below:

1   Lack of an optimum sources of funds. Due to poor planning, the enterprises *do not maintain a desirable combination of sources of funds*. This leads to shortage of equity and then they depend too much on borrowed capital. Hence, sound financial planning is required for an optimal financial structure.

2   Inadequate combination of assets. This results in the problem of either shortage or excess of assets for the business. This is more pertinent to current assets, like inventories and receivables. For a manufacturing undertaking, these problems need an immediate check by adopting appropriate working capital techniques.

3   **Inaccurate projection of revenue and cost.** This results in improper investment in inventories, receivables, and plant capacity. These factors ultimately result in poor earnings of the enterprise. So, there should be an efficient and effective profit planning for better utilisation of resources and enhanced earnings.

4   **Absence of stable dividend policy.** In the absence of a definite and stable dividend policy, the shareholders discontinue from the company. So, there should be a sound dividend policy and dividend payments should be more regular and consistent in proportion to the paid-up capital.

5   **Unprofessional management.** If there is incompetent management, it leads to instability in the organisation. The enterprise should be managed by *professionally competent, qualified* and *experienced personnel* for better result orientation.

Points to remember

- Financial management is the process of acquisition and disbursement of funds. It consists of three elements, *(i) investment decision, (ii) financing decision, and (iii) dividend decision.*
- The main objectives of financial management are: *(i) profit maximisation, (ii) wealth maximisation, (iii) liquidity, and (iv) solvency.*
- The main functions of financial management are: *(i) estimating financial requirements, mobilization of funds, (iii) proper utilisation of finance, (iv) distribution of profits, (v) cash management, and (vi) financial control.*
- Traditionally, a single manager would manage the entire operations of a business. With business going global, the finance function has become a specialised function. Since liberalisation in 1991, the face of Indian corporate has changed tremendously, making finance as the essence of every business. Today every company has specialist set of people shouldering the responsibility of finance managers in their organisation.
- The financial management problems faced by corporate enterprises are: *(i) lack of desirable sources of funds, (ii) inadequate combination of assets, (iii) inaccurate projection of revenues and costs, (iv) absence of stable dividend policy and (v) unprofessional management.*

Note

1 Emery, Douglas R., et al. 1998. *Principles of Financial Management.* Englewood Cliffs, NJ: Prentice Hall, p. 2.

13 Capital budgeting
Concept and application

The capital budgeting decision is about investment in long-term assets. Capital budgeting is often used interchangeably with terms like capital expenditure or capital investment. It involves large cash outlays and huge risk for generating future return of the company, which makes a capital budgeting decision irreversible. Therefore, proper analysis and evaluation of the proposed capital budgeting decision is required for the success of the project. This involves the application of capital budgeting techniques in order to determine which projects will yield the maximum return over a given period of time.

Meaning of capital budgeting

The capital budgeting decision refers to the investment in a fixed asset whose returns are expected over a long period of time. 'It is the process of identifying, analysing and selecting investment projects whose returns (cash flows) are expected to extend beyond one year'.[1] Any expenditure that generates a cash flow benefit for more than one year is capital expenditure. *For example*, the purchase of a new machine, acquiring another company, research and development and so forth.

Box 13.1   Types of capital budgeting decisions

The capital investment decisions are classified as follows:

1   *Replacement decision*: It is the most routine decision of an undertaking which involves the decision of replacing an old asset with the new asset. This is essential to ensures smooth level of business operations.

2 *Expansion/modernisation decision*: This decision is about increasing the production capacity of business or modernisation of the existing facilities for meeting growing demands by introducing new men, machines, or/and methods.

3 *Diversification decision*: This is deciding to entering into new lines of business either related or unrelated based on the company's growth plans and competitive conditions. Such decisions result in increasing requirement of fixed assets.

The capital investment decision is the most difficult and important decision for the business as it determines the success of an enterprise in the long run.

In a 'capital investment decision', the major criterion for selection of a project is its viability and impact on shareholder value. The two most important parameters for arriving at a project decision are the *project's expected cash inflows* and *cash outflows*. They determine whether the returns meet a sufficient target benchmark or not.

The capital budgeting decision basically can be grouped into:

a. Allocation of long-term funds into fixed assets
b. Risk analysis of capital investment decisions
c. Measurement of the cost of capital.

Capital budgeting process

The capital budgeting process consist of the following steps:

1 **Identifying investment needs:** The identification of the need for capital investment is the first step. This involves the evaluation of various available opportunities by the management on the basis of both financial and non-financial factors. The key criterion is the 'risk-return trade-off'.

2 **Project feasibility study:** The next step is to evaluate the proposal for its feasibility at various levels of economic viability, commercial viability, technical viability, and the financial viability.

3 **Capital project evaluation:** After deciding on the proposed project, its evaluation is done regarding its viability using both qualitative and quantitative methods. The estimated cash flows, target cost of capital, and potential risks are identified for the evaluation. Calculating appropriate discount rate is a critical part of this process.

Factors used for the evaluation

1 *Initial cash outflows* – It is the amount of cash flows to be invested initially in the project.
2 *Net cash inflows from operations*- It is the amount of cash inflows to be generated from the capital investment decision.
3 *Terminal cash flows (salvage value)* – It is the salvage value of an existing asset at the end of the life.
4 *Depreciation* – The usage charge of an asset.
5 *Income tax effect* – Tax shield on account of sale of an asset.
6 *Discounting rate* – The funding rate in computation of cash flows.
7 *Risk considerations* – Political risk, monetary risk, and other risks should be considered in the evaluation process.

Finally, various capital budgeting techniques are applied to test its feasibility (discussed later in the chapter).

4 **Capital investment implementation:** Once the proposed project is deemed viable, the project team executes it.

Capital budgeting projects

The capital investment projects are categorised as follows:

1 **Independent projects:** These are the projects whose selection do not affect the selection of any other project, i.e. they are independent of other projects. *For example, you have Rs. 50,000. You decide to buy a water purifier that costs about Rs. 10,000 and a new laptop for your house that costs around Rs. 20,000. The decision to buy the purifier does not affect the decision to buy the laptop – they are independent decisions.*

2   **Dependent projects or contingent projects:** The acceptance of these projects is dependent upon the acceptance of other project. *For example, procurement of furniture due to the construction of new office is a case of dependent project. Here, the usage of new furniture is dependent upon the new office.*

3   **Mutually exclusive projects:** These projects are one where the investment in one project affects other projects because only one project can be undertaken. *Taking the first example further, let us assume that you had decided to buy only water purifier. You looked at two different brands of purifiers, one is A and the other is B. So, when you decide to buy B, you have also decided you are not going to buy A.*

Project feasibility

Project feasibility or project appraisal is 'assessing, in advance, whether a project is viable to be undertaken or not'. Therefore, before deciding on a project, one must evaluate its 'feasibility'. *The feasibility study can be conducted for smaller projects as well, but generally on account of time and efforts involved, it is conducted for bigger projects.*[2]

A *feasible capital project* is one which generates adequate operating cash inflows, withstands all the risks and lasts for its predetermined life to meet the desired goals.

Types of project feasibility

Following types of feasibility studies are conducted to analyse the viability of a project:

I Market feasibility

The *market feasibility* is helpful in identifying the business opportunities for the proposed project. Based on the opportunities found, the project should proceed further.

This analysis uses several tools to determine feasibility:

> *Demographic analysis* – This involves analysis of demographic trends that are occurring in a particular market area, based on indicators like age, education and income level. The demographic analysis is helpful in providing key inferences on demand changes occurring in the market.
>
> *Industry analysis* – This analysis examines and identifies industries trends that are presently occurring in the market place and thereby helps in identifying what industries are most appropriate for the area by estimating industry supply and industry competition.
>
> *Retail sales analysis* – Retail sales analysis focuses on purchasing trends of the existing population within a market area and whether there is an opportunity for new retail to capture a portion of the existing market.

II Technical feasibility

Technical feasibility enables to determine the technical requirements of men, machines and materials of the proposed project. Accordingly, the organisation finds out whether it has sufficient technical resources to undertake the project or not. It may think of taking help from outside if there is lack of internal technical know-how.

The tools used to determine technical feasibility are:

> *Technology analysis* – This is assessing the type of technology required for the project and the constraints involved in the implementation. Thus, it determines the reliability and competitiveness of technology for the project.
>
> *Resource analysis* – Based on the technology, the requirement of men, material and other inputs needed to produce a product or service are listed. This provides the information about the operations of your business.
>
> *Environmental analysis* – This consists of analysing the environmental impacts of the business. It evaluates the category of business with its potential impact on traffic, water reserves and other significant natural resources.

III *Financial/economic feasibility**

The *financial feasibility* is the most important part of any feasibility study as this determines the commercial viability of the project. A project is considered to be financially feasible if its probable revenues exceed the total costs. This assessment typically involves a 'cost-benefit analysis' of the project based on which necessary financial resources are allocated.

The following tools are used to determine financial feasibility:

1 *Cost analysis* – This analysis determines the possible cost structure of the project. Questions about operating and other related costs are answered at this stage for determining the economic viability of the project.
2 *Revenue analysis* – In order to ensure the success of a project, you need to know your business will make profits. Therefore, 'revenue projection' is done to find out the expected revenue, profit margin and expected net profit of the project.
3 *Capital analysis* – This provides information about the funds required to start the project and keep it running until it is self-sustaining. You should include enough capital funds to run the business.

IV *Organisational feasibility*

The *organisational or managerial feasibility* aims at determining the managerial capability to undertake the project. The most viable projects on all parameters fail out sometimes due to incompetent management.

This applies the following tools:

1 *Organisation structure analysis* – This study identifies the proposed legal structure of the business with all the stakeholders involved. The availability of skilled and experienced business managers is identified to ensure the professional handling of the project.
2 *Performance analysis* – The formal review process of the project with all parties involved at periodic interval is necessary for achieving the desired results of the project. The review fixes the responsibility of individuals for the job.

---

* Generally, both financial and economic feasibility of the project are done combined, though economic feasibility can be conducted separately as well.

Capital investment analysis of DLF, Unitech and Parsvnath Developers

The analysis of capital budgeting practices of three major players in the Indian realty sector, namely, DLF Ltd., Unitech Ltd. and Parsvnath Developers Ltd. is discussed below.

Indian realty sector

The real estate sector in India is one of the most globally recognised sectors and is the second largest employer after agriculture. DLF has over 60 years of track record of sustained growth and its primary business is development of residential, commercial and retail properties. Unitech, established in 1972, is today a leading real estate developer in India. Parsvnath has emerged as one of the most progressive and multi-faceted real estate and construction entities in the country over the years. These companies have global presence. Therefore, the analysis of their capital investment practices will be useful worldwide. The data has been taken from the annual reports of companies.

1. Investment pattern

The trend of investment in long-terms assets of the units is analysed to find out whether they are growing or not? It is further evaluated to determine the risk strategy of the management in the environment within which they operate.

(A) DLF LTD

The investments of DLF for five years are given in Table 13.1.

Table 13.1 Investment pattern of DLF

Year	2007	2008	2009	2010	2011
Investments (in Rs. crores)	769.17	1,839.83	2,956.32	6,558.88	7,037.24

Note: Rs. 1 crore = Rs. 10 million

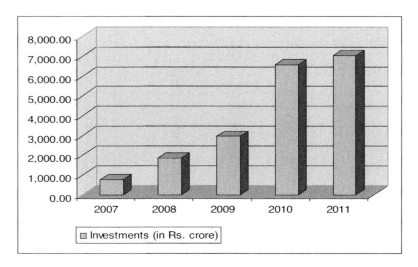

Figure 13.1 Investment trend of DLF

It is clear that the investments by DLF have been increasing every year. DLF unlocked about Rs. 1,270 crore during 2010–11 by divesting certain non-core assets and businesses. The overall divestment target for non-core assets increased to Rs. 10,000 crore, implying that between Rs. 6,000–7,000 crores would be realised through divestments over the next couple of years. The cash flow from divestment would be utilised primarily for debt reduction.

(B) UNITECH LTD
The investments of Unitech for a span of five years are given in Table 13.2.

Table 13.2 Investment pattern of Unitech

Year	2007	2008	2010	2010	2011
Investments (in Rs. crores)	518.92	1,397.99	1,954.94	1,654.15	2,054.02

Note: Rs. 1 crore = Rs. 10 million

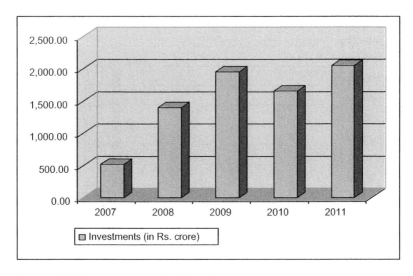

Figure 13.2 Investment trend of Unitech

As it can be seen from the data that the company's investments increased in 2009 and have been almost constant since then. The company is exposed to specific risks in connection with the management of investments and the environment uncertainties. The company needs to measure and monitor these risks and ensure that it adheres to the policies and procedures for mitigating them.

(C) PARSVNATH DEVELOPERS LTD
The investments of Parsvnath Developers for the five years are given in Table 13.3.

Table 13.3 Investment pattern of Parsvnath

Year	2011	2010	2009	2008	2007
Investments (in Rs. crores)	82.86	80.57	99.34	220.83	428.22

Note: Rs. 1 crore = Rs. 10 million

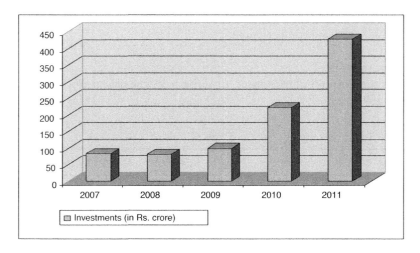

Figure 13.3 Investment trend of Parsvnath

It is clear here that over the past five years, investment in the company has been building up and gaining a real momentum, particularly in Tier I cities.

2. Operating risk

Operating risk indicates the resources' sufficiency for the required growth of business units. To measure the degree of operating risk, the current assets/fixed assets (CA/FA) ratio has been used, as it determines the availability of resources to the business according to the nature of industry.

(A) DLF LTD

The composition of total assets of DLF for the time period is given in Table 13.4.

Table 13.4 Assets composition of DLF

	Mar, 07	Mar, 08	Mar, 09	Mar, 10	Mar, 11
Net current assets (Rs. in cr.)	5,679.57	14,588.51	15,618.55	15,521.99	17,955.29
Net fixed assets (Rs. in cr.)	328.57	1,474.37	1,815.53	1,729.02	1,743.10
Current assests to fixed assets ratio (times)	17.29	9.89	8.60	8.98	10.30

Note: Rs. 1 crore = Rs. 10 million

The 'current to fixed asset ratio' is quite low, meaning the company's operating risk is on a higher side. It does not have adequate current resources to support its growth.

(B) UNITECH LTD
The composition of total assets of Unitech for the time period is given in Table 13.5.

Table 13.5 Assets composition of Unitech

Ratio	Mar, 07	Mar, 08	Mar, 09	Mar, 10	Mar, 11
Net current assets (Rs. in cr.)	4,176.75	7,862.74	8,430.43	11,006.33	12,626.15
Net fixed assets (Rs. in cr.)	69.63	100.73	107.84	107.07	104.49
Current assets to fixed assets ratio (times)	59.98	78.06	78.18	102.80	120.84

Note: Rs. 1 crore = Rs. 10 million

The 'current to fixed asset ratio' is very high, meaning the company has resources to fund the business growth but it also signals low availability of capital resources, particularly in 2010 and 2011.

(C) PARSVNATH DEVELOPERS LTD
The composition of total assets of Parsvnath Developers for the time period is given in Table 13.6.

Table 13.6 Assets composition of Parsvnath

Ratio	Mar, 07	Mar, 08	Mar, 09	Mar, 10	Mar, 11
Net current assets (Rs. in cr.)	2,281.64	3,207.32	3,351.44	3,218.23	3,144.57
Net fixed assets (Rs. in cr.)	71.29	119.47	127.24	106.94	149.02
Current assets to fixed assets ratio (times)	32.01	26.85	26.34	30.09	21.10

Note: Rs. 1 crore = Rs. 10 million

The 'current to fixed asset ratio' is adequate around 30:70 (current assets to fixed assets), meaning the company's level of operating risk is almost negligible. It indicates availability of adequate mix of resources for the required growth.

Points to remember

- Capital budgeting decision is the decision of investment in fixed assets/long-term assets whose returns are expected over a long period of time.
- The capital investment decisions can be of following types: replacement, expansion and diversification.
- The capital budgeting process includes following steps: identifying investment needs, project feasibility study, project evaluation and project implementation.
- The capital investment projects are of following types: independent, dependent or mutually exclusive projects.
- Project feasibility or project appraisal is 'assessing, in advance, whether a project is worthwhile to be undertaken or not'.
- Market feasibility is conducted to determine the viability of the project in the marketplace. The market assessment helps in identifying the business opportunities for the product.
- Technical feasibility identifies the technical requirements of men, machines and materials of the proposed project.
- Financial feasibility is the most important part of any feasibility study, as this determines the commercial viability of the project.
- Organisational feasibility determines the managerial capability to undertake the project.

Notes

1 Van Horne, James C., et al. 1996. *Fundamentals of Financial Management*, Ninth Edition. New Delhi: Prentice-Hall of India Private Limited, p. 314.
2 Goel, Sandeep. 2015. *Capital Budgeting*. New York: Business Expert Press, p. 19.

14 Time value of money

The time value of money (TVM) is an important concept in capital budgeting decision. It is primarily used to compare the investment alternatives of various types for the current power of money. The capital budgeting decision should duly consider the time value of money, otherwise it would be impractical if it is not duly incorporated in the capital budgeting analysis.

What is time value of money?

Time value of money describes the relationship between the 'value of rupee today' and 'value of rupee in future'. It refers to the purchasing power of money exercised by an individual with the changing times.[1] TVM is based on the concept that a rupee that you have today is worth more than the promise or expectation that you will receive a rupee in the future. The money held today is more valuable because you can invest it and earn interest.

For instance, you can invest your rupee for one year at 7% annual interest rate and accumulate Rs. 1.07 at the end of the year. The *future value* of the rupee after one year is Rs. 1.07 @ 7% interest rate and the *present value* of Rs. 1.07 to be received in one year is only Rs. 1. This example is illustrated in the following figure.

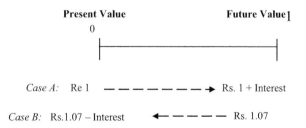

Figure 14.1 TVM principle

> **The money has time preference on account of the following key factors:**
>
> (i) Risk/uncertainty
> (ii) Preference for consumption
> (iii) Investment opportunities.[2]

Methods of valuation

The two methods of accounting used for time value of money are compounding and discounting. *Compounding* denotes the future value of present sum of money. *Discounting* implies the present value of a future sum of money.

A. Compounding – 'future value' (FV)

(a) Future value of an amount of rupee

$$FV(A) = P \times (1 + r)$$

Here, A = Future value of the lump sum at the end of the period
P = Amount invested today
r = Interest rate

Illustration 14.1: Mr. Smith decides to invest Rs. 5,000 in a term deposit account at an annual interest rate of 7%. What is the compounded value after 5 years?

Solution

A (FV) = P $(1 + r)^n$
So, A = Rs. 5,000 $(1 + .07)^5$
= Rs. 5,000 × 1.403*
= Rs. 7,015

Hence, the compounded value of Rs. 5,000 will be Rs. 7,015.

Note*: Using compound value of Re 1 tables, we get the compound value factor of Re 1 at 7% per annum at the end of 5 years as 1.403.

(b) Future value of an annuity series of cash flows

If same amount is invested every year, it is termed an 'annuity'.

$$A(FV) \;=\; P\left[\frac{(1+r)^n - 1}{r}\right]$$

Here, A = Future value of the annuity at the end of the period
P = Amount invested at regular intervals
r = Annual rate of interest
n = Number of years of annuity

Illustration 14.2: Mr. Jack plans to buy an equipment after three years. He plans to deposit Rs. 2,000 at the end of each year into a bank savings account paying a fixed rate of interest of 7%. How much will he get after three years?

Solution

$$A(FV) \;=\; P\left[\frac{(1+r)^n - 1}{r}\right]$$

$$A(FV) \;=\; 2,000\left[\frac{(1+.07)^3 - 1}{.07}\right]$$

So, A = Rs. 2,000 × 3.215*
= Rs. 6,430

Hence, the compounded value of an annuity of Rs. 2,000 will be Rs. 6,430.

Note*: Using compound value annuity tables, we get the compound value factor of Re 1 at 7% per annum at the end of three years as 3.215.

Box 14.1   Interest rate determination

The present or future value of cash inflows are calculated using an interest rate or discount rate (also known as 'cost of capital'). This rate is determined on the basis of various factors, such as:

(i) *Inflation rate*: The higher the inflation rate, the higher the return expected by the investors on their investment.

(ii) *Interest rate*: The higher the interest rate on deposits, the greater the loss of interest income on future cash inflows leading to demand for higher return on investment by the investors.

(iii) *Risk premium*: The higher the risk of a project, the higher the return expectations of an investor.

B. Discounting – 'present value' (PV)

(a) Present value of a future amount

$$PV(P) = \frac{A}{(1+r)}$$

Here, P = Present value of the lump sum today
A = Amount received a year after
r = Interest rate

Illustration 14.3: Mr. James plans to get Rs. 1,000 after three years at the rate of 8%. What is the present value of future cash inflows?

Solution

$$PV = \left[\frac{A}{(1+r)^n}\right]$$

So,

$$PV = \left[\frac{1,000}{(1+.08)^3}\right]$$

$$= \text{Rs. } 1,000 \times 0.794^*$$
$$= \text{Rs. } 794$$

Hence, the present value of Rs. 1,000 will be Rs. 794.

Note*: Using present value tables, we get the present value factor of Re 1 at 8% per annum at the end of three years as 0.794.

(b) Present value of an annuity

$$PV = A \times \frac{1}{r}\left[1 - \frac{1}{(1+r)^n}\right]$$

Here, P/PV = Present value of the instalments today
A = Instalment at the end of each period
r = Rate of discount
n = Number of years of annuity

Illustration 14.4: Mr. Anil has won a competition and is expecting to receive Rs. 5,000 at the end of each year for the next 40 years. What is the present value of Rs. 5,000 due to be received at the 7% discount rate?

Solution

$$PV = A \times \frac{1}{r}\left[1 - \frac{1}{(1+r)^n}\right]$$

So,

$$= \text{Rs. } 5,000 \times 13.332^*$$
$$= \text{Rs. } 66,660$$

Hence, solving the equation above, the present value of Rs. 5,000 annuity comes out to be Rs. 66,660.

Note*: Using, present value annuity tables, we get the present value factor of annuity of Re 1 at 7% per annum at the end of 40 years as 13.332.

Points to remember

- The time value of money (TVM) refers to relationship between the value of a rupee today and the value of a rupee in future. It refers to the purchasing power of money exercised by an individual with the changing times.
- Money has a time preference on account of following key factors: *(i) risk / uncertainty, (ii) preference for consumption, and (iii) investment opportunities.*

- TVM is an important part of capital budgeting decision. A capital budgeting decision would not be viable if the time value of money is not duly incorporated in the capital budgeting analysis.
- There are two methods of accounting for time value of money, *(i) compounding*, and *(ii) discounting*. *Compounding* refers to the future value of a present sum of money. *Discounting* denotes the present value of a future sum of money.

Notes

1 Goel, Sandeep. 2015. *Capital Budgeting*. New York: Business Expert Press, p. 47.
2 Goel, Sandeep. 2015. *Capital Budgeting*. New York: Business Expert Press, p. 47.

15 Estimation of cash flows

The capital budgeting decision is a 'cash-flow concept' rather than a profit-based concept, as capital investment decision has to take place today, not in future. Cash flows are the guiding factor in a capital investment decision. They provide the direction to the management while investing in a project. Therefore, the correct computation of cash flows is important for the success or failure of any investment decision. Thus, it is imperative to know the process of determination of cash flows for capital investment decisions.

Cash flows estimation

Cash flow can arise from a revenue or expense stream that changes a cash account over a given period.[1] **Cash inflows** are expected returns from the operating activities, whereas **cash outflows** are an outcome of the investing activities. This process of cash flows determines the liquidity position of the business and its capacity to undertake the required project. Therefore, estimation of cash inflows and outflows correctly is vital for the continued existence and the growth of business in future. Incorrect forecasting of cash flows could lead to the acceptance of an unprofitable project or rejection of profitable projects.

> Cash inflows expected from a project are 'after-tax operating cash flows', as the project is supposed to generate cash returns from its core activities and that too after the corporate tax has been provided for. They denote the real return for the shareholders (owners) of the business.

The estimation of future cash flows is not easy for the management due to uncertainty element of the future. *For example*, in case of project of similar nature in the past, it is relatively easier to estimate the cash flows for the management than in case of complete new project.

The following factors must be kept in mind while estimating cash flows.

1. Relevant cash flows

The cash flows considered for capital budgeting decisions should always be 'relevant' cash flows.

Relevant cash flows are determined keeping in view the following factors.

(a) Sunk costs

It is a cash outflow associated with the project which has already occurred in the past and will not be affected by the decision to undertake the investment. *For example*, a firm incurs Rs. 50,000 for the ground inspection of project before any decision about its acceptance or rejection. This amount of Rs. 50,000 will be an outflow irrespective of the final decision. Thus, it is a sunk cost.

This cost should not be included in the capital budgeting analysis because it is not a relevant cash flow for the project decision-making. So, all cost and cash outflows of such nature should not be considered in the capital budgeting decision.

(b) Incidental capital expenses (transportation and installation costs)

These costs generally are not included in the purchase price of an asset, but they are essential for using the asset. *For example*, the firm buys an equipment for Rs. 10,000 and spends another Rs. 2,000 on its installation. The additional Rs. 2,000 will be added to the total capital cost of the equipment, that is the total capital expenditure will be Rs. 12,000.

The depreciable cost of an asset will include the purchase price plus all the commissioning expenses incurred to make the asset operational. In the above case, the depreciation will be charged on Rs. 12,000.

(c) Inflation

The inflation factor, as discussed earlier, has an important bearing on the interest rate. Therefore, it should be duly incorporated while estimating the future cash flows associated with a project; otherwise it might result in a wrong decision.

2. Incremental cash flows

The next important factor is that cash flows in capital budgeting decision should always be 'incremental' cash flows associated with the asset. *Incremental* implies the 'net benefit'.[2] This means that only those cash flows should be considered which get affected by the capital investment.

The *incremental factor* in cash flows arises due to the concept of 'opportunity cost'.* This implies that every investment decision has at least two alternatives. Let's understand this with the following scenarios:

Scenario 1:   Replacement of an old asset
Scenario 2:   Investment choice between two projects, Project A or Project B
Scenario 3:   Investment in a Project

In these three scenarios, there is a second alternative available. Even in the third case of investment in a single project, there is a choice available whether to invest or not to invest. So, for rational decision cash flows to be considered for capital investment should be 'incremental cash flows' instead of absolute cash flows.

Components of cash flows (Incremental cash flows)

There are three components of cash flows which are required for capital budgeting decision:

1   *Initial cash outflows /Initial investment*
2   *Annual (average) cash inflows from investment*
3   *Terminal cash flows (salvage value).*

    (i)   *Initial cash outflows.* This is the investment outlay on the asset which that occur at the beginning of the life of project. These

---

* Opportunity cost is the next best return sacrificed if the funds are not invested in the proposed capital budgeting project. Refer Chapter 6, 'Cost Concepts and Classification', for a detailed explanation.

cash flows include the purchase price of the asset, additional capital expenses, the changes in net working capital, the cash flows from the disposal of the old asset (in case of replacement), and the tax implications.

The item *'changes in net working capital'* refers to the possible change in any item of current asset/current liability (working capital) on account of the capital investment. For example, if the new machine improves the production efficiency, thereby consuming less raw material (inventory) as compared to the old machine, then this will result in saving of cash.

This implies decrease in working capital, that is the change in net working capital will be positive and will be deducted from the total cash outflows above and vice versa.

How to calculate cash outflows?

Initial cash outflow

       Purchase price of new asset (s)/project (s)
+ Incidental capital expenses
       (e.g. transportation costs, installation costs, etc.)
+(−) Increase/decrease in net working capital
− Net proceeds from the sale of old asset
+(−) Increase in taxes/tax savings due to the disposal of old asset
       (if the investment is a replacement decision)

= Initial cash outflow

Illustration 15.1: Initial cash outflows

Friends Ltd. plans to replace their old painting machine.

From the following information, calculate the net cash outflow required by for such replacement:

    Cost of the old machine is Rs. 20,000 with a book value of Rs. 3,000
    Life of the old machine is seven years

Purchase price of the new machine is Rs. 70,000
Shipping expenses incurred on its transportation are Rs. 10,000
Sale proceeds of old machine are Rs. 5,000
Additional working capital requirement is Rs. 2,000
Corporate tax rate is 25%

Solution

	Rs.
Cost of the new machine	70,000
Add: Shipping expenses	10,000
Add: Additional working capital required	2,000
Add: Income tax liability (2,000 × 25/100)*	500
	82,500
Less: Sale proceeds of old machine	5,000
Net cash outflow	77,500

(ii) *Operating cash inflows after tax.* These are the expected returns to be generated from the use of the asset during its life.

The incremental operating cash flows can be computed using the following equation:
Incremental operating cash flow t = Δ Cash revenues t – Δ Cash expenses t – Δ Taxes t = Δ NIt – Δ Taxes t
where Δ represents a change and Δ NIt is the change in net income associated with the project.

Calculation of operating cash inflows

Operating cash inflows over a project's life

Profit after tax (PAT)
+ Depreciation
  (Non-cash charges)
+ Interest after tax
  (Non-operating items)

= Annual cash inflows

Box 15.1   Cash inflows versus PAT

Cash inflows are preferred over profits because cash flows are necessary to undertake the investment and meeting operational expenses, not the accounting profit. Cash flows are based on 'time value of money', not the income. The computation of accounting income often includes non-cash items, such as depreciation and provisioning.

Therefore, 'operating cash inflows after taxes' are used in the calculation because that is the amount which represents the amount to be enjoyed by the shareholders.

(iii) *Terminal cash flows.* These are the cash flows that occur only at the end of the life of the asset. They denote the scrap value/ salvage value of the asset.

Box 15.2   Checklist for calculating cash flows:

- Consider incremental cash flows
- Focus on relevant cash flows
- Ignore sunk cost
- Ignore any other irrelevant cost.

Illustration 15.2: Incremental cash flows

A firm has on old fabrication plant with a remaining life of another three years. It is estimated to generate cash flows of Rs. 20,000, Rs. 10,000 and Rs. 5,000 during the next three years. Its book value is Rs. 50,000 and the market value is Rs. 20,000.

The firm is planning to replace it with the new machine for Rs. 70,000. The new machine is estimated to generate cash flows of Rs. 50,000, Rs. 45,000 and Rs. 35,000 for the next three years. Both old and new equipment have zero resale value after three years. Taxes are assumed to be zero.

What are the incremental cash flows which will occur if the old machine is replaced?

Solution

Cash flows computation (Rs.)

	0	1	2	3
Cash flows from new machine (1)	−70,000	50,000	45,000	35,000
Less: Cash flows from old machine (2)	20,000	20,000	10,000	5,000
Incremental cash flows (1–2)	−50,000	30,000	35,000	30,000

After spending Rs. 50,000 of incremental cash outflows, the firm enjoys Rs. 95,000 of incremental cash inflows, ignoring the time value of money.

Note: The book value of Rs. 50,000 of the old machine is not considered as it is not relevant here.

It is 'sunk cost'.

Illustration 15.3: Tax implications

A company purchased a water cooler for its office staff a few years ago for Rs. 20,000. It wants to replace this with the new one in the market for Rs. 30,000. The company is subject to income tax @ 25%. The present book value of the old asset is Rs. 5,000.

Calculate the net initial cash outflow if the company decides to replace the old water cooler, and it is sold for:

(a) Rs. 5,000
(b) Rs. 10,000
(c) Rs. 3,000.

Solution

		Rs.
1	Cash outflow on the new asset	30,000
	Less: Cash proceeds from the sale of old asset	5,000
	Net cash outflow	**25,000**
2	Cash outflow on the new asset	30,000
	Less: Cash proceeds from the sale of old asset	10,000
		20,000
	Add: Income tax liability on profit from the sale of old asset $(5,000 \times 25/100)$	1,250
	Net cash outflow	**21,250**
3	Cash outflow on the new asset	30,000
	Less: Cash proceeds from the sale of old asset	3,000
		27,000
	Less: Income tax saving on loss from the sale of old asset $(2,000 \times 25/100)$	500
	Net cash outflow	**26,500**

Points to remember

- Cash inflows are expected returns from the operating activities, whereas cash outflows are an outcome of the investing activities.
- The following factors must be kept in mind while estimating cash flows: *(i) relevant cash flows*, and *(ii) incremental cash flows*. In relevant cash flows, ignore sunk costs, consider additional capital expenses and inflation factor.
- There are three types of incremental cash flows: *(i) initial cash outflow, (ii) operating cash inflows*, and *(iii) terminal cash flows*.
- The item 'changes in net working capital' refers to the change or affect in current asset/current liability when a new asset is purchased and added to the firm or when an old machine is replaced by a new machine.
- Cash inflows are preferred over income because cash flows are necessary to undertake the investment and meeting operational expenses, not the accounting profit. Cash flows are based on the 'time value of money', not the income.
- Operating cash flows after taxes are used in capital budgeting decision because that is the amount which represents the amount to be enjoyed by the shareholders.

Notes

1 Goel, Sandeep. 2015. *Capital Budgeting*. New York: Business Expert Press, p. 51.
2 Goel, Sandeep. 2015. *Capital Budgeting*. New York: Business Expert Press, p. 54.

16 Capital budgeting appraisal methods

Capital budgeting appraisal is one of the most important tasks as the success of a project is based on its evaluation results. There are various techniques which are used to evaluate the project, comprising based on time-value and others. The capital investment appraisal methods are selected, depending on the nature and objective of the project in addition to the long-term growth of the business and shareholders' wealth maximisation.

The capital budgeting techniques are grouped into the following two categories:

(a) Capital budgeting techniques not based on 'time value of money'
(b) Capital budgeting techniques based on 'time value of money'.

These techniques are categorised into following two groups:

I Non-discounted cash flow techniques

(i) Payback period (PBP)
(ii) Accounting rate of return (ARR)

II Discounted cash flow (DCF) techniques

(i) Discounted payback
(ii) Net present value (NPV)
(iii) Profitability index (PI)
(iv) Internal rate of return (IRR)

I Non-discounted cash flow techniques

1. Payback period

The 'payback period' is the conventional method used in capital budgeting decision. It is the simplest and the most widely used method for appraising capital budgeting project.

It is defined as 'the time period required to recover the initial investment of the project'. The project with the shortest payback period is selected.

It is computed as:

$$\frac{\text{Initial investment}}{\text{Annual cash inflow}}$$

Acceptance/Rejection rule

If payback period > predetermined period/cut-off rate, reject the project and vice versa.

Illustration 16.1:
Scenario 1: **Even cash inflows**

A project requires Rs. 40,000 as initial investment. The annual cash inflows generated is Rs. 5,000 for ten years. Calculate the payback period.

Solution

Payback period =

$$\frac{\text{Initial investment}}{\text{Annual cash inflow}}$$

$$\frac{Rs.\ 40,000}{Rs.\ 5,000} = 8\ Years$$

Scenario 2: **Uneven cash inflows**

A project requires Rs. 25,000 as initial investment. The annual cash inflows for five years are Rs. 10,000, Rs. 9,000, Rs. 7,000, Rs. 4,000, and Rs. 2,000. Calculate the payback period.

Solution

Initial investment = Rs. 25,000

Year	Cash inflows	Cumulative cash inflows
1	Rs. 10,000	Rs. 10,000
2	9,000	19,000
3	7,000	26,000
4	4,000	30,000
5	2,000	32,000

In two years, Rs. 19,000 has been recovered. Rs. 6,000 is left to be recovered.

In the third year, the cash inflow is Rs. 7,000.

So, the payback period = 2 years + 6,000/7,000
= 2.85 years

> The payback method has the biggest limitation that it does not consider time value of money. On account of the above limitations and limited suitability, 'discounted payback period' is preferred over payback period. It is discussed under DCF techniques.

2. Accounting rate of return (ARR)

The 'accounting (average) rate of return' (ARR) is the ratio of average net profit of the project to the assets employed for the project. It measures the rate of return on the project *using accounting profit* information. Therefore, it is closely related to ROI performance measure. The return from the project is compared with target ARR based on the firm's cost of capital for arriving at a decision.

It is computed as:

$$\frac{Average\ profit\ after\ tax}{Average\ investment/Original\ investment} \times 100$$

> ### Acceptance/rejection rule
>
> If ARR > required rate of return, accept the project and vice versa.

Illustration 16.2: AB Ltd. is planning to invest in a project. The initial investment required for the project is Rs. 30,000. The expected earnings before interest, taxes and depreciation (EBITDA) during next three years is given below.

Year	EBITDA for Project (Rs.)
1	12,000
2	15,000
3	18,000

The project is entirely funded by equity, so the interest is zero. Tax rate is 30%. Depreciation is charged on a straight-line basis. The scrap value is nil. Should the firm accept this project, if the minimum accounting rate of return required by the company is 15%?

Solution

Years	1	2	3	Average
EBITDA	Rs. 12,000	15,000	18,000	15,000
Less: Depreciation	10,000	10,000	10,000	
EBIT	2,000	5,000	8,000	5,000
Less: Interest	–	–	–	
EBT	2,000	5,000	8,000	5,000
Less: Tax @ 30%	600	1,500	2,400	
PAT	1,400	3,500	5,600	3,500

$$\text{So, Accounting Rate of Return} = \frac{3,500}{30,000} \times 100$$
$$= 11.67\%$$

The company cannot accept this project, as its ARR is less than the minimum or standard rate of return.

II Discounted cash flow (DCF) techniques

Following steps are used in using the DCF methods:

i.   Calculate the cash outflows and cash inflows.
ii. Discount the cash flows by 'discount factor'.
iii. Compare the discounted cash inflows with cash outflows to arrive at decision.

1. Discounted payback period

One of the major limitations of the payback method is that it does not consider the 'time value of money'. That's why 'discounted payback' is preferred over the payback method, as it overcomes this problem by discounting the cash flows and then calculating the payback period. It is a discounted version of the payback method.

Thus, *discounted payback period* is the time period taken in recovering the investment outlay on present value basis. But, it fails to consider the cash flows beyond the payback period.

Illustration 16.3: A project requires investment of Rs. 20,000. The cash flow generated by it for three years is as follows.

Years	0	1	2	3
Cash flows	(20,000)	12,000	8,000	5,000

The discounting factor is 8%. Calculate the payback and discounted payback.

Solution

The simple payback of the project is two years while discounted payback is 2.51 years, which is longer than simple payback because the discounted payback uses cash flows after discounting it with the cost of capital.

Years	0	1	2	3	Simple Payback	Discounted Payback
Cash flows	−20,000	12,000	8,000	5,000		
Cumulative cash flows		12,000	20,000	25,000	2 years	
PV factor @ 8%		0.926	0.857	0.794		
PV of cash flows		11,112	6,856	3,970		
Cumulative PV of cash flows		11,112	17,968	21,938		2.51 years

2. Net present value (NPV)

NPV is one of the most popular and widely used DCF methods. It discounts the future cash inflows and outflows using the target cost of capital. Simply, NPV is the difference between 'the present value of future cash inflows and the present value of cash outflows'. A positive value implies that the project is profitable and vice versa.

It is calculated as:

> NPV = PV of cash inflows – PV of cash outflows

Mathematically, it is expressed as:

$$NPV = \left[\frac{C_1}{(1+k)} + \frac{C_2}{(1+k)^2} + \frac{C_3}{(1+k)^3} + \text{.......} + \frac{C_n}{(1+k)^n} \right] - C_0$$

$$NPV = \sum_{t=1}^{n} \frac{C_t}{(1+k)^t} - C_0$$

Here, $C_1, C_2 \ldots C_n$ represent future cash inflows

C_0 represents cash outflows
k is the discounting rate
t = time period

Acceptance/rejection rule

If NPV > 0, accept the project and vice versa.

Illustration 16.4:
Scenario 1: *Annuity cash flows*

A handloom project requires an initial investment of Rs. 10,000. It provides a net cash inflow of Rs. 5,000 each year for five years. If the cost of funds is 8%, calculate the net present value.

Solution

Net Present Value = PV of cash inflows – PV of cash outflows
PV factor of an annuity of Re 1 for 5 years at 8% per annum interest is Rs. 3.993
So, Present value of cash inflows = 5,000 × 3.993 = Rs. 19,965
Hence, NPV = 19,965 – 20,000 = –Rs. 35

The company should not undertake the project as the NPV is negative; in other words, the benefits associated with the investment are less than the costs associated with it.

Scenario 2: *Mixed stream cash flows*

Young Brothers Ltd. is planning to buy software for manufacturing iPhones. The cost of the software is Rs. 60,000. Following are the cash flows associated with the project over its life period of five years.

Year	Cash Flows After Tax
1	Rs. 15,000
2	Rs. 20,000
3	Rs. 24,000
4	Rs. 22,500
5	Rs. 8,000

Determine whether the software should be invested in or not using NPV criteria, if the target return on capital is 9%.

Solution

Net present value = present value of inflows – present value of outflows

Present value of inflows =

$$\frac{15,000}{(1+0.09)} + \frac{20,000}{(1+0.09)^2} + \frac{24,000}{(1+0.09)^3} + \frac{22,500}{(1+0.09)^4} + \frac{8,000}{(1+0.09)^5}$$

Alternatively, using present value tables we get:

Year	1	2	3	4	5
PV at 9%	.917	.842	.772	.708	.650

Present value of inflows

$$= 15,000 \times .917 + 20,000 \times .842 + 24,000 \times .772 + 22,500 \times .708$$
$$+ 8,000 \times .650$$
$$= 13,755 + 16,840 + 18,528 + 15,930 + 5,200 = \text{Rs. } 70,253$$

Hence, NPV = 70,253 – 60,000 = Rs. 10,253.

The company can purchase the software as the NPV is positive, in other words the benefits associated with the investment are greater than the costs associated with it.

3. Profitability index (Pi)/benefit-cost ratio (B /C ratio)

It is the ratio of 'present value of future cash inflows and the present value of cash outflows' at the required rate of return. The index is used instead of net present value in case of evaluating mutually exclusive proposals with different costs.

It is calculated as:

$$PI = \frac{\text{Present value of cash inflows}}{\text{Present value of cash outflows}}$$

Acceptance/rejection rule

If PI > 1, accept the project and vice versa.

Example

Taking the example of Young Brothers Ltd. in the above illustration of NPV,

PI will be:

$$PI = \frac{\text{Present value of cash inflows}}{\text{Present value of cash outflows}}$$
$$= Rs. \frac{70,253}{60,000}$$
$$= 1.17$$

Since the profitability index is more than one, the project can be invested in.

4. Internal rate of return (IRR)

It is the rate of return at which NPV is zero, i.e. the rate at which 'PV of cash inflows = PV of cash outflows'. It can also be called the break-even rate of discounted cash flows. This rate of return is then compared with the budgeted rate of return to decide on the acceptance of the project.

Algebraically, it is expressed as:

$$C_0 = \frac{C_1}{(1+r)} + \frac{C_2}{(1+r)^2} + \frac{C_3}{(1+r)^3} + \ldots + \frac{C_n}{(1+r)^n}$$

$$C_0 = \sum_{t=1}^{n} \frac{C_t}{(1+r)^t}$$

$$= \sum_{t=1}^{n} \frac{C_t}{(1+r)^t} - C_0 = 0$$

Here, C_1, C_2 ... C_n represent future cash inflows
C_0 represents cash outflows
r is the Internal rate of return to be calculated
t = time period

Acceptance/rejection rule

If IRR > required rate of return, accept the project and vice versa.

Illustration 16.5: Bright Industries Ltd. want to expand its business by investing either in project A or in project B. Both the projects involve an outlay of Rs. 10,000 and have a lifespan of three years. The cash flows after tax associated with projects A and B are as follows:

Year	Project A (Rs.)	Project B (Rs.)
1	2,000	4,000
2	4,000	4,000
3	6,000	4,000

Based on the IRR criterion, determine which project the company should invest in.

Solution

IRR FOR PROJECT A
Let r represent the IRR of project A:

$$10,000 =$$
$$\frac{2,000}{(1+r)} + \frac{4,000}{(1+r)^2} + \frac{6,000}{(1+r)^3}$$

i.e. $10,000 = 2,000 \times \text{PVIF}_{(r\%,\ 1\ \text{year})} + 4,000 \times \text{PVIF}_{(r\%,\ 2\ \text{years})} + 6,000 \times \text{PVIF}_{(r\%,\ 3\ \text{years})}$

The value of the right-hand side of the equation at 9% is Rs. 9,834. The value of the right hand side of the equation at 8% is Rs. 10,044.

Hence, r will lie between 8% and 9%. Interpolating these two values we get,

$$r = 8\% + (9\% - 8\%) \times \frac{(10,044 - 10,000)}{(10,044 - 9,834)}$$
$$= 8.21\%.$$

IRR FOR PROJECT B

Let r represent the IRR of project B:

$$10,000 =$$
$$\frac{4,000}{(1+r)} + \frac{4,000}{(1+r)^2} + \frac{4,000}{(1+r)^3}$$

The PVIFA at 9% is 2.531 and PVIFA at 10% is 2.487.

NPV at 9% $= 4,000 \times 2.531 - 10,000 = 10,124 - 10,000 = 124$
NPV at 10% $= 4,000 \times 2.487 - 10,000 = 9,948 - 10,000 = -52$

Hence r will lie between these two values.
    Interpolating the two values, we get:

$$r = 9\% + (10\% - 9\%) \times \frac{(10,124 - 10,000)}{(10,124 - 9,948)} = 9.70\%.$$

Comment: IRR for Project B is higher and hence, more profitable than A.

Box 16.1   NPV vs. IRR

NPV is considered to be a better method for capital budgeting decision than IRR for the following reasons:

1   *Reinvestment of Cash Flows*: The NPV method assumes that the project's cash inflows are reinvested to earn the discounting rate, whereas the IRR assumes that the cash inflows are reinvested to earn the IRR. The NPV's assumption is more realistic in most situations because discounting rate is the financing cost whose recovery is the main criterion. IRR recovery is more of an interpolation.

2   *Multiple IRRs:* It is possible to have multiple IRRs for the same project. If the cash flows are non-conventional (e.g. positive cash flow in one year, negative cash flow in the next year), the IRR method will have more than one solution. The NPV method does not have this problem.

Case: Indian Cloth Mills Ltd.

Indian Cloth Mills (ICM) is situated in the east. They want to expand in the west, and therefore wish to acquire a cloth mill for Rs. 5,000 million. The additional equipment required for the project is Rs. 1,000 million. The mill has a time horizon of five years.

The corporate planning department of the company has done the profit forecasting for the mill's operation as given in the following table.

Table: Profitability Projections

	(Rs. in million)				
	Year				
	1	2	3	4	5
Sales	5,500	5,800	6,500	6,000	5,000
Materials and consumables	200	250	280	300	250
Wages and salaries	1,500	1,800	2,000	1,400	1,200
Selling and distribution costs	800	750	1,000	500	650
Depreciation (WDV@ 20%)	1,200	960	768	614	492
Corporate office costs	200	200	200	200	200
Profit (loss) before tax	1,600	1,840	2,252	2,986	2,208
Less: tax @ 30%	480	552	676	896	662
Profit after tax	1,120	1,288	1,576	2,090	1,546

There is a survey cost of Rs. 5 million incurred in the first year of the project. Corporate office costs incurred is Rs. 200 million per annum and half is for the project. The mill is sold for Rs. 3,200 million.

Financing of the project

The company proposes to finance the project:

(i)   50% by internal financing @ cost of 11%
(ii) 50% by raising a five-year 7% after-tax interest (10% before tax) loan from a financial institution.

Discussion question

Should the project be accepted and financed? Advise using the suitable capital evaluation techniques.

Solution

Step 1: Calculate 'Initial cash outflows'

	(Rs. mn.)
Cost of mill	5,000
Cost of equipment	1,000
Total capital investment/Total cash outlay	6,000

Step 2: Calculate 'Cash inflows'

(a)   Calculation of PAT

	(Rs.mn.)					
	0	*1*	*2*	*3*	*4*	*5*
Sales		5,500	5,800	6,500	6,000	5,000
Less: Materials and consumables		200	250	280	300	250
Wages and salaries		1,500	1,800	2,000	1,400	1,200
Selling and distribution costs		800	750	1,000	500	650
Depreciation (WDV) @ 20%		1,200	960	768	614	492
Corporate office costs		100	100	100	100	100
Survey costs		5	–	–	–	–
Total expenses		3,805	3,860	4,148	2,914	2,692
Profit (loss) before tax		1,695	1,940	2,352	3,086	2,308

		(Rs.mn.)				
	0	*1*	*2*	*3*	*4*	*5*
Less: tax @ 30%		509	582	706	926	693
Profit after tax		**1,187**	**1,358**	**1,646**	**2,160**	**1,616**

Notes:

1. Out of corporate office costs of Rs. 200 mn, only half is incurred for the project. Thus, the 'Relevant cost' of Rs. 100 million is charged to the project above.
2. The cost of 9% is 'weighted average cost of capital'* (WACC), arrived at as:

(Weights of debt × cost of debt after tax + Weights of equity × cost of equity)/ Weights

$(wd \times kd + we \times ke)$/weights

$= (11\% + 7\%)/2 = 9\%$

(b)   Calculation of cash inflows from PAT

To arrive at 'cash inflows', depreciation is added back to PAT.						
				(Rs. mn.)		
	0	*1*	*2*	*3*	*4*	*5*
Sales		5,500	5,800	6,500	6,000	5,000
Less: Materials and consumables		200	250	280	300	250
Wages and salaries		1,500	1,800	2,000	1,400	1,200
Selling and distribution costs		800	750	1,000	500	650
Depreciation (WDV) @ 20%		1,200	960	768	614	492
Corporate office costs		100	100	100	100	100
Survey costs		5	–	–	–	–
Total expenses		3,805	3,860	4,148	2,914	2,692
Profit (loss) before tax		1,695	1,940	2,352	3,086	2,308
Less: tax @ 30%		509	582	706	926	693
Profit after tax		1,187	1,358	1,646	2,160	1,616
Plus: depreciation		1,200	960	768	614	492
CFO		**2,387**	**2,318**	**2,414**	**2,774**	**2,107**

* For detailed discussion on WACC, refer to the next chapter on 'Cost of Capital'.

Step 3: Calculate NPV, IRR and payback

	0	1	2	3	4	5
	(Rs. mn.)					
Sales		5,500	5,800	6,500	6,000	5,000
Less: Materials and consumables		200	250	280	300	250
Wages and salaries		1,500	1,800	2,000	1,400	1,200
Selling and distribution costs		800	750	1,000	500	650
Depreciation (WDV) @ 20%		1,200	960	768	614	492
Corporate office costs		100	100	100	100	100
Survey costs		5	–	–	–	–
Total expenses		3,805	3,860	4,148	2,914	2,692
Profit (loss) before tax		1,695	1,940	2,352	3,086	2,308
Less: tax @ 30%		509	582	706	926	693
Profit after tax		1,187	1,358	1,646	2,160	1,616
Plus: depreciation		1,200	960	768	614	492
CFO		2,387	2,318	2,414	2,774	2,107
Cash outlay	–6,000					
Salvage value						3,200
Book value (Cost – Accum. Dep.)						1,966
Profit on Sale						1,234
Tax loss on Profit (SV – BV)						–370
Net cash flows	–6,000	2,387	2,318	2,414	2,774	4,937
NPV at 9%	5,179					
IRR	35%					
Cumulative cash flows	6,000	2,387	4,705	7,119	9,893	14,830
Payback (years)			2.54			

Note: The 'last year cash inflows' consist of annual cash inflows, terminal cash flows and tax saving.

Comment: In the above case, NPV is positive, that is Rs. 5,179 million and the IRR is higher than the discounting rate of 9%. So, it is advisable to purchase the cloth mill.

The payback period is just 2.54 years.

WORKING

The computation of 'NPV' is discussed below:

	1	2	3	4	5
Discounting factor @ 9%	0.917	0.842	0.772	0.708	0.650
PV of cash inflows	2,188.88	1,951.76	1,863.61	1,963.99	3,209.05

(*Net cash flows × discounting factor*)

NPV Cash inflows = Rs. 111,77.29 million
PV cash outflows = Rs. 6,000 million
NPV = Rs. 5,177.29 million.

Similarly, IRR can be computed using the methodology as discussed earlier in the chapter.

Points to remember

- Capital budgeting techniques are grouped in the following two categories: *(i) capital budgeting techniques not based on 'time value of money,'* and *(ii) capital budgeting techniques based on 'time value of money.'*
- The payback period is the traditional method of capital budgeting. It is defined as 'the time period required to recover the initial investment of the project'. The project with the shortest payback period is selected.
- The accounting rate of return (ARR) is the ratio of the average net income from the project to the assets of the project. It measures the rate of return on the project *using accounting profit* information.
- Discounted payback period is the time period taken in recovering the investment outlay on present value basis. It is an improved version of the payback method as it considers time value of money.
- Net present value method (NPV) is based on the time value of money and is a popular DCF method. It is the difference between the present value of net cash inflows and present value of cash outflows. A positive value implies that the project is profitable and vice versa.
- Profitability index (PI) is the ratio of present value of cash inflows and the present value of cash outflows at the required rate of return.

- Internal rate of return (IRR) is the rate of return at which NPV is zero, that is the rate at which PV of cash inflows = PV of cash outflows. This rate of return is then compared with the budgeted rate of return to determine the viability of the capital project.
- NPV is considered to be better than IRR on account of *(i) reinvestment of cash flows*, and *(ii) problem of multiple IRRs*.

17 Cost of capital

The financing of a project is the next important task after project selection. The discounting rate used in the capital budgeting decision can determine the success or failure of the project. The most common sources of finance which are used for financing the project are equity and debt. These financing options are used depending upon their risk-return trade-off. The discounting rate depends on the type of financing used for the project.

What is cost of capital?

It is 'the cost of acquiring funds for investment in a project'. It is also referred to as *discounting rate, cut-off rate, hurdle rate* or *target rate of return*. In this context, 'total cost of capital' and 'weighted average cost of capital' (WACC) are used interchangeably.

The computation of cost of capital is important on account of following reasons:

(i) *Capital investment decision*: The cost of capital is used as yardstick by the management to decide on the selection of a project.
(ii) *Capital structure decision*: The cost of various sources of finance is used as the factor for selecting the optimum mix of funds for financing the project.

Classification of costs

The costs of sources of finance can be classified into following two categories:

1 *Explicit costs*: These are the fixed costs that are paid by the firm to procure a source of finance. They consist of:

   (a) *Debt*
   (b) *Preference shares.*

2 *Implicit costs*: These costs are not fixed and assured like explicit cost. They are an opportunity cost. They consist of:

(a) *Equity shares*
(b) *Retained earnings.*

Computation of cost of capital

The process of computation of cost of capital comprises the following steps:

1 Compute 'Specific Costs'

(i)   *Cost of debt*
(ii) *Cost of preference shares*
(iii) *Cost of equity*
(iv) *Cost of retained earnings.*

2 Assign 'Weights to Specific Costs'

(i) Book value weights vs. market value weights.

3. Multiply (1) by (2) to get the 'cost of capital' (WACC)

$$ko = kdwd + kpwp + kewe + krwr$$

I Computation of specific costs

1. Cost of debt

The debt or loan component has an explicit cost as mentioned above. The cost of debt provides tax benefit to the company for interest payments, i.e. interest paid by the company on debt is tax deductible. *(See the example below.)*

Tax shield on interest example

	30% tax rate	
	A (Zero debt)	B (Rs. 3,000 debt @10%)
EBIT	5,000	5,000
Less: Interest	–	300
EBT	5,000	4,700
Less: Tax	1,500	1,410
PAT	3,500	3, 290

Effective interest rate   7%

Effective rate = $I(1 - T) = 10(1 - 0.30) = 7\%$

So, tax reduces the effective rate of debt for the company.

It is calculated as follows:

$$\text{Cost of debt}(kd) = \frac{I}{NP}(1-t)$$

Here, I = Annual interest payment
NP = Sale proceeds of debentures (par value − discount +
        premium − floatation cost)
t = Tax rate

Illustration 17.1: A company issues 10% irremediable debentures of Rs. 2 million at a face value of Rs. 1,000.

The company is in 30% tax bracket. Calculate the cost of debt (after tax) if the debentures are issued at (i) par, (ii) 10% discount and (iii) 10% premium.

Solution

1   Issued at par

$$kd = \frac{I}{NP}(1\text{-}t) = \frac{100}{1,000}(1-0.30) = 0.07(7\%)$$

2   Issued at discount

$$kd = \frac{I}{NP}(1-t) = \frac{100}{900}(1-0.30) = 0.077(7.7\%)$$

3   Issued at premium

$$kd = \frac{I}{NP}(1-t) = \frac{100}{1,100}(1-0.30) = 0.063(6.3\%)$$

2. Cost of preference capital

Like debt capital, preference share also has an explicit cost as the rate of dividend on preference share is fixed and known. But, the dividend paid to preference shareholders is not tax deductible so there is no tax benefit to the company.

It is calculated as follows:

$$\text{Cost of preference share}(kp) = \frac{D}{NP}$$

Here, D = Preference dividend
    NP = Sale proceeds of preference shares (par value – discount + premium – floatation cost)

Illustration 17.2: A company raises preference share capital for perpetuity of 1 million by issue of 10% preference shares of Rs. 100 each. The company is in 30% tax bracket. Calculate the cost of preference capital when they are issued at (i) par, (ii) 10% discount and (iii) 10% premium.

Solution

1 Issued at par

$$kp = \frac{D}{NP} = \frac{10}{100} = 0.1 \,(10\%)$$

2 Issued at discount

$$kp = \frac{D}{NP} = \frac{10}{90} = 0.11 \,(11\%)$$

3 Issued at premium

$$kp = \frac{D}{NP} = \frac{10}{110} = 0.090 \,(9.0\%)$$

3. Cost of equity capital

It is an imputed cost as there is no fixed rate of return paid to equity shareholders. The dividend paid to equity shareholders is variable. In addition, the return to equity shareholders also consist of market returns. Thus, the cost of equity capital (COEC) is the rate of return that the firm must earn to meet equity shareholders' expectations for maximising their wealth. It is commonly calculated by the *Capital Asset Pricing Model (CAPM)*.

Box 17.1 Capital Asset Pricing Model (CAPM)[1]

The CAPM is the most widely used method to calculate 'cost of equity'. It describes 'risk-return' trade-off for securities, implying thereby 'the higher the risk involved of a stock, the higher will be the return expected by shareholders'. It is based on the following assumptions:

(i)   Efficiency of security markets
(ii)   Investors' preferences for an optimum mix of risk-return.

CAPM classifies the 'investment risk' into two categories:

(i)   *Diversifiable/Unsystematic risk* (risk which can be reduced and controlled)
       (e.g. compensation policy of the company, strikes and lockouts)
(ii)   *Non-diversifiable/Systematic risk/Market risk* (risk which is uncontrollable)
       (e.g. interest rate changes, inflation)

The investors are sensitive to the 'systematic risk'. So, the measurement of non-diversifiable/systematic risk is relevant for an investment decision-making. Measurement of non- diversifiable risk/systematic risk of an investment/security is measured by the 'beta' coefficient.

$$\boxed{\text{CAPM Equation: } ke = Rf + b\,(km - Rf)}$$

Here,
   ke = Cost of equity capital
   Rf = the risk free rate of return
   km = expected market return, i.e. return expected on the market portfolio of shares
   $km - Rf$ = risk premium (difference between the expected market return and risk-free rate of return)
   b = beta of the firm's share (systematic risk of an equity share in relation to the market)

Beta coefficient and its application

" 'Beta' (β) is a measure of the volatility or sensitivity of a security's return in relation to changes in the return of the stock market".

Categories of beta

(i)   **Aggressive beta:** Shares with beta more than 1 are considered as aggressive beta stocks. They are relatively more risky to other stocks.

Example: Beta for State Bank of India (SBI) for July 2014 to June 2015 was 1.28. In the same sector (banking sector), the Beta of Axis Bank Ltd. was higher than SBI at 1.83.[2]

This shows greater volatility, being aggressive beta stocks. Further, this proves that there can be two stocks in the same sector but with different risks.

(ii) **Neutral beta:** Shares with beta equal to 1 are considered average beta stocks.
(iii) **Conservative/defensive beta:** Shares with beta less than 1 are considered defensive beta stocks. They are less risky to other stocks.

Example: Beta of Maruti Suzuki India Ltd. (MSIL) for July 2014 to June 2015 was 0.81 which indicates lower volatility. But in the same sector (automobile sector), Beta for Tata Motors Ltd. was 1.41, indicating greater volatility than Maruti.[3]

This again shows that there can be two stocks in the same sector but with different risks. For example, Maruti is a defensive beta stock, whereas Tata Motors is an aggressive beta stock.

Calculation of beta

$$\beta_j = \frac{\text{Covariance}\, i\; m}{\text{Variance}\, m}$$

= Co-movements of individual stock and market Index volatility

$$\beta_j = \frac{\text{Covar}_{j,m}}{\sigma_m^2}$$

$$= \frac{\sigma_j \sigma_m \text{Cor}_{j,m}}{\sigma_m \times \sigma_m} = \frac{\sigma_j}{\sigma_m} \times \text{Cor}_{j,m}$$

Illustration 17.3: The financial manager of New Ventures applies the CAPM to determine the firm's cost of equity capital. The financial analyst of the firms provides the following information about the equity funds:

> Risk free rate is currently 7%
> Market return is 11%
> Firm's beta is 1.4.

Solution

$$ke = Rf + \beta\ (Km - Rf)$$
$$= 7\% + 1.4\ (11\% - 7\%)$$
$$= 7\% + 1.4\ (4\%)$$
$$= 12.6\%$$

4. Cost of retained earnings

Like equity, retained earnings (reserves and surplus) also have an implicit cost as they do not involve any explicit payments by the management.

Cost of retained earnings is the return sacrificed by the equity shareholders. In other words, the cost of retained earnings is *the opportunity cost* of retained earnings which is equal to the cost of equity as follows:

> So $kr = ke$

II Assigning weights to specific costs

At this stage, the proportion of each source of fund is determined in the total capital structure of the company.

The weights assigned may be either:

(a) *Historical weights*

These weights are assigned with the current capital structure as the basis. The weights here can again be:
(i)   *book value weights*
(ii) *market value weights.*

Market value weights are usually preferred over book value weight for assigning weights in calculating WACC.

(b) *Marginal weights*

These weights are assigned in the ratio of new capital to be raised. So the weights here are for the new capitals structure.

III Multiply specific costs with weights to get total cost

This is the last stage of computing total cost of capital. The costs arrived at stage (1) are multiplied with the respective weights in stage (2) to arrive at 'WACC'.

Weighted average cost of capital (WACC)

$ko = \Sigma\ wiki$
$ko = kd\ (1 - t)wd + kewe + kpwp$

Here, ko = WACC

wd, we, wp = weights of each fund in the total capital structure

---

Illustration 17.4: Aspirations Ltd. is a one-year-old company. Following is its capital structure for 2015. Calculate the total cost of capital of the firm for business valuation, using (a) book value weights and (b) market value weights:

Source	Book Value (Rs.)	Market Value (Rs.)
Equity Share Capital (Rs. 10 shares)	30,000	40,000
Preference Share Capital	10,000	10,000
Debentures	10,000	11,000

The after-tax cost of different sources of finance is as follows:

Equity Share Capital: 14%; Preference Share Capital: 9%; Debentures: 7%.

Solution

(a) *WACC (Book Value Weights)*

Source (1)	Amount (Rs.) (2)	Proportion/ Weight (3)	After Tax Cost (4)	Weighted Cost (3) × (4)
Equity Share Capital	30,000	0.6	14%	8.4%
Preference Share Capital	10,000	0.2	9%	1.8%
Debentures	10,000	0.2	7%	1.4%
	50,000			11.6%

Here, Weighted Average Cost of Capital (ko) = **11.6%**

(b) *WACC (Market Value Weights)*

Source (1)	Amount (Rs.)(2)	Proportion/ Weight (3)	After Tax Cost (4)	Weighted Cost (3) × (4)
Equity Share Capital	40,000	0.655	14%	9.17%
Preference Share Capital	10,000	0.16	9%	1.44%
Debentures	11,000	0.18	7%	1.26%
	61,000			11.87%

Here, Weighted Average Cost of Capital (ko) = **11.87%**

Comment: WACC according to market value weights is higher than the WACC as per book value weights.

Points to remember

- Cost of capital is the cost of acquiring the funds for investment in a project. It is often referred to as *discounting rate, cut-off rate, hurdle rate* or *target rate of return*. It helps in *(i) capital investment decision,* and *(ii) capital structure decision.*
- Explicit costs are the fixed costs that are paid by the firm to procure a source of finance. They consist of: *(i) debt,* and *(ii) preference shares.*
- Implicit costs are not an assured cost like explicit cost. They are an opportunity cost. They comprise of: *(i) equity shares* and *(ii) retained earnings.*
- The process of computation of cost of capital comprises the following steps: *(i) compute specific cost, (ii) assign weights, to specific costs,* and *(iii) multiply them to get WACC.*
- Cost of equity capital (COEC) is usually calculated by the *Capital Asset Pricing Model* (CAPM).

- CAPM describes the 'risk-return trade-off' for securities. According to it, the measurement of non-diversifiable/systematic risk is relevant for an investment decision-making. Measurement of non-diversifiable risk/systematic risk of an investment/security is measured by 'beta' coefficient.
- 'Beta' (β) is a measure of the volatility or sensitivity of a security's return in relation to changes in the return of the stock market.
- There are three categories of beta: *(i) aggressive beta (ii) neutral beta,* and *(iii) defensive beta.*

Notes

1 Goel, Sandeep. 2015. *Capital Budgeting*. New York: Business Expert Press, p. 122.
2 BSE, www.bseindia.com/indices/betavalues.aspx (accessed on 5 June 2017).
3 BSE, www.bseindia.com/indices/betavalues.aspx (accessed on 5 June 2017).

18 Capital structure planning

After computing the cost of capital, the firm decides about its 'capital structure' as a part of financing policy. The weighted average cost of capital (WACC) is helpful in the capital structure decision. It is used as the basis for evaluating various sources of finance and thus helps the company whether it should procure the required source of finance or not. Every firm tries to minimise its WACC by employing a suitable capital mix, as a firm with lower WACC can pass on higher profits to its owners. In short, a firm aims to have an optimum capital mix of debt and equity for shareholders' wealth maximisation.

The 'financing decision' of a firm involves a consideration of three principal responsibilities of the finance manager. These are:

(a) Estimation of total financial requirements for the business enterprise
(b) Identification of sources of finance and determining the financing mix
(c) Exploring sources of finance and raising the required finance.

In other words, 'financing decision' of a project or enterprise covers two inter-related aspects:

(a) Determination of an appropriate 'financial/capital structure'
(b) Raising the required amount of funds.

Capital structure defined

The resources' requirement of a firm can be financed either by owners' equity or creditors' funds. The owners' funds comprise ordinary shares or retained earnings; the creditors' funds denote borrowings.

The various means of financing represent the financial structure of an enterprise. The 'liability plus equity' side of the balance sheet represents the 'financial structure' of a company.

Box 18.1   Financial structure vs. capital structure

The 'financial structure' refers to the total amount of funds of an enterprise. Traditionally, short-term borrowings are excluded from the list of methods of financing the firm's capital expenditure, and therefore, the long term claims are said to form the 'capital structure' of the enterprise.

Capital structure is the composition of debt and equity. Determination of an optimal capital structure is a significant managerial decision. It influences the shareholder's return and risk. Consequently, the market value of the shares may be affected by the capital structure decision.

Types of business finance

Finance used in business is of the following kinds.

1. Long-term finance

Long-term finance refers to that category of funds whose repayment is generally more than a ten-year period. It is raised from shareholders, debenture holders, financial institutions and retained earnings.

Such type of finance is used for investment in fixed assets, such as land, buildings, plants, machinery, furniture, fixtures and so forth. Long-term finance is used for meeting the permanent needs of business. Such finance cannot be taken out of the business without closing down the firm or without reducing the scale of operations.

2. Medium-term finance

Medium-term/intermediate-term finance is that category of finance whose repayment can be projected within a planning cycle of reasonable length of time. It is raised for a period of more than one year but less than ten years from debenture holders, financial institutions, public deposits and commercial banks. This type of finance is required for investment in permanent working capital and for repayment of assets.

3. Short-term finance

Short-term finance is that category of finance which is employed by an enterprise for day-to-day operations. It is used for meeting obligations of time period of year or less. It is raised from trade credit and commercial banks and so represented by current liabilities and provisions. It is invested in current assets which is also known as 'working capital'.

Instruments of finance*

A business form can raise funds from two main sources: owned funds and borrowed funds.

Owned funds refer to the funds provided by the owners. In a *proprietorship*, the proprietor himself provides the owned funds from his personal resources. In a *partnership form*, the ownership funds are contributed by partners jointly. In a *joint stock company*, owned funds are raised through the issue of shares and reinvestment of earnings.

Borrowed funds refer to the borrowings of a business firm. In a company, borrowed funds consist of the funds raised from debenture holders, financial institutions, public deposits and commercial banks. Thus, the various instruments of finance may be divided as shown in Figure 18.1.

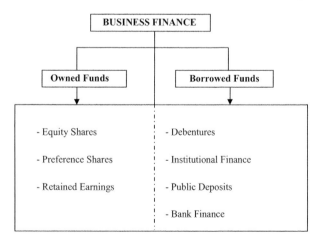

Figure 18.1 Instruments of finance

* Refer to Chapter 9, 'Financial Markets', for further discussion on instruments of finance.

1. Shares

The issue of shares is the most important source of raising long-term finance. The 'share' indicates the interest of a shareholder in the assets and profits of a company. Shares can be issued in the following forms:

(a) Equity (ordinary) shares

Equity shares are real owners of a company as they are paid in the last after everyone has been paid out of profits of the company. They do not carry any special or preferential rights in the payment of annual dividend or repayment of capital.

(b) Preference shares

Preference shares are those shares which carry certain special or preferential rights in the payment of dividend and repayment of capital as compared to equity shareholders.

2. Retained earnings

Retained earnings, also referred to as 'reserves and surplus', are the profits which have not been distributed as dividends but have been kept for reinvestment in business.

3. Debentures

Debentures represent the borrowings of a company for a fixed rate of interest to be paid to the debenture holders and repayment to them before anything is paid to other fund providers.

4. Institutional finance

Institutional finance consists of financing from the central and state level financial institutions to the business firms, for example *IFCI* and state finance corporations *(SFCs)*.

5. Public deposits

Public deposits refer to the deposits received by a company from the public as loan or debt.

6. Bank finance

Bank finance refers to the finance raised from commercial banks. Commercial banks are an important source of short-term and medium-term finance for business.

Factors affecting capital structure

There are various factors which govern the capital structure decision. They should be duly considered before taking any rational decision regarding capital structure. They are as follows.

1. Profitability

It is logically the first step in the direction of designing a firm's capital structure. The profitability status of the company affects the choice among debt or equity for capital mix. This analysis is based on the 'Earnings before Interest and Tax – Earnings per Share (EBIT – EPS)' relationship as EBIT should be higher than the interest payment on debt funding for stability of the company. EPS is a measure of a firm's performance, therefore the EBIT/EPS analysis information is extremely useful to the finance manager in arriving at an appropriate financing decision.

2. Liquidity

The analysis of the liquidity of the firm is an important factor in capital structure planning in addition to profitability analysis. It is significant in the context of the risk of insolvency as interest payments on debt capital affect the cash flows of the company.

3. Cost of raising capital

The cost of raising finance has an important influence on the capital mix. The cost of equity share capital is higher than that of debenture and preference share capital. Debentures are a cheaper source of finance because the interest payable on debentures entitles the tax benefit to the company.

4. Nature of enterprise

The nature of the enterprise is one of the important factors affecting the capital structure of an enterprise. Business concerns with stable earning may raise funds by issues of debentures or preference shares because they will not feel the burden of fixed cost. On the other hand, the companies with fluctuating earnings rely more on equity share capital for raising their funds.

5. Control

The control factor also determines the type of capital to be raised. If the management is not prepared for the dilution of control, it will prefer to raise capital through borrowings, as the creditors cannot participate in the management of the company. If the management is prepared, it may go for the equity capital.

6. Flexibility of financial structure

Flexibility means the firm's ability to change its capital structure to the needs of the changing conditions. A capital structure is flexible if it is possible to acquire additional capital either through owned capital or through borrowed capital. So, if a company wants greater flexibility, it must have enough scope for addition to capital either through owned capital or borrowed capital.

7. Capital market conditions

Capital market conditions also affect the availability of a particular type of capital. In the case of a boom, people will like to invest in shares as they expect increasing profits; during a depression, they will like to invest in debentures so that they do get a given return on their investment.

8. Legal requirements

The state regulations regarding the issue of securities also have a bearing on the capital structure of a company. This is particularly true in the case of Indian banking companies which have to abide by the provisions of the Banking Regulation Act, 1949 for issuing the securities.

Concept of leverage

Leverage refers to any method or technique followed by a firm to multiply its gains. In other words, it is the employment of an asset or source of funds for which the firm has to pay a fixed cost or return. It is used by the company to maximise shareholders' value.

The leverage can be either 'operating' leverage or 'financial' leverage. The use of fixed operating costs by a firm to magnify EBIT is called *operating leverage*. The use of fixed financing costs by a firm to magnify EPS is termed as *financing leverage*.

Leverage ratio

This ratio is used to calculate the amount of fixed obligations involved in a company's structure and its ability to meet those obligations. As mentioned above, the leverage ratios are of two types: operating leverage ratio and financial leverage ratio.

1   *Operating leverage ratio*: It is the degree of fixed operating costs involved in a project. So, a firm with lower sales is a highly leveraged firm and affirm with higher sales is a low leveraged firm. It is calculated as:

$$DOL = \frac{\text{Percentage change in EBIT}}{\text{Percentage change in sales}}$$

Here, DOL = Degree of operating leverage

The higher the degree of operating leverage, the greater the operating risk and vice versa.

2   *Financial leverage ratio*: It is the degree of total debt involved in the financial structure of a firm. It is also called the 'debt to equity ratio'. Its accepted norm is 2:1. A high financial leverage ratio indicates risk of payment of interest and repayment of principal. It is calculated as:

$$DFL = \frac{\text{Percentage change in EPS}}{\text{Percentage change in EBIT}}$$

DFL = Degree of financial leverage

The higher the degree of financial leverage, the higher the financial risk and vice versa.

Box 18.2   Financial Leverage* and Shareholder's Wealth

The primary motive of a company in using 'financial leverage' is to magnify the shareholder's returns, given the fact that the fixed-financial cost is lower than the firm's rate of return (ROI). So, the difference between the earnings generated by assets financed by the fixed charges funds and costs of these funds is distributed to the shareholders as wealth in the form of higher EPS.

Measures of leverage:** The ratios which measure how financially sound a company is to meet its long term obligations are known as 'leverage or solvency ratios'. There are three common solvency ratios:

- Debt-Equity Ratio = Debt/Equity
- Interest Coverage Ratio = EBIT/Interest on long-term loans
- Debt Service Coverage Ratio = CFO/Interest + Instalments

Factors determining financial leverage

The financial leverage or 'trading on equity' is subject to the following factors:

1   **Adequate return.** A company can have trading on equity only when the rate of return on total capital employed is more than the rate of interest/dividend on debentures/preference shares.
2   **Stable earnings.** Trading on equity is beneficial only for those companies which have stable earnings. The reason being is that both interest and preference dividend impose a recurring burden on the company. In the absence at stable profits, the company may face serious financial difficulties in case of trade depression.
3   **Security.** There must be sufficient fixed assets to offer as security to lenders for trading on equity.

---

* Financial leverage is also referred to as 'trading on equity'.
** Refer to Chapter 5, 'Financial Analysis', for detailed discussion on the measures of leverage.

4 **Risk consideration.** Every rupee of extra borrowings increases the risk. This results in an increase in the expected rate of interest by the subsequent lenders. Thus, borrowings become costlier, ultimately leading to reduction in profits available for equity shareholders.

Box 18.3   Capital structure analysis

The overall financial structure of an undertaking can be analysed from the point of view:

(i) Duration of time
(ii) Trading on equity.

> *Duration of time*: The study of financial structure is done initially from the point of view of the length for which funds are needed with their respective ownership. As a matter of fact, an enterprise needs funds for financing *long-term, medium-term* and *short-term requirements.*
>
> *Trading on equity*: It is analysed with respect to the debt-equity funding in the capital structure and the return enjoyed by equity shareholders.

Capital structure analysis of Ashok Leyland, Maruti Suzuki and Bajaj Auto

---

The present section analyses capital structure of the leading companies in the 'Indian automobile sector' on a comparative basis. This will provide practical insights into the different financing policies of companies in the sector.

These companies are multinationals (MNCs), therefore their analysis will be relevant global level. The data of the companies has been taken from their annual reports.

Indian automobile sector

The Indian auto industry is one of the largest in the world and is a prominent auto exporter.

Ashok Leyland Ltd. started in 1948 and is the second largest manufacturer of commercial vehicles in India. Maruti Suzuki Ltd. is India's leading automobile manufacturer and the market leader in the car segment. Bajaj Auto Ltd. is the leading two- and three-wheeler manufacturing company in India and ranked as the world's fourth largest in the segment.

Parameters for analysis

- 'Debt to equity ratio' of the units has been analysed to study their *financing policy.*
- *Degree of financial leverage* has been further calculated to measure 'the level of financial risk' of the units.
- The correlation has been studied between D/E ratio and ROE or RONW to find the *impact of leverage on shareholder's wealth.*

1. Ashok Leyland

The financing mix of Ashok Leyland is given in Table 18.1.

Table 18.1 Ashok Leyland's financing analysis

Types	Parameters	2008–2009	2009–2010	2010–2011
Financial Leverage Ratios	Debt/Equity (in times)	0.67	0.95	0.97
	Debt/Total Assets (in times)	0.36	0.38	0.39
	ICR (in times)	2.30	6.35	5.24
Shareholder's Wealth Ratios	ROE or RONW (%)	8.97	19.06	25.29
	EPS (Rs.)	1.26	2.94	4.42
Degree of Financial Leverage	EBIT (Rs. in crores)	368.77	646.62	990.72
	% change in EBIT		75.34	53.21
	EPS (Rs.)	1.26	2.94	4.42
	% change in EPS		133.33	50.34
	Degree of Financial Leverage		1.77	0.95
Correlation	0.95	Positive Correlation		

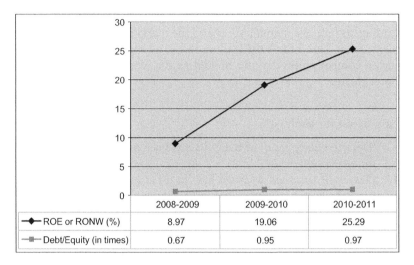

	2008-2009	2009-2010	2010-2011
ROE or RONW (%)	8.97	19.06	25.29
Debt/Equity (in times)	0.67	0.95	0.97

Figure 18.2 Ashok Leyland's financing trend

In the case of Ashok Leyland, it can be observed that there is positive correlation between D/E and ROE and both have been increasing for the years under study. This indicates that Ashok Leyland has been able to increase its shareholders' wealth by leveraging debt.

So, it's always better to choose debt option if EBIT is increasing and higher than the interest component.

2. Maruti Suzuki

The financing mix of Maruti is given in Table 18.2.

Table 18.2 Maruti's financing analysis

Types	Parameters	2008–2009	2009–2010	2010–2011
Financial Leverage Ratios	Debt/Equity (in times)	0.09	0.07	0.04
	Debt/Total Assets (in times)	0.07	0.06	0.02
	ICR (in times)	29.91	108.24	125.35
Shareholder's Wealth Ratios	ROE or RONW (%)	12.08	23.58	17.81
	EPS (Rs.)	41.57	85.43	77.98
Degree of Financial Leverage	EBIT (Rs. in crores)	1,726.80	3,626.00	3,133.80
	% change in EBIT		109.98	–13.57
	EPS (Rs.)	41.57	85.43	77.98
	% change in EPS		105.51	–8.72
	Degree of Financial Leverage		0.96	0.64
Correlation	–0.39	Negative Correlation		

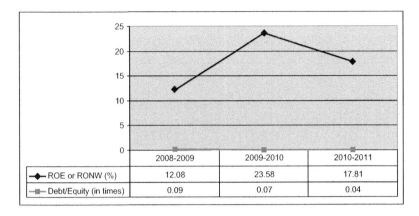

Figure 18.3 Maruti's financing trend

In case of Maruti Suzuki, it is found that there is negative correlation between D/E and ROE. D/E has been decreasing for consecutive years but on other hand ROE has been fluctuating, first it increased sharply in 2010 and in same fashion it fell sharply in the next year. In such condition, it is difficult to establish the impact of leverage on shareholder's wealth.

3. Bajaj Auto Limited

The financing mix of Bajaj Auto is given in Table 18.3.

Table 18.3 Bajaj's financing analysis

Types	*Parameters*	*2008–2009*	*2009–2010*	*2010–2011*
Financial Leverage Ratios	Debt/Equity (in times)	0.84	0.61	0.21
	Debt/Total Assets (in times)	0.46	0.31	0.06
	ICR (in times)	54.32	403.61	2,119.19
Shareholder's Wealth Ratios	ROE or RONW (%)	44.50	70.98	70.16
	EPS (Rs.)	41.50	111.05	108.92
Degree of Financial Leverage	EBIT (Rs. in crores)	974.22	2,413.59	4,349.44
	% change in EBIT		147.74	80.21
	EPS (Rs.)	41.50	111.05	108.92
	% change in EPS		167.59	–1.92
	Degree of Financial Leverage		1.13	–0.02
Correlation	–0.76	**Negative Correlation**		

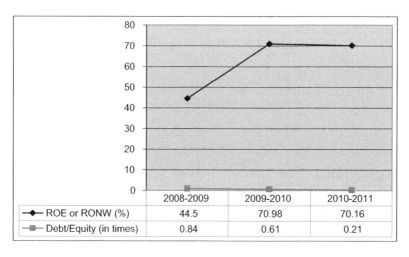

	2008-2009	2009-2010	2010-2011
◆ ROE or RONW (%)	44.5	70.98	70.16
■ Debt/Equity (in times)	0.84	0.61	0.21

Figure 18.4 Bajaj's financing trend

In case of Bajaj Auto, there is negative correlation between D/E and ROE. D/E has been decreasing over the years, but on other hand ROE has been fluctuating. It increased from 44.50% in 2008–09 to 77.98% in 2009–10 and then declined to 70.16% in 2010–11. In this case, it is again difficult to establish the impact of leverage on shareholder's wealth.

Points to remember

- The financing policy decision is deciding about the capital structure of the firm. A firm tries to have an optimum capital mix of debt and equity for shareholders' wealth maximisation.
- *Financial structure* is the total amount of funds of an enterprise. *Capital structure* is the composition of debt and equity.
- Finance used in business is of the following types, *(i) long-term finance, (ii) medium-tem finance,* and *(iii) short-term finance.*
- A business form can raise funds from two main sources: *(i) owned funds,* and *(ii) borrowed funds.*
- *Equity shares* are those shares which do not carry any special or preferential rights in the payment of annual dividend or repayment of capital. *Preference shares* are those shares

which carry certain special or preferential rights in the payment of dividend and repayment of capital as compared to equity shareholders. *Retained earnings* refer to the profits which have not been distributed as dividends but have been kept for reinvestment in business.

- *Debentures* are known as creditor ship securities because debenture holders are the creditors of a company. *Institutional finance* includes central and state level financial institutions to provide funds to the business firms. *Public deposits* refer to the deposits received by a company from the public as loan or debt. *Bank finance* refers to the finance raised from commercial banks.

- There are various key factors which govern the capital structure decisions, such as *(i) profitability, (ii) liquidity, (iii) cost of raising capital, (iv) nature of enterprise, (v) control, (vi) flexibility of financial structure, (vii) capital market conditions,* and *(viii) legal requirements.*

- 'Leverage' refers to the employment of an asset or source of funds for which the firm has to pay a fixed cost or return. The use of fixed operating costs by a firm to magnify EBIT is called *operating leverage.* The use of fixed financing costs by a firm to magnify EPS is termed as *financing leverage.*

- 'Leverage ratio' is used to calculate the amount of fixed obligations involved in a company's structure and its ability to meet those obligations. Leverage ratios are of two types: *(i) operating leverage ratio,* and *(ii) financial leverage ratio.*

- The financial leverage is subject to the following factors: *(i) adequate return, (ii) stable earnings, (iii) security,* and *(iv) risk considerations.*

- The overall financial structure of an undertaking can be analysed from the point of view: *(i) duration of time,* and *(ii) trading on equity.*

19 Working capital management

The term 'working capital' has several meanings in business and economic development finance. From a *financing perspective*, working capital refers to 'the firm's investment in short-term resources for running the business smoothly without any interruptions'. The goal of working capital management is to ensure that a firm is able to continue its operations and it can meet its day-to-day expenses and short-term debt as and when they arise. The management of working capital involves managing current resources, such as inventories, accounts receivable and payable, and cash. The sustainability and long-term growth of an organisation is linked to a sound and efficient working capital management.

Meaning of working capital

In simple words, working capital means 'the capital used to carry out the day-to-day operations of a business'. This indicates whether a company has enough short-term assets to cover its short-term debt. Anything below 1 indicates negative working capital (W/C), while anything over 2 means that the company is not investing excess assets. Most believe that a ratio between 1.2 and 2.0 is sufficient.

The capital required for a business can be classified under two main categories:

- *Fixed capital*
- *Working capital*

Every business needs funds for two purposes: for its establishment and to carry on its day-to-day operations.

'Long-term funds' are required to create production facilities through purchase of fixed assets, such as plant and machinery, land, building, furniture and so forth. Investment in these assets represents that part of firm capital, which is blocked on a permanent or fixed basis called **fixed capital**.

The funds are also needed for 'short-term purposes', that is for the purchase of raw material, payment of wages and other day-to-day operations of business. These funds are known as **working capital**. In other words, working capital refers to that firm's capital, which is required for short-term assets or current assets. Funds thus invested in current assets keep revolving last and being constantly converted into cash and this cash flow is again converted into other current assts. Hence it is known as 'circulating or short-term capital'.

The working capital requirement of an organisation is dependent on its 'working capital cycle or operating cycle' as it is commonly referred to (Figure 19.1). The shorter the length of the cycle, the lower would be the working capital requirement and vice versa.

Box 19.1   Operating cycle and Cash cycle

'Operating cycle' is the number of days taken by a company in realising its inventories in cash. It is the total of the time taken in selling inventories and the time taken in collecting cash from trade receivables. The length of the operating cycle determines the amount of investment required in working capital of an organisation. Operating cycle is a measure of the operating efficiency and working capital management of a company. A short operating cycle is good, as it indicates that the company's cash is tied up for a shorter period.

It is calculated as:

Operating cycle = Inventory conversion period + Debtors conversion period

Inventory conversion period is the average number of days taken by the company to sell its inventory. *Debtors conversion period* is the time taken to realise receivables in cash.

Example: Assume 60 days are taken to deliver and process the raw material, and sell the finished goods to the customers. Customers take a further 40 days on average to pay.

Operating cycle = 60 inventory days + 40 debtor days = 100 days

'Cash cycle' (also called the cash conversion cycle) is another useful measure used to assess the operating efficiency of a company. It denotes the actual cash requirement to run the business operations.

Cash cycle = Operating cycle – Payment period to suppliers

Example: Taking the above example further, if the firm receives 30 days' credit from its suppliers.

Cash conversion cycle = 100 days – 30 creditor days = 70 days

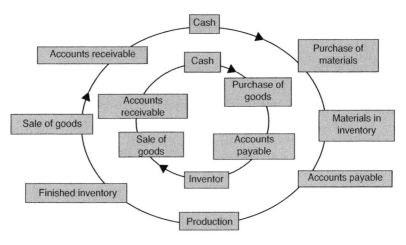

Figure 19.1 Operating cycle (working capital cycle)

Concept of working capital

1. Gross working capital

It refers to the firm's investment in 'total current assets' needed to operate over a normal business cycle. This implies the required investment in inventory, accounts receivable receivable, cash and other items listed as current assets on the firm's balance sheet.

2. Net working capital

Net working capital represents the difference between current assets and current liabilities. It may be positive or negative. Positive net working capital is that when current assets are more than current liabilities. But when current liabilities become more than current assets, then it is negative working capital. In this context, working capital financing concerns how a firm finances its current assets.

It is calculated as:

Working capital = Current assets – Current liabilities

How it works – example

Following is the sample balance sheet of ABC Company.

Balance Sheet of ABC Company as of 31 March 2015

	Amount (Rs.)		Amount (Rs.)
Cash	20,000	Accounts Payable	10,000
Marketable Securities	10,000	Bank Overdraft	20,000
Accounts Receivable	20,000	Accrued Expenses	10,000
Inventory	30,000	Cash Credit	20,000
Total Current Assets	80,000	**Total Current Liabilities**	60,000

Figure 19.2 Balance sheet of ABC Company

Using the working capital formula and the above information, we can see that ABC Company's working capital is:

Rs. 80,000 – Rs. 60,000 = Rs. 20,000

Constituents of working capital*

Following are the components of working capital.

A. Current assets

These assets are reasonably expected to be converted into cash within one year in the normal course of business. They include *cash and bank,*

* For further discussion on current assets and current liabilities, refer to Chapter 2, 'Fundamentals of Accounting'.

accounts receivable, inventory, prepaid expenses and other liquid assets that can be readily converted to cash.

1. Cash and bank

Cash is an asset that is in money form. It typically includes bank accounts and money market funds. Marketable securities, such as government securities/treasury bills, certificate of deposits are easily converted into cash within a short-period of time and are thus called 'cash equivalents'.

2. Accounts receivable

Accounts receivable (A/R) are amounts owed by customers for goods and services a company sold them on credit.

3. Inventory

Inventory includes raw material, semi-finished goods and finished goods lying unsold.

4. Prepaid expenses

These assets arises on a balance sheet as a result of business making payments for goods and services to be received in the nearby future. While prepaid expenses are initially recorded as assets, their value is expensed over time as the benefit is received onto the income statement, because unlike conventional expenses, the business will receive something of value in the near future.

B. Current liabilities

These are the company's debts or obligations that are due within one year. Current liabilities appear on the company's balance sheet and include *short term debt, accounts payable, accrued liabilities* and other debts.

1. Short-term debt

Short-term debt includes any debt incurred by a company that is due within one year. The debt in this account is usually made up of short-term bank loans taken out by the company.

2. Accounts payable

Accounts payable (A/P) are amounts owed to suppliers and other creditors for goods and services bought on credit.

3. Accrued liabilities

Accrued liabilities are expenses that a business has incurred but has not yet been paid. A company can accrue liability for any number of items, like a pension account that will pay retirees in the future. Accrued liabilities are recorded as either short- or long-term liabilities on a company's balance sheet, depending upon the time period.

Estimation of working capital

The working capital requirement of an organisation is based on its 'operating cycle'. The different factors included here are *the conversion period in the production process, the holding period of inventory, the collection period to customers, the payment period from suppliers* and so forth.

   How working capital is computed is explained below with the help of the following illustration.

Illustration 19.1: Following are the details about the operating cycle of a typical manufacturing company.

Estimated Production	3,00,000 units p.a.		
Cost Break Up (per unit in Rs.):		*Holding/ Process /Collection Period:*	
Raw Material	20	Raw Material	2 months
Labour	15	WIP	1/2 month
Manufacturing Overheads	5	Finished Goods	1 month
Depreciation	5	Debtors	1 month
Selling Overheads	5	Creditors	2 months
Total Cost	50		
Profit	10	Cash Balance	Rs. 5,00,000
Selling Price	60		

Calculate the monthly working capital requirement in the present case.

Solution

A. Calculation of requirement of each component of working capital

	Rs.
1. Raw Material	
Annual Consumption (3,00,000 × Rs. 20)	60,00,000
Monthly Consumption	5,00,000
Average Holding (5,00,000 × 2 months)	10,00,000
2. WIP	
Annual Production Cost (3,00,000 × Rs. (20 + 15 + 5)	120,00,000
Monthly Production	10,00,000
Average Holding (10,00,000 × 1/2 month)	5,00,000
3. Finished Goods	
Annual Production (3,00,000 × Rs. (20 + 15 + 5)	120,00,000
Monthly Production	10,00,000
Average Holding (10,00,000 × 1 month)	10,00,000
4. Debtors	
Annual Cost of Sales (3,00,000 × Rs. (20 + 15 + 5 + 5)	135,00,000
Monthly Cost of Sales	11,25,000
Average Debtors (11,25,000 × 1 month)	11,25,000
5. Sundry Creditors	
Annual Consumption (3,00,000 × Rs. 20)	60,00,000
Monthly Consumption	5,00,000
Average Creditors (5,00,000 × 2 months)	10,00,000

Note: Depreciation is not considered in the above computation, being a non-cash operating expenditure.

B. Calculation of Net Working Capital

	Rs.
I. Current Assets:	
Cash	5,00,000
Raw Material	10,00,000
WIP	5,00,000
Finished Goods	10,00,000
Debtors	11,25,000
Total	41,25,000
II. Current Liabilities:	
Sundry Creditors	10,00,000
Net Working Capital (I-II)	31,25,000

Types of working capital

The following are the different types of working capital required in an organisation.

1. Permanent working capital

As the operating cycle is a continuous process so the need for working capital also arises continuously. But the magnitude of current assets needed is not always same; it increases and decreases over time. However there is always a minimum level of current assets. This level is known as '*permanent or fixed working capital*'. It refers to the core current assets which are essential to run a business. Therefore, it is also called 'core working capital'.

2. Temporary working capital

The extra working capital needed to support the changing production and sales activities, is called '*variable or temporary working capital*'. These are shown in Figure 19.3.

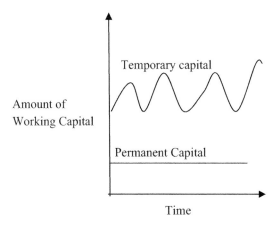

Figure 19.3 Types of working capital

Determinants of working capital

The working capital requirement depends upon various factors which are discussed below, though the importance of influence of theses determinants on working capital may differ from firm to firm.

1. Nature and size of business

The working capital of a firm basically depends upon nature of its business, *for example* public utility undertakings like electricity; water supply needs less working capital because they offer deals in cash revenues, whereas trading and financial firms have very less investment in fixed assets but require a large sum of money invested in working capital.

The size of business also determines working capital requirement and it may be measured in terms of scale of operations. The greater the size of operations, the larger will be the requirement of working capital.

2. Manufacturing cycle

The manufacturing cycle also creates the need of working capital. Manufacturing cycle starts with the purchase and use of raw material and completes with the production of finished goods. If the manufacturing cycle will be longer, more working capital will be required and vice versa.

3. Production policy

Production policy also determines the working capital level of a firm. If the firm has steady production policy, it may require need of continuous working capital. But if the firms adopt a fluctuating production policy means to produce more during the lead demand season, then more working capital may be required at that time but not in other periods during a financial year. So the different production policies lead to need for different types of working capital.

4. Firm's credit policy

The firm's credit policy directly affects the working capital requirement. If the firm has a liberal credit policy, the more credit period will be provided to the debtors, so this will lead to more of a working capital requirement. With the liberal credit policy, operating cycle length increases and vice versa.

5. Sales growth

Working capital requirement is directly related with sales growth. If the sales are growing, more working capital will be needed due to need of more raw materials, finished goods and credit sales.

6. Business cycle

Business cycle refers to alternate expansion and contraction in general business. In a boom period, larger amount of working capital is required, whereas in a period of depression, a lesser amount of working capital is required.

Types of working capital policy

Following are the different type of working capital financing policy adopted by an organisation.

1. Aggressive working capital policy

This is 'high risk, high return policy'. It involves keeping a low amount of current assets by the enterprise. It finances the current assets by short-term sources. Therefore, it is risky and results in 'negative working capital'.

Here, the strategy is to defer the payments to the suppliers the maximum possible extent and to collect from the customers sooner. So a business uses very little of its own cash, paying the creditors as late as it possibly can. It is a high-risk arrangement because if your creditors ask for their payments and, for some reason, you don't have enough money to pay them off; you might land up in trouble.

> "More risky, less costly"

Box 19.2   Negative working capital

Negative working capital occurs when current liabilities exceed current assets, which can lead to bankruptcy. In another scenario, negative working capital is a sign of managerial efficiency in a business with low inventory and accounts receivable (which means they operate on an almost strictly cash basis).

Negative working capital good or bad?

'Ordinarily, having negative anything is not a good thing, but with operating working capital it can be'.

Negative working capital is good if the following conditions are satisfied:

1   If payment of all short term liabilities is on time
2   With good sales and profit margin
3   With proper inventory management.

If the above conditions are fulfilled, the working capital is funded by cash profits generated from normal operating cycle and there is no strain on payment.

2. Conservative working capital policy

This is the opposite of the aggressive approach. In this policy, you finance your current assets by long-term sources and keep a safety net for future uncertainty. This results in 'positive working capital'. So, this is the policy with the lowest risk, but it is less profitable as well as it reduces the money used in increasing the production.

"Less risky, more costly"

3. Matching working capital policy

This policy is an arrangement where the current assets of the business are used perfectly to match the current liabilities. It is a medium risk proposition. *For example*, if the creditor is due to be paid in five months, the company will ensure that there is enough cash to pay the creditor five months hence. It is also called a 'hedging approach'.

The following table lists the working capital policy of top ten Sensex companies. There is a mix of companies with positive and negative working capital as discussed above. It verifies that the working capital policy of a company is not sector specific.

Table 19.1 Working capital policy of top ten Sensex companies as of March
         2016

Company	Industry	Market capitalisation	Working Capital (Rs. in crores)
Adani Ports and Special Economic Zone Ltd.	Port	Large Cap	−564.33
Asian Paints Ltd.	Paints	Large Cap	1,431.72
Axis Bank Ltd.	Bank – Private	Large Cap	–
Bajaj Auto Ltd.	Automobile Two & Three Wheelers	Large Cap	1,665.23
Bharti Airtel Ltd.	Telecommunication-Service Provider	Large Cap	−16,486.10
Cipla Ltd.	Pharmaceuticals & Drugs	Large Cap	3,382.7
Coal India Ltd.	Mining & Minerals	Large Cap	4,399.24
Dr. Reddy's Laboratories Ltd.	Pharmaceuticals & Drugs	Large Cap	5,296.20
GAIL(India) Ltd.	Industrial Gases & Fuels	Large Cap	−126.43
HDFC Ltd.	Bank – Private	Large Cap	−1,03,832.92

Sources: 1. List of companies is taken from www.bseindia.com/sensexview/indexview_new.aspx?index_Code=16&iname=BSE30.

2. Working capital figure is taken from 'Moneycontrol database' (www.moneycontrol.com).

Note: Rs. 1 crore = Rs. 10 millions.

Working capital management

Working capital management involves the relationship between a firm's short-term assets and its short-term liabilities. The management of working capital is concerned with the problems that arise in attempting to manage the current assets, current liabilities and the inter-relationship that asserts between them.

The basic goal of working capital management is to manage current assets and current liabilities of a firm in such a way that a satisfactory of 'optimum level of working capital' is maintained, that is it is neither inadequate nor excessive. This is so because both inadequate as well as excessive working capital position is bad for business.

Effective working capital management encompasses several aspects of short term finance:

(i)   Maintaining adequate levels of cash
(ii) Converting short term assets (i.e. accounts receivable and inventory) into cash
(iii) Controlling outgoing payments to vendors, employees, and others.

To do this successfully, companies invest short-term funds in working capital portfolios of short dated, highly liquid securities, or they maintain credit reserves in the form of bank lines of credit or access to financing by issuing commercial paper or other money market instruments.

Effective execution requires managing and coordinating several tasks within the company, including managing short-term investments, granting credit to customers and collecting on this credit, managing inventory, and managing payables. It also requires reliable cash forecasts, as well as current and accurate information on transactions and bank balances.

The scope of working capital management includes transactions, relations, analyses and focus:

(i)   *Transactions* include payments for trade, financing and investment relations with financial institutions and trading partners must be maintained to ensure that the transactions work effectively.
(ii) *Analysis* of working capital management activities are required so that appropriate strategies can be formulated and implemented.
(iii) *Focus* requires that organisations of all sizes today must have a global viewpoint with a strong emphasis on liquidity.

Equally important is to note that that working capital needs vary from industry to industry, especially considering how different industries depend on expensive equipment.

Significance of working capital management

Working capital is the lifeblood of business. It is very essential to maintain smooth running of a business. No business can run successfully without an adequate amount of working capital. The main advantages or importance of working capital are as follows.

1. Sound liquidity

Working capital is a common measure of a company's efficiency, liquidity and overall health. Positive working capital indicates that the company is able to pay off its short-term liabilities immediately, whereas negative working capital indicates that a company is unable to do so. This is why any decrease in working capital suggests that a company is becoming overleveraged and struggling to sustain. Therefore, an efficient working capital management is of crucial importance for maintaining sound liquidity in the current state of business.

2. Smooth business operations

Working capital helps to operate the business smoothly without any financial problem for making the payment of short-term liabilities. Purchase of raw materials and payment of salary, wages and overhead can be made without any delay. Any day-to-day financial requirement can be met without any shortage of fund and interrupting flow of production.

3. Increase in goodwill

Sufficient working capital enables a business concern to make prompt payments and hence helps in creating and maintaining goodwill. Goodwill is enhanced because all current liabilities and operating expenses are paid on time.

4. Ease of obtaining loan

A firm having adequate working capital, high solvency and a good credit rating can arrange loans from banks and financial institutions in easy and favourable terms.

5. Risk management

Adequate working capital enables a firm to face business crises in emergencies such as depression. Working capital shortage can cause business to fail even though it may actually turn out to have profit. Therefore, the timing of payment, collection policies and asset purchases play an important role in mitigating risk of business shut-down.

Working capital analysis of Nestle India and Dabur India

The working capital practices of leading fast-moving consumer goods (FMCG) sector companies in India, *Nestle India* and *Dabur India* are discussed here on comparative basis. **They operate globally; therefore their analysis will be relevant for all.** This will also provide an insight into *the trend of positive and negative working capital and its 'impact on profitability'.* **The data has been taken from the annual reports of companies.**

Indian FMCG sector*

Nestle and *Dabur's* analysis of working capital practices is discussed below.

Table 19.2 Indian FMCG – working capital position

Nestle India (Negative Working Capital)					
	Dec '08	*Dec '09*	*Dec '10*	*Dec '11*	*Dec '12*
Net Current Assets (Rs. in crores)	–423	–598	–657	–884	–1,065
Net Sales (Rs. in crores)	4,329	5,142	6,260	7,491	8,327
Profit before Depreciation and Tax (PBDT)%	20%	20%	20%	21%	22%
Current Ratio (in times)	0.66	0.60	0.62	0.42	0.54
Quick Ratio (in times)	0.29	0.24	0.27	0.24	0.22
Inventory Turnover Ratio (in times)	11.39	11.61	12.33	11.60	11.55
Debtors Turnover Ratio (in times)	87.37	93.68	98.22	83.83	82.04
Average Raw Materials Holding Period (days)	25	31	22	30	–
Average Finished Goods Holding Period (days)	26	22	23	22	–
Number of Days in Working Capital	–35	–42	–38	–42	–46

Note: Rs. 1 crore = Rs. 10 millions.

* Refer to Chapter 5, 'Financial Analysis', for Indian FMCG sector and companies' overview.

Dabur India (Positive Working Capital)					
	Mar '08	Mar '09	Mar '10	Mar '11	Mar '12
Net Current Assets (Rs. in crores)	–34	276	30	243	360
Net Sales (Rs. in crores)	2,094	2,408	2,867	3,274	3,759
Profit before Depreciation and Tax (PBDT)%	19%	19%	20%	20%	17%
Current Ratio (in times)	0.91	1.19	0.93	0.99	1.15
Quick Ratio (in times)	0.58	0.99	0.68	0.78	0.85
Inventory Turnover Ratio (in times)	12.52	10.94	11.31	8.65	7.19
Debtors Turnover Ratio (in times)	25.94	22.63	23.62	19.67	17.62
Average Raw Materials Holding Period (days)	46	45	53	63	86
Average Finished Goods Holding Period (days)	20	21	22	29	28
Number of Days in Working Capital	–6	41	4	27	34

Note: Rs. 1 crore = Rs. 10 millions.

Comment: Nestle is with negative WC and Dabur is with positive WC. In this case, Nestle with negative working capital is more profitable then Dabur with positive working capital. On comparing the current ratio of both the companies, we find that current ratio of Nestle is less than 1, implying that it is more risky for the creditors as compared to Dabur, whose current ratio is approximately around 1. But this negative working capital is leveraged by Nestle to its advantage and contributing to higher profits.

Points to remember

- In simple words working capital means 'the capital used to carry out the day-to-day *operations of a business*'.
- The capital required for a business can be classified under two main categories: *fixed capital*, or the investment in permanent or fixed assets; and *working capital*, or the funds needed for 'short-term purposes'.
- 'Operating cycle' is the number of days taken by a company in realising its inventories in *cash*. *The length of the operating cycle determines the amount of investment required in working capital of an organisation. 'Cash cycle' (also called the cash conversion cycle) denotes the actual cash requirement to run the business operations.*
- *Gross working capital* refers to the firm's investment in 'total current assets' needed to operate over a normal business cycle. *Net working capital* represents the difference between current assets and current liabilities.
- The constituents of working capital are **current assets and current liabilities**. Current assets include *cash and bank, accounts receivable, inventory* and *prepaid expenses*. Current liabilities consist of *short-term debt, accounts payable* and *accrued liabilities*.
- There are two types of working capital required in an organisation: *permanent working capital*, or the core current assets which are essential to run a business; and *temporary working capital*, or the extra working capital needed to support the changing production and sales activities.
- The working capital requirement depends upon various factors, including *nature and size of business, manufacturing cycle, production policy, firm's credit policy, sales growth* and *business cycle*.
- Working capital financing policy adopted by an organisation can be aggressive, conservative or matching. An *aggressive policy* is a 'high risk, high return' policy. It involves keeping a low amount of current assets by the enterprise. It finances the current assets by short-term sources. Therefore, it results in 'negative working capital'. A *conservative policy* involves financing the current assets by long-term sources, which results in 'positive working capital'. In a *matching policy*, the current assets of the business are used perfectly to match the current liabilities. It is a medium-risk proposition.

- Working capital management involves the relationship between a firm's short-term assets and its short-term liabilities. The basic goal of working capital management is to manage current assets and current liabilities of a firm in such a way that a satisfactory 'optimum level of working capital' is maintained.

- The main advantages or importance of working capital are as follows: *sound liquidity, smooth business operations, increase in goodwill, ease of obtaining loan* and *risk management*.

20 Dividend policy

'Shareholders' wealth maximisation' implies magnifying the returns to shareholders by outperforming the accepted benchmarks. The returns comprise of both dividend yield and capital yield. *Dividend yield* arises when the company regularly pays dividend to shareholders in proportion to the increasing surplus. *Capital yield* arises when the company shows sound business performance which is reflected in the market returns of shareholders. The market performance of the company is not within the control of the management, but the dividend payments are decided by them. Therefore, an adequate dividend policy plays an important role in the shareholders' wealth maximisation.

Dividend policy: overview

It is the management decision about amount of profits to be distributed as cash dividends and the remaining profits to be reinvested for future growth. It also involves deciding about the payment in the form of stock dividends to the shareholders. The meeting of shareholders' expectations about dividends by the management influences in determining the share value, therefore, dividend policy is a significant decision by the management of a company.

Types of dividends

The dividend is paid by the company in various *direct* and *indirect forms* as follows

1   **Cash dividend.** This is the most common form of dividend payment by the company. It is the dividend which is paid in cash in the form of final dividend or interim dividend.

2 **Bonus shares.** 'Bonus shares' are also called 'stock dividend', as these are shares which are issued free of cost to the shareholders of a company, by capitalising a part of the company's reserves.

'Bonus issue' implies issues of 'extra' shares to existing share-holders. Bonus shares are issued to the shareholders in proportion to their holdings. For example, the bonus issue of 1:2 means company will issue one bonus share for every two shares held.

Bonus issue is also called *'book entry'* because it increasers the number of shares on one hand and decreases profits on the other hand. So, it does not affect the net worth in total. Post bonus issue, the share price usually falls in proportion to the bonus issue, thereby making no difference to the personal wealth of the shareholder in short run.

---

3 **Stock split.** A 'stock split' is a division of the stock into multiple shares with lower face value. It increases the number of shares in a public company. This is done by the company to make shares more affordable for the investors. It allows shareholders to enjoy higher dividends in future.

In the immediate run, the price in split is so adjusted that the before and after market capitalisation of the company remains the same and dilution does not occur.

For example, a company with 100 shares of stock priced at Rs. 10 per share. The market capitalisation is 100 × Rs. 10 = Rs. 1,000.

The company goes for a 1 to 2 stock split. There are 200 shares now and each shareholder holds twice the shares. The price of each share is adjusted to Rs. 5. The market capitalisation is 200 × Rs. 5 = Rs. 1000, which the same as before the split.

---

4 **Share buyback.** 'Share repurchase' occurs when a company buys back its own shares from the market and reduces the number of shares outstanding. This is considered as an alternative to the dividend payment as cash is returned to the investors through another way.

A buyback is a *'controlling tool'* which is used by the promoters or the management of the company to retain/increase control in their hands. Generally, companies buyback for probable takeovers or when they find their own shares to be undervalued or when they have surplus idle cash. Stock buybacks also increase the market valuation.

5   **Rights issue.** A 'rights issue' is an issue of new shares to the existing shareholders in order to raise capital. As a matter of right, the new shares are first offered to existing shareholders in proportion to their current shareholding.

Procedure for cash dividend payment

A company which intends to declare and pay dividend adopts the following procedure. Further, if the company's shares are listed on the stock exchanges, additional requirements relating to 'listing agreements' are to be followed.

1. Recommendation by board of directors

Dividend can be declared only on the recommendation of the board of directors of the company. The shareholders do not have any power to declare any dividend. the board of directors, after considering and approval of the financial statements of the company, determines the rate of dividend to be declared and then recommend the same to the shareholders. For this purpose, a board meeting is convened to pass the resolution for:

(a) *Rate of dividend and the amount of dividend to be paid*
(b) *Book closure date for dividend purposes*
(c) *Date of annual general meeting*
(d) *Bank with which the account shall be opened for the purpose of remittance of dividend*

2. Approval by the shareholders

The dividend recommended by the board of directors is declared by a resolution passed at the annual general meeting by the shareholders. The declaration of dividend should form part of an ordinary business item to be transacted in the notice of the annual general meeting. While approving the rate of dividend at the annual general meeting, the share-holders have power to declare a lower rate of dividend than what is recommended by the board but they have no power to increase the amount or the rate of dividend so recommended by the board of directors.

3. Dividend-interim dividend

After the Companies (Amendment) Act, 2000, interim dividend is now recognised as a part of final dividend (clause 14A of Section 2). An interim dividend can be declared by the board of directors and they have authority to do so. Further, the provisions contained in Section 205, 205A, 205C, 206, 206A and 207[1] shall apply to interim dividend.

4. Dividend to be deposited in a separate bank account

The company should deposit the dividend amount (including interim dividend) within five days of its declaration in the separate bank account opened for this purpose. It means that the interim dividend will have to be deposited in a bank account within five days of the board meeting, whereas the final dividend will have to be deposited within five days from the date of the annual general meeting in which it was approved by the shareholders. Also Section 205 (1B)[2] stipulates that the amount so deposited shall be used only for the purpose of payment of dividend (whether interim or final).

Determinants of dividend policy

An optimum dividend policy of an enterprise is determined after taking into consideration the following factors:

(i) *External factors*
(ii) *Internal factors*

A. External factors

Following are the external factors which affect the dividend policy of the firm.

1. General state of economy

The general state of economy affects to a great extent the management's decision to retain or distribute earnings of the firm. In case of uncertain economic and business conditions, the management may like to retain the whole or a part of the firm's earnings for future uncertainties.

2. Capital market access

In case a firm has an easy access to the capital market, it can follow a liberal dividend policy. However, if the firm has difficulty in accessing the capital market, it is likely to adopt a more conservative dividend policy.

3. Legal restrictions

A firm may also be legally restricted from declaring and paying dividends. *For example*, in India the Companies Act, 2013 and 1956 have laid down several provisions to be followed for the declaration and payment of dividends.

4. Contractual restrictions

The lenders of the firm generally put restrictions or covenants on dividend payment to protect their interests. *For example*, it may be provided in a loan agreement that the firm shall not declare any dividend so long the liquidity ratio is less than 1:1 or else.

5. Tax policy

The tax policy of the government also affects the dividend policy. The management's inclination to retain a larger amount of the firm's earnings or to pay liberal dividends are guided by the tax factor.

B. Internal factors

The following are the internal factors which affect the dividend policy of a firm.

1. Desire of the shareholders

The desire of the shareholders cannot be overlooked by the directors while deciding about the dividend policy. The shareholders expect two forms of return from their capital investment, namely, *capital gains* and *dividends*. In most cases, the shareholders' desire to get dividends take priority over the desire to earn capital gains because of the less uncertainly and sometimes due to the need for current income.

2. Financial needs of the company

The financial needs of the company may conflict with the desires of the shareholders. The management will give more weight to the financial needs of the company. However, retained earnings should be used as a source of financing only when the company has profitable investment opportunities.

3. Nature of earnings

A firm having stable income can afford to pay higher amount of dividends as compared to a firm with instable earnings.

4. Desire of control

Dividend policy is also influenced by the desire of shareholders or the management to retain control over the company. The issue of additional equity shares for procuring funds dilutes control. So, this factor also needs to be considered before arriving at a dividend decision.

5. Liquidity position

It is also important for the management to take into account the cash position and overall liquidity position of the firm before and after payment of dividends while taking the dividend decision.

Dividend policies

Various companies adopt different kinds of dividend policies. These policies are determined on the basis of factors, as discussed above. So, each of the dividend policies may exist across industries.

Following are the various dividend policies followed by companies.

I Constant dividend per share policy

In this policy, companies payout a constant DPS irrespective of their EPS, that is a change in their PAT (whether increase or decrease) would not affect the dividend paid out to shareholders. This kind of policy generally is an indication of the fact that the company does not prioritise shareholders' payout in the current run.

This type of policy is usually resorted to by companies which have minimum growth potential and little scope for any large expansion. Table 20.1 and Figure 20.1 present an example of such policy. Here, Apollo Tyres has paid a fixed amount of dividend of Rs. 4.50 per share irrespective of changing EPS throughout the years.

Table 20.1 Dividend policy of Apollo Tyres

	2003	2004	2005	2006	2007
EPS (Rs. per share)	33.05	18.37	17.64	20.39	27.14
DPS (Rs. per share)	4.50	4.50	4.50	4.50	4.50

Source: Annual Reports of Apollo Tyres

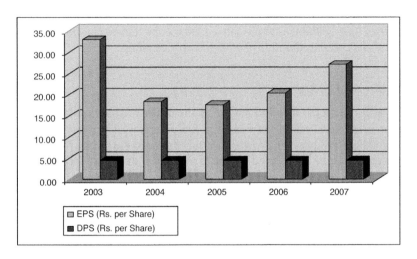

Figure 20.1 Dividend trend of Apollo Tyres

II Constant dividend payout policy

A 'constant dividend payment policy' means that a corporation establishes a certain dividend payout ratio and applies this to earnings every year, that is the fraction of earnings is paid out as dividends every year.

This policy ensures that retentions as well as dividends fluctuate with earnings, but with given investment plans. In such case, the outside finance will sometimes be required and reserves are affected by the dividend policy.

Table 20.2 and Figure 20.2 present an example of such policy, whereby Bharat Electronics Ltd. (BEL), an Indian public sector undertaking (PSU), has paid a constant payout of around 20% throughout the time period.

Table 20.2 Dividend policy of Bharat Electronics Ltd.

	March '11	March '12	March '13	March '14	March '15
EPS (Rs. per share)	107.69	103.74	111.23	116.45	145.90
DPS (Rs. per share)	21.60	20.80	22.30	23.30	29.20
D/P Ratio (%)	20.06	20.05	20.05	20.01	20.01

Source: Annual Reports of Bharat Electronics

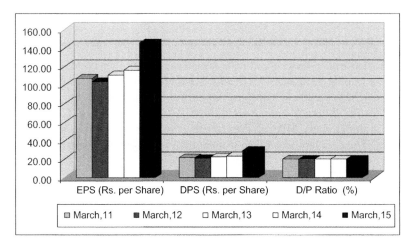

Figure 20.2 Dividend trend of Bharat Electronics Ltd.

III Long-run residual dividend policy

A 'long-run residual dividend policy' is designed to give shareholders reasonable confidence in the payment of dividends. Such a policy is created by the corporation by *first* forecasting the relevant variables, such as earnings, investment needs, interest charges and taxation, for a given period, usually five years.

Then the dividends from a pure residual policy are determined, total dividends for all years are compared with total earnings over the same period. *Lastly*, an average dividend payout ratio is determined. This is then applied to each year's earnings to fix the dividends.

IV Hybrid dividend policy

A 'hybrid dividend policy' encompasses a combination of the above policies as seen appropriate by the company. Using this approach, the companies view the debt/equity ratio as a long-term rather than a short-term goal.

As these companies generally experience business cycle fluctuations, they will generally have one set dividend, which is set as a relatively small portion of yearly income and can be easily maintained. On top of this set dividend, these companies will offer another extra dividend paid only when income exceeds general levels.

Dividend policy of HUL and Dabur India

The 'dividend policies' of Indian fast-moving consumer goods (FMCG) sector leading companies, *HUL and Dabur* are analysed here for providing an insight to the readers into the nitty-gritty of different types of dividend policies by different companies within the same sector. These companies are multinationals (MNCs), therefore their analysis is relevant at the global level. The data has been taken from annual reports of the companies.

Indian FMCG sector[*]

The dividend analysis of the above companies is explained below.

1. Cash dividend

(A) HUL

The company's dividend trend shows 'constant dividend policy' with few exceptions. For the year 2011, Hindustan Unilever has declared an equity dividend of 700% amounting to Rs. 7.00 per share. The company has shown a good dividend track by consistently declaring dividends for the period of five years.

Table 20.3 Dividend at a glance of HUL

Announcement Date	Effective Date	Dividend Type	Dividend %	Remarks
17–10–2011	04–11–2011	Interim	350	–
09–05–2011	08–07–2011	Final	350	–
14–10–2010	01–11–2010	Interim	300	–
25–05–2010	08–07–2010	Final	350	–
15–10–2009	06–11–2009	Interim	300	–
11–05–2009	12–06–2009	Final	400	–
15–07–2008	04–08–2008	Interim	350	–
13–02–2008	17–03–2008	Final	300	–
23–10–2007	07–11–2007	Interim	300	Dividend (Platinum Jubilee)
23–07–2007	07–08–2007	Interim	300	–
20–02–2007	20–04–2007	Final	300	AGM
10–07–2006	08–08–2006	Interim	300	–
14–02–2006	28–04–2006	Final	250	AGM

[*] Refer to Chapter 5, 'Financial Analysis', for Indian FMCG sector and companies' overview.

Dividend payout ratio (%)

- For 2008–2009: 76.47
- For 2009–2010: 75.20
- For 2010–2011: 71.20

(B) DABUR
The company has good dividend record and consistently declared dividends for the period of 2006 to 2011.

The board endeavours to maintain the dividend payout ratio around 50% according to:

(a) The company's need for capital for its growth
(b) The availability of adequate cash flow

Dividend payout ratio (%)

- For 2008–2009: 47.41
- For 2009–2010: 46.89
- For 2010–2011: 49.43

Table 20.4 Dividend at a glance of Dabur

Announcement Date	Effective Date	Dividend Type	Dividend (%)	Remarks
14–10–11	04–11–11	Interim	55.00	–
27–04–11	29–06–11	Final	65.00	–
13–10–10	02–11–10	Interim	50.00	–
18–06–10	03–08–10	Final	125.00	–
14–10–09	30–10–09	Interim	75.00	–
29–04–09	29–06–09	Final	100.00	–
13–01–09	02–02–09	Interim	75.00	–
30–04–08	19–06–08	Final	75.00	AGM
10–10–07	29–10–07	Interim	75.00	–
05–03–07	16–03–07	Interim	75.00	–
09–10–06	03–11–06	Interim	100.00	–
25–04–06	21–06–06	Final	100.00	AGM

2. Bonus issue

(A) HUL
The last bonus announced by Hindustan Unilever in 1991 was in the ratio of 1:2. This led to the quoting of share ex-bonus from 19 July 1991.

Table 20.5 Bonus issue of HUL

Announcement Date	Bonus Ratio	Record Date	Ex-Bonus Date
30–09–1991	1:2	21–08–1991	19–07–1991
22–06–1987	1:1	–	–
22–06–1983	3:5	–	–
22–06–1979	1:3	–	–

(B) DABUR
1 The bonus announced by Dabur in 2010 was 1 share for each share.
2 Like HUL, Dabur has also been liberal in bonus issue during the period.

Table 20.6 Bonus issue of Dabur

Announcement Date	Bonus Ratio	Record Date	Ex-Bonus Date
26–07–2010	1:1	10–09–2010	08–09–2010
31–10–2006	1:2	29–01–2007	25–01–2007
24–10–2005	1:1	20–01–2006	19–01–2006
30–09–1993	4:1	01–12–1993	16–11–1993

3. Stock split

(A) HUL
Hindustan Unilever had split the face value of its shares from Rs. 10 to Rs. 1 in the year 2000. The result was the quoting of share on an ex-split basis from 3 July 2000.

Table 20.7 Stock split of HUL

Announcement Date	Old Face Value	New Face Value	Ex-Split Date
05–07–2000	10	1	03–07–2000

(B) DABUR
Dabur India had split the face value of its shares from Rs. 10 to Rs. 1 in 2000. The effect on the share was quote on an ex-split basis from 27 November 2000.

Table 20.8 Stock split of Dabur

Announcement Date	Old Face Value	New Face Value	Ex-Split Date
03–11–2000	10	1	27–11–2000

Corporate cases

The corporate India cases in the *power sector* are discussed in this section for further insight into the subject. The financials of the companies have been taken from their annual reports. **The companies analysed here have global operations. So, their analysis will be relevant at the intentional level.**

Indian power sector

India's power sector is one of the most diversified in the world. The sources of power generation range from conventional sources such as coal, lignite, natural gas, oil, hydro and nuclear power to viable non-conventional sources such as wind, solar, and agricultural and domestic waste. India ranks third, just behind US and China, among 40 countries with a renewable energy focus.[3]

Here, we will discuss leading power units in India on comparative basis in public sector vs. private sector. *NTPC Ltd.*, set up in 1975, is India's largest power generation company in the public sector. It is one of the most diversified power major with presence in the entire value chain of the power generation business. *NHPC Ltd.* is a hydropower generation company in the public sector in India. *Tata Power Ltd., a part* of the Tata Group, is an electric utility company engaged into electricity generation and distribution. *Power Grid Corporation of India Ltd. (PGCIL)* is a state-owned company into the transmission and distribution of energy. *Torrent Power Ltd.* is engaged in electricity generation and distribution and also into hydroelectricity, wind power and so forth.

Analysis

The *dividend trend* of the units has been analysed with the help of the 'dividend payout ratio'.

The *earning potential* has been evaluated by examining their 'EPS trend'. This helps to find out the interrelationship among these two indicators for shareholders' interest.

1. NTPC

From the data it is evident that the numbers of shares are fixed, or constant. For the two years, 2010 and 2011 the dividend paid is constant, and thus DPS (dividend per share) is same for these two years. For the year 2012 there is an increase in the dividend paid, increasing the DPS. As PAT (profit after tax) has shown an increasing trend continuously from 2010 to 2012, EPS has also been increasing. So the company is doing well in terms of profit. But the payout ratio is almost constant for all the three years.

Table 20.9 Dividend picture of NTPC

Year	Dividend paid	PAT (Rs. crores)	No. of shares	DPS (%)	EPS (%)	Payout Ratio (%)
2010	3,133.20	8,728.2	82454.64	3.8	10.59	35.88
2011	3,133.26	9,102.59	82454.64	3.8	11.04	34.42
2012	3,298.73	9,223.73	82454.64	4	11.19	35.74

Note: Rs. 1 crore = Rs. 10 million

2. NHPC

From the data, it is clear that the numbers of shares are fixed, or constant. During the years 2010, 2011 and 2012 the dividend paid has been increasing continuously and thus DPS (dividend per share) has been increasing for these years. PAT (profit after tax) slightly increased from 2010 to 2011. In the year 2012, there is good increase in PAT and thus EPS is very high because the numbers of shares is constant. This is a very good sign for a company because the number of shares is constant and PAT has increased. But the payout ratio has shown a fluctuating trend during the period.

Table 20.10 Dividend picture of NHPC

Year	Dividend paid	PAT (Rs. crores)	No. of shares	DPS (%)	EPS (%)	Payout Ratio (%)
2010	676.54	2,090.5	123007.43	0.55	1.7	32.35
2011	738.04	2,166.67	123007.43	0.6	1.76	34.09
2012	861.06	2,771.77	123007.43	0.7	2.25	31.11

Note: Rs. 1 crore = Rs. 10 million

3. TATA POWER

It is clear that the numbers of shares are constant. From 2010 to 2011 the dividend paid has increased and so the DPS (dividend per share) increased during these two years. For 2012, the dividend paid did not increase but DPS changed as a *stock split* took place, thus increasing the numbers of shares. PAT (profit after tax) slightly decreased from 2010 to 2011 and therefore EPS also decreased, though PAT increased from 2011 to 2012. The payout ratio increased from 2010 to 2011, but decreased sharply in 2012.

Table 20.11 Dividend picture of Tata Power

Year	Dividend paid	PAT (Rs. crores)	No. of shares	DPS (%)	EPS (%)	Payout Ratio (%)
2010	285.05	947.65	2373.07	12	39.93	30.05
2011	296.92	941.49	2373.07	12.5	39.67	31.5
2012	296.92	1,169.7	23730.72	1.25	4.93	25.35

Note: Rs. 1 crore = Rs. 10 million

4. POWER GRID

The numbers of shares have been constant throughout. The dividend paid increased during the period, resulting in an increase in DPS (dividend per share). PAT (profit after tax) has also shown a continuous increasing trend during the period, resulting in an increasing EPS. The payout ratio is more or less constant around 30% during the years, indicating the securing payment to shareholders.

Table 20.12 Dividend picture of Power Grid

Year	Dividend paid	PAT (Rs. crores)	No. of shares	DPS (%)	EPS (%)	Payout Ratio (%)
2010	631.34	2,040.94	46297.3	1.36	4.40	30.91
2011	810.23	2,696.89	46297.3	1.75	5.83	30.02
2012	976.89	3,254.95	46297.3	2.11	7.03	30.01

Note: Rs. 1 crore = Rs. 10 million

5. TORRENT POWER

The numbers of shares are fixed during the period. For all the three years, the dividend paid has been increasing and thus DPS (dividend per share) has also been increasing for these years. PAT (profit after tax) also increased continuously from 2010 to 2012 and so the EPS. The payout ratio considerably increased from 16.93% in 2010 to 24.81% in 2012, signifying that company is sharing the increasing profits with the shareholders.

Table 20.13 Dividend picture of Torrent Power

Year	Dividend paid	PAT (Rs. crores)	No. of shares	DPS (%)	EPS (%)	Payout Ratio (%)
2010	141.73	836.55	4724.48	3	17.71	16.93
2011	259.85	1,065.72	4724.48	5.5	22.56	24.37
2012	307.08	1,237.46	4724.48	6.5	26.19	24.81

Note: Rs. 1 crore = Rs. 10 million

Conclusion

From the analysis of the companies, it is found that their payout ratios are in the range of 25%–35%. It is considerably a good ratio. The companies are distributing one-third of their earnings generated as dividend and the rest is retained as surplus.

But there is no fixed pattern found in the distribution of dividend of these companies, whereas a stable dividend pattern is always considered to be positive from the shareholders' point of view.

Points to remember

- Dividend policy is the decision by the management about the profits to be distributed as cash and part to be reinvested for future growth.
- The dividend is paid by the company in various forms as follows: *cash dividend, bonus shares, stock split, shares buyback* and *right issue*.
- 'Cash dividend' is the most common form of dividend payment by the company.
- 'Bonus shares' are shares which are issued free of cost to the shareholders of a company, by capitalising a part of the company's reserves.

- A 'stock split' is a division of the stock into multiple shares with lower face value. This is done by the company to make shares more affordable for the investors.
- 'Share buyback' occurs when a company buys back its own shares from the market and reduces the number of shares outstanding. This is considered as an alternative to the dividend payment.
- A 'rights issue' is an issue of new shares to the existing shareholders in order to raise capital.
- A company which intends to declare and pay dividend adopts the following procedure: *(i) recommendation by board of directors, (ii) approval by the* shareholders, *(iii) dividend decision – interim dividend and (iv) deposit of dividend in a separate bank account.*
- An optimum dividend policy of an enterprise is determined after taking into consideration the following factors: **external factors and internal factors.** External factors include *state of economy, access to capital market, legal restrictions, contractual restrictions* and *tax policy.* Internal factors include *desire of the shareholders, financial needs of the company, nature of earnings, desire of control* and *liquidity position.*
- 'Constant dividend per share policy' implies that companies payout a constant DPS irrespective of their EPS.
- **'Constant payout policy' means a corporation establishes a certain dividend payout ratio and applies this to earnings.**
- 'Long-run residual dividend policy' is created by the corporation by first forecasting the relevant variables and then the dividends from a pure residual dividend policy are determined.
- 'Hybrid dividend policy' means that the companies will generally have one set dividend and will offer another extra dividend paid only when income exceeds general levels.

Notes

1 Companies Act, 1956, www.mca.gov.in/Ministry/pdf/Companies_Act_1956_13jun2011.pdf (accessed on 21 February 2013).
2 Companies Act, 1956, www.mca.gov.in/Ministry/pdf/Companies_Act_1956_13jun2011.pdf (accessed on 21 February 2013).
3 Power Sector in India – IBEF, www.ibef.org/industry/power-sector-india.aspx (accessed on 18 September 2016).

Part VI
Value-based management

21 Economic value added

'Value creation' is the ultimate objective of any corporate organisation. The most successful organisations understand that the purpose of any business is to create value for its customers, employees, investors and most importantly, its shareholders. There are many companies that are not managed to their full potential value. Their managers act as value destroyers with their misguided actions. 'Managing for value creation' provides the basis for a comprehensive and integrated *value-based management* system that not only helps in evaluating the business performance for all the stakeholders but also enables the management in taking sound business decisions for future growth.

What is value creation?

'Value creation' is a corporation's **raison d'être**, the ultimate measure by which it is judged. Debate has focused on what is the most appropriate type of value for the corporation to create. Is it:

- *The value of the company in the stock market gives the company (its market value)?*
- *The value shown in its balance sheet (the accounting or book value of its assets minus its liabilities)?*
- *The value based on its expected future performance – profits or cash?*
- *None of these?*[1]

From the *financial perspective*, value is said to be created when a business earns revenue more than expenses, that is when its return on capital exceeds the cost of capital.

Economic value added (EVA): the shareholders' value

The shareholders are the most important stakeholders of a company, being the owners of the company. Therefore, the main emphasis of the management is on creating value for shareholders.

I Traditional measures

Traditional approaches to measuring 'shareholder's value creation' have used parameters such as *earnings capitalisation, market capitalisation and others.*

1. Market price

In the 1990s, the measure which was prominently used for analysing shareholders' value was the *'company's market price'*. The presumption was that shareholders look for capital gains from their investments. But measure based on stock market value is subject to the same wild fluctuations as the market itself. In a rising tide, all boats are raised. But when the macroeconomic changes force up-markets, it does not mean that the value of every company in that market rises. The markets are moved by sentiment that has little to do with the underlying value of individual corporations.[2]

2. Earnings Per Share (EPS)

The limitation of market value, as discussed above, was evident in the form of dotcom frenzy at the end of the 1990s. So, a group of scholars favoured *'earnings per share (EPS)'* as the real measure of shareholders' value. But, the accounting measures are not carved in stone. They can (and do) differ from country to country and have their own set of accounting limitations. They are not free from biases of the management.

II Economic value added (EVA) measure

A measure developed to overcome these problems is called EVA (economic value added). It is the professedly managed innovation in the field of internal and external performance measurement. Stern Stewart, a UK-based consulting firm, unveiled EVA (economic value added) in the year 1990, but its origin as economic profit dates back to the early 1900s. *EVA is the financial performance measure that captures the true economic profit of an enterprise.* This is the reason why EVA has been successfully employed in nearly 400 companies worldwide, including well-known firms as Coca-Cola, Siemens and Sony.[3]

EVA computation

This is the measure of output (taken as operating profit after tax and some other adjustments) less input (taken as the annual charge on the total capital employed, both debt and equity). In simple terms, EVA is the profits generated by any economic entity over its cost of capital employed. If the difference between the above two parameters is positive than the entity is said to be creating wealth for its stakeholders. A negative EVA on the other hand indicates the company is a destroyer of value.[4]

EVA = Net Operating Profit after Tax (NOPAT) – Cost of Capital Employed (COCE)*

Where NOPAT is the profits generated from the core operations of the company.

It is calculated as: Profit before Tax + Non-operating items (including Interest) – Tax.

Cost of Capital Employed is calculated as: Weighted average cost of borrowings and equity (WACC) × Average Capital employed. It is the total invested capital in the business.

Thus, the real test of the management is to generate return higher than the investment from core activities for shareholders' wealth maximisation. According to Mr. Roberto Goizueta, the former chairman and CEO of the Coca-Cola Company and an ardent believer in the maximisation of shareholders' wealth: *'Management doesn't get paid to make shareholders comfortable. We get paid to make the shareholders rich'.*[5]

Example: How is value created?

Young India Company (YIC) is a leading software company in India. In year 2015, YIC's net assets generated pre-tax operating profits of Rs. 240 million, as reported in its income statement. The corporate tax rate is 30%.

---

* Refer to Chapter 17, 'Cost of Capital', for a detailed discussion on WACC and its computation.

The company employed Rs. 1,000 million of capital as shown in the balance sheet for 31 March 2015. YIC's weighted average cost of capital (WACC) is 10%.

EVA = Net Operating Profit after Tax (NOPAT) – Weighted Average Cost of Capital

(i) NOPAT = Rs. 240 million – Rs. 72 million (30 % tax amount)
          = Rs. 168 million
(ii) WACC = Rs. 100 million (10% * Rs. 1,000 million)
   So EVA = Rs. 168 million – Rs. 100 million
          = Rs. 68 million

YIC generated Rs. 168 million of after-tax operating profit (NOPAT) but consumed Rs. 100 million of funds in the process. Therefore, YIC generated a positive EVA of Rs. 68 million in year 2015. As long as YIC keeps generating positive EVA, it will create value.

How to grow EVA?

EVA will increase if:

(a) Operating profits are increased with less capital, that is greater efficiency of resources is there.
(b) Return on capital invested in additional projects is more than the cost of obtaining new capital, that is profitable growth is achieved.
(c) Capital is used in activities that cover the cost of capital, that is productive usage is done.

Case: EVA of Hindustan Unilever Limited (Sector – FMCG)

Hindustan Unilever Limited (HUL) is a leading fast-moving consumer goods (FMCG) company in India. It is more than 100 years old company in the sector in India with brands like Dove, Lux, Lipton, and Lifebuoy among others.

The company has been following EVA for years. In HUL, the goal of sustainable long-term value creation for our shareholders is well understood by all the business groups. This can be seen in Table 21.1 and Figure 21.1.

Table 21.1 EVA reporting of HUL

(Rs. in crores)

Particulars	2011–12	2012–13	2013–14	2014–15	2015–16
Cost of Capital Employed (COCE)					
1 Average Debt	0	0	0	0	0
2 Average Equity	3,462	4,018	3,715	4,338	4,603
3 Average Capital Employed: [1] + [2]	3,462	4,018	3,715	4,338	4,603
4 Cost of Debt, post-tax %	6.20	6.02	6.36	5.56	5.43
5 Cost of Equity %	10.10	10.07	11.62	10.91	11.99
6 Weighted Average Cost of Capital % [WACC]	10.10	10.07	11.62	10.91	11.99
7 COCE : [3] × [6]	350	405	432	474	552
Economic Value Added (EVA)					
7 Profit After Tax (PAT), before exceptional items	2,599	3,314	3,555	3,843	4,078
8 Add: Interest, after taxes	1	0	24	11	0
9 Net Operating Profits After Taxes [NOPAT]	2,600	3,314	3,579	3,854	4,078
10 COCE, as per [7] above	350	405	432	474	552
11 EVA: [10] – [11]	**2,250**	**2,926**	**3,147**	**3,380**	**3,526**

Source: Hindustan Unilever Limited. 2016. 'Economic Value Added', Annual Report 2015–16, www.hul.co.in/Images/annual-report-2015-16_tcm1255-482421_en.pdf (accessed on 5 August 2016).

Note: Rs. 1 crore = Rs. 10 million

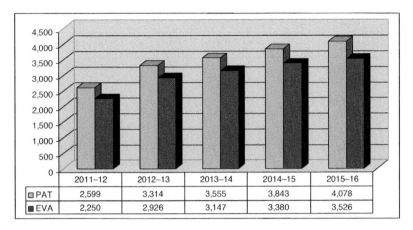

	2011–12	2012–13	2013–14	2014–15	2015–16
☐ PAT	2,599	3,314	3,555	3,843	4,078
■ EVA	2,250	2,926	3,147	3,380	3,526

Figure 21.1 EVA trend of HUL

Note: Rs. in crores

Calculation of COCE

1 *Cost of debt* is taken at the effective rate of interest applicable to a AAA-rated company like HUL for a short term debt, net of taxes. They have considered a pre-tax rate of 8.22% for 2015–16 (8.42% for 2014–15).

2 *Cost of equity* is the return expected by the investors to compensate them for the variability in returns caused by fluctuating earnings and share prices.

Cost of equity = Risk-free return equivalent to yield on long-term government bonds (taken at 7.47% for 2015–16).

+

Market risk premium (taken at 6.43%) × Beta variant for the Company, (taken at 0.704) where Beta is a relative measure of risk associated with the Company's shares as against the market as a whole.

Thus HUL's cost of equity = 7.47% + 6.43% × 0.704 = 11.99%

ANALYSIS

HUL has shown considerable improvement in EVA (from Rs. 2,250 crores in 2012 to Rs. 3,526 crores in 2016). The company has been able to bring down the cost of capital (COCE) significantly, to become a zero debt company, thereby improving EVA performance. Therefore, the difference between PAT and EVA is not very huge, a positive sign for the shareholders.

How to measure value creation?
Market value added (MVA)

As known, the core objective of financial management is 'value creation'. This means that before making a business decision, managers should always ask themselves the key question: *will the decision raise the value of their firm?*

The key question can be answered with the help of the fundamental finance principle, 'when the return on invested capital exceeds the cost of capital', that is 'EVA'.

EVA and growth

Goel (2012) found that the companies in India which were reporting positive EVA for 2004 to 2009 had grown at much faster pace compared to SENSEX vis-à-vis the companies reporting negative EVA.

The companies which were not reporting EVA had underperformed with respect to SENSEX.[6]

Market Value Added (MVA)

EVA is directly linked to the growth of the company, and that is expressed by 'market valued added' (MVA). If MVA is positive, the firm is creating real value because the market value of its capital exceeds the amount of capital invested in it. If MVA is negative, the firm is destroying the value.

The real measure of determining the value of a company is EVA with positive MVA. To find out whether management has created or destroyed value as of a particular point in time, the *market value* of the firm is compared with its total capital (both equity and debt capital) to the amount of capital that shareholders have invested in the firm (the firm's capital employed).

Market value added (MVA) = Market value of capital – Capital employed

Example: EVA vs. MVA

Considering the earlier example of Young India Company, a leading software company in India, let us understand the implication of MVA.

The company employed Rs. 1,000 million of capital as shown in the balance sheet for 31 March 2015. It consisted of Rs. 700 million of equity and Rs. 300 million of debt. The market value of that capital as on the date was Rs. 1,500 million.

> MVA = *Market value of capital – Capital employed*
> = Rs. 1,500 million – Rs. 1,000 million
> = Rs. 500 million

So, MVA is positive with Rs. 500 million, indicating that YIC has created Rs. 500 million of real value as of 31 March 2016 with a positive EVA of Rs. 68 million.

How to estimate the market value of capital?

(i) *For public listed companies*: The market value of capital can be obtained from the financial markets, at least for firms whose equity and debt capital are publicly traded in the form of securities.

(ii) *For private companies*: If the firm is not publicly traded, its market value is unobservable and its MVA cannot be calculated. It can be calculated based on its purchase price, that is if someone makes an offer to buy the firm, then it could be estimated on that offer price.

Points to remember

• Value creation is the primary objective of any business entity. From a *financial perspective*, value is said to be created when a business earns revenue more than expenses, that is when its return on capital exceeds the cost of capital.

• Traditional approaches to measuring 'shareholder's value creation' have used parameters such as earnings capitalisation, market capitalisation and others.

- EVA (economic value added) *is the financial performance measure that captures the true economic profit of an enterprise.* It was unveiled by Stern Stewart, a UK-based consulting firm. EVA is the profits generated by any economic entity over its cost of capital employed.
- EVA will increase if: *(i) operating profits can be increased with less capital, (ii) return on capital invested in additional projects is more than the cost of obtaining new capital* and *(iii) capital is used in activities that cover the cost of capital.*
- EVA is directly linked to growth of the company and that is expressed by 'market value added' (MVA). If MVA is positive, the firm is creating value and if MVA is negative, the firm is destroying value. MVA is defined as *the market value of its capital over the amount of capital invested in it.*
- The companies in India which were reporting positive EVA for 2004 to 2009 had grown at much faster pace compared to SENSEX vis-à-vis the companies reporting negative EVA. The companies which were not reporting EVA had underperformed with respect to SENSEX.

Notes

1 *The Economist*. 2009. Value Creation, 'The Ultimate Measure By Which a Company Is Judged', 20 November, www.economist.com/node/14301714# (accessed on 5 September 2016).
2 *The Economist*. 2009. Value Creation, 'The Ultimate Measure By Which a Company Is Judged', 20 November, www.economist.com/node/14301714# (accessed on 5 September 2016).
3 Goel, Sandeep. 2012. 'EVA Reporting in India: The Market Analogy', *Singapore Management Review*, 34 (2): 18–29.
4 Goel, Sandeep. 2012. 'EVA Reporting in India: The Market Analogy', *Singapore Management Review*, 34 (2): 18–29.
5 Shapiro, A. 1990. *Modern Corporate Finance*. Basingstoke: The Macmillan Company, p. 333.
6 Goel, Sandeep. 2012. 'EVA Reporting In India: The Market Analogy', *Singapore Management Review*, 34 (2): 18–29.

22 Human resource valuation

'Value creation' is a total effort-based approach to the management which requires that managers at all levels of the organisation should manage their firm's resources efficiently and thereby contribute in the accomplishment of the ultimate objective of maximising a firm's value. Shareholders' value creation should be compatible with other stakeholders as well; including the loyal customers, suppliers and the dedicated work force, that is *'human resource'*. It is the most vital input on which the success and failure of the organisation largely depends upon. In the era of knowledge and technology, only those organisations can survive and succeed which can effectively manage their human resources. The motivated employees are the real assets of any organisation who can take it to greater heights. Therefore, their valuation and contribution to the organisation need to be recognised.

Human valuation: meaning

Human resource valuation (HRV) or human resource accounting (HRA) is a specialised branch of accounting that provides significant information about the cost, value and performance of the human resources in an organisation and helps in the effective human resource management.

Human resource accounting (HRA) has been defined by the Committee on Human Resource Accounting of the American Accounting Association as *'the process of identifying and measuring data about human resources and communicating this information to interested parties'.*[1]

Human resource is one of the most important 'M' in 4M's associated with any organisation, that is **money, machines, materials** and **men.** But the surprising fact is that the first three are recognised and find a place in the assets side of the balance sheet of organisation. But the fourth 'M' (men) has universal ambiguity prevalent about its treatment in the financial statements, despite being the most important element of an organisation. The International Accounting Standards Board (IASB) and the Accounting Standards Board (ASB) in India have not been able to formulate any specific accounting standard for measurement and reporting of human resource.

The companies that report their human resource value do so in the form of additional information in the notes and not as an integral part of the financial statements.

Box 22.1   Indian Accounting Standard (Ind AS) 38 – Intangible Assets

Ind AS 38, which deals with intangible assets, states that human resources cannot be treated as intangible assets as they are not under the 'control' of the company.

Paragraph 15 of Ind AS 38 is reproduced below:

An entity may have a team of skilled staff and may be able to identify incremental staff skills leading to future economic benefits from training. The entity may also expect that the staff will continue to make their skills available to the entity. However, an entity usually has insufficient control over the expected future economic benefits arising from a team of skilled staff and from training for these items to meet the definition of an intangible asset. For a similar reason, specific management or technical talent is unlikely to meet the definition of an intangible asset, unless it is protected by legal rights to use it and to obtain the future economic benefits expected from it, and it also meets the other parts of the definition.[2]

Importance of human resource valuation

'Human resource value' is often considered as a useful component of an 'enterprise value', especially in service industries, where manpower is the single largest input for generating income. In recent years, a number of companies in the information technology sector have included such valuation in their annual reports, although a number of public sector units in the manufacturing sector have been reporting these numbers for long.

The benefits of adopting HRA are manifold, as discussed below.

1   **Better decision-making.** It helps an organisation to take managerial decisions based on the availability and the necessity of human resources. The valuation of human resource provides a true insight to various stakeholders into the organisation and its future potential.
2   **Effective control.** The company can determine whether its human asset is appreciating over the years or not. This information becomes important particularly for knowledge-based industries as their success depend solely on the knowledge of the employees.
3   **Proper compensation.** This information can be used by the company internally to compare the performance and productivity of employees in various departments. Accordingly, it can decide the compensation of employees.
4   **Growth potential.** The company can identify and retain valuable employees for future growth.

To sum up, HRA helps an organisation in identifying the right person for the right job, based on the person's knowledge, skills, capabilities and experience.

Disadvantages of human resource valuation

Human resource valuation is not free from limitations. These are as follows:

1   **Inter-comparison difficult.** Different companies might be using different HRA models and comparing two companies using two different models is difficult and not meaningful.
2   **Misuse of HRA.** The companies can misuse HRA to enhance their image. A company can use the assumptions in human valuation to its benefit in order to keep the values positive.
3   **Models not full proof.** The human valuation methods are based on various assumptions which are in themselves subjective. Hence figures could be totally ambiguous. There could be a concern of the creditability of the numbers reported.

Human valuation methods

Various methods and models developed for valuing human resource methods are based on *'cost or economic value of human resources'*. Under these methods human resources of an organisation are translated into a common denominator, that is money on which organisational decisions are taken. The value of human asset can be shown on a conventional balance sheet and profit and loss account.

These methods are discussed as follows:

1 **Historical cost method.** This method was developed by Rensis Likert. Under this method, all actual costs incurred on recruitment, training, selection and so forth are capitalised. Then, the capitalised cost is amortised (written off) over the period an employee serves in the organisation. In case the employee leaves the organisation before his expected service period, the remaining amount is written off completely in that particular year of his/her leaving the organisation.

2 **Replacement cost method.** 'Replacement cost' refers to the cost of replacing an existing employee with other employee rendering equivalent services. This method values the human resource on the basis of his replacement cost, that is the cost of recruitment, training and development, opportunity cost for the period till the new recruit attains the same efficiency level as of the old (to be replaced) employee.

3 **Opportunity cost method.** This method is used to value those employees who possess specific skills and, thus, are rare in availability. A 'bid price' is offered by the managers for acquiring such scarce employees. This bid price becomes the investment in such employees. The bid price is arrived at calculating actual or expected rate for capitalisation of the potential earnings to be earned by such employees. This method has the drawback of absence of a well-justified criterion to decide the amount of the bid.

4 **Economic value method.** Under this method, human asset is valued on the basis of the contribution they will make to the organisation till their retirement from the jobs. The payments made to them in the form of salary, allowances, benefits and so forth are estimated and then discounted to arrive at the present economic value of the individuals. This is also called the 'Discounted net present value of future earnings' method.

Box 22.2 The Lev and Schwartz model

The most commonly used method by Indian companies is the Lev and Schwartz model, which values human resources in the form of discounted present values of all future payments to the employees.

The Lev and Schwartz model states that, '*the human resource of a company is the summation of value of all the Net present value (NPV) of expenditure on employees*'.

Under this model, the following steps are adopted to determine HR value:

(a) Classification of the entire labour force into certain homogeneous groups, like skilled, unskilled, semiskilled etc. and in accordance with different class and age wise. *For example* at *Infosys, the classification is based on software professionals and support staff* and so forth.
(b) Construction of average earning stream for each group. *For example* at Infosys, incremental earnings based on group/age have been considered.
(c) Discounting the average earnings at a predetermined rate in order to get present value of human resources of each group.
(d) Aggregation of the present value of different groups which represent the capitalised future earnings of the concern as a whole,

$$Vr = I(t)/[(1 + r)^\wedge(t - r)]$$

Where, Vr = the value of an individual r years old
$\quad\quad$ I (t) = the individual's annual earnings up to retirement
$\quad\quad\quad$ t = retirement age
$\quad\quad\quad$ r = a discount rate as per the cost of capital to the company.

This model has its own limitations as well.

Human resource accounting: the industry practice

The first attempt to value human beings in monetary terms was made by Sir William Petty (1623–1687).[3] He treated human being as an element of wealth.

For the first time, HRA was implemented in 1967 by R. G. Barry Corporation, a footwear manufacturing company in Ohio (US).[4]

Indian scenario

In India, the importance and value of human assets got momentum in the early 1990s when there was a major increase in employment in firms in service, technology and other knowledge-based sectors. In these knowledge-based firms, the intangible assets, especially human resources, contributed significantly to the building of shareholder value.

'It was first introduced in India by Bharat Heavy Electrical Ltd. (BHEL), a leading public enterprise, during the financial year 1973–74'.[5]

Later it was also adopted by other leading public and private sector organisations in the subsequent years. Some of them are Hindustan Machine Tools Ltd. (HMT), Oil and Natural Gas Corporation Ltd. (ONGC), National Thermal Power Corporation Ltd. (NTPC), Associated Cement Company Ltd. (ACC), Tata Engineering and Locomotive Company Ltd. (TELCO) and Infosys Technologies Ltd. (ITL).

However, different companies adopted different models for human resource valuation and also different discount rates and disclosure pattern, that is either age-wise, skill-wise and so forth. This makes it clear, that there has been no uniformity among Indian enterprises regarding human resource accounting disclosure.

Case: Human resource valuation at Infosys Technologies Ltd.

In the financial year 1995–96, Infosys Technologies (Infosys) became the first software company to value its human resources in India. The company used the Lev and Schwartz model and valued its human resources assets at Rs. 1.86 billion. Infosys had always given utmost importance to the role of employees in contributing to the company's success.

Mr. Narayana Murthy, the then chairman and managing director of Infosys, said: *'Comparing this figure over the years will tell us whether the value of our human resources is appreciating or not. For a knowledge intensive company like ours, that is vital information'.*[6]

Use of the Lev and Schwartz method to value HR in Infosys

As mentioned above, Infosys have used the Lev and Schwartz model for human resource valuation. The evaluation is based on the present value of future earnings of employees.

1. Assumptions

The assumptions made by Infosys in the evaluation are:

(a) Employee compensation includes all direct and indirect benefits earned both in India and overseas.
(b) The incremental earnings based on group/age has been considered.
(c) The future earnings have been discounted at the cost of capital of 11.21% (previous year 10.60%).

2. Methodology

The methodology used by Infosys in the process is as follows:

- All the employees of Infosys were divided into five groups, based on their average age. Each group's average compensation was calculated.
- Infosys also calculated the compensation of each employee at retirement by using an average rate of increment.
- The increments were based on industry standards, and the employee's performance and productivity.
- Finally, the total compensation of each group was calculated. This value was discounted at the rate per annum which was the cost of capital at Infosys to arrive at the total human resources of Infosys.

The HRV figures of Infosys are given in Table 22.1 and its HRV reporting is given in Table 22.2.

Table 22.1 Human resource valuation at Infosys for 2011

in ₹ crore, unless stated otherwise		
	2011	2010
Employees (no.):		
Software professionals	1,23,811	1,06,864
Support	7,009	6,932
Total	1,30,820	1,13,796
Value of human resources:		
Software professionals	1,22,539	1,06,173
Support	12,566	7,114
Total	1,35,105	1,13,287

in ₹ crore, unless stated otherwise		
	2011	2010
Total income[1]	27,501	22,742
Total employee cost[1]	14,856	12,093
Value-added	25,031	20,935
Net profit[1]	6,823	6,219
Ratios:		
Value of human resources per employee	1.03	1.00
Total income/human resources value (ratio)	0.20	0.20
Employee cost/human resources value (%)	11.0	10.7
Value-added/human resources value (ratio)	0.19	0.18
Return on human resources value (%)	5.1	5.5

(1) As per IFRS (audited) financial statements

Note: Rs. 1 crore = Rs. 10 million

Table 22.2 Balance sheet of Infosys including intangible assets as of 31 March 2011

in ₹ crore		
	2011	2010
ASSETS		
Current assets:		
Cash and cash equivalents	16,666	12,111
Available-for-sale financial assets	21	2,518
Investment in certificates of deposit	123	1,190
Trade receivables	4,653	3,494
Unbilled revenue	1,243	841
Derivative financial instruments	66	95
Prepayments and other current assets	917	641
Total current assets	23,689	20,890
Non-current assets:		
Property, plant and equipment	4,844	4,439
Goodwill	825	829
Intangible assets		
Brand value	40,509	36,907
Human resources value	1,35,105	1,13,287

in ₹ crore		
	2011	2010
Other intangible assets	48	56
Available-for-sale financial assets	23	38
Deferred income tax assets	378	346
Income tax assets	993	667
Other non-current assets	463	347
Total non-current assets	1,83,188	1,56,916
Total assets	2,06,877	1,77,806
LIABILITIES AND EQUITY		
Current liabilities:		
Trade payables	44	10
Current income tax liabilities	817	724
Client deposits	22	8
Unearned revenue	518	531
Employee benefit obligations	140	131
Provisions	88	82
Other current liabilities	2,012	1,707
Total current liabilities	3,641	3,193
Non-current liabilities:		
Deferred income tax liabilities	–	114
Employee benefit obligations	259	171
Other non-current liabilities	60	61
Total liabilities	3,960	3,539
Equity:		
Share capital	286	286
Share premium	3,082	3,047
Retained earnings	23,826	20,668
Capital reserves-intangible assets	1,75,614	1,50,194
Other components of equity	109	72
Total equity attributable to equity holders of the company	2,02,917	1,74,267
Total liabilities and equity	2,06,877	1,77,806

Notes: The figures above are based on IFRS financial statements.[7]

Rs. 1 crore = Rs. 10 million

ANALYSIS

Infosys has shown human resource as 'intangible asset' under its balance sheet of 2011, given in Table 22.2.

1   The total number of employees increased from 1,06,864 in 2010 to 1,23,811 in 2011; an increase of 15.86%. The increase is clear both in the number of software professionals and support staff.
2   The total human resource value has shown an increasing trend from Rs. 1,13,287 crores in 2010 to Rs. 1,35,105 crores in 2011, showing an increase of approximately 20%. This is a positive sign for human resources' contribution in the company's profits.

It is evident that the human resource value has increased at a faster rate than the number of employees, indicating better productivity of employees.

Points to remember

• Human resource valuation (HRV) or human resource accounting (HRA) is a specialised branch of accounting that provides significant information about the cost, value and performance of the human resources in an organisation and help in effective human resource management.
• The companies that report their human resource value do so in the form of additional information in the notes and not as an integral part of the financial statements.
• The benefits of adopting HRA are manifold as *better decision-making, effective control, proper compensation* and *growth potential.*
• The limitations of human resource valuation are *difficult inter-comparison, misuse,* and *the models are not full proof.*
• The 'historical cost method' was developed by Rensis Likert. Under this method, all actual costs incurred on recruitment, training, selection and so forth are capitalised.
• The 'replacement cost method' considers the cost of replacing an existing employee with another employee rendering equivalent services.
• The 'opportunity cost method' is used to value those employees who possess specific skills and, thus, are rare in availability.
• The 'economic value method' value the human resource on the basis of the contribution they will make to the organisation

till their retirement from the jobs. This is also called '*Discounted net present value of future earnings*' method.

- The Lev and Schwartz model values human resources in the form of discounted present values of all future payments to the employees.
- The first attempt to value human beings in monetary terms was made by Sir William Petty (1623–1687). For the first time, HRA was implemented in 1967 by R. G. Barry Corporation, a footwear manufacturing company in Ohio (US).
- In India, the importance and value of human assets gained momentum in the early 1990s when there was a major increase in employment in firms in service, technology and other knowledge-based sectors.
- It was first introduced in India by BHEL (Bharat Heavy Electrical Ltd), a leading public enterprise, in its annual report during the financial year 1974–75. In subsequent years it was also adopted by other leading public and private sector organisations.
- In the financial year 1995–96, Infosys Technologies (Infosys) became the first software company to value its human resources in India.

Notes

1 American Accounting Association. 1973. 'Report of the Committee on Human Resource Accounting', *The Accounting Review*, 48 (Supplement): 169.
2 Indian Accounting Standard (Ind AS) 38 – Intangible Assets, http://mca.gov.in/Ministry/pdf/INDAS38.pdf (accessed on 1 July 2018).
3 Suresh, R. 2006. 'Human Resource Accounting: A Behavioural Approach', *The Management Accountant*, February: 91.
4 Brummet, G.M., Flamholtz, M.C. and Pyle, C.R. 2009. 'Human Resource Accounting: A Tool to Increase Managerial Effectiveness', *Management Accounting*: 12–15.
5 Kashive, Neeraj. 'Importance of Human Resource Accounting Practices and Implications of Measuring Value of Human Capital: Case study of Successful PSUs in India', *XIMB Journal of Case Research*, 4 (2), http://home.ximb.ac.in/~jcr/cases/Case03-HRA-DEC2013.pdf (accessed on 27 August 2017).
6 Rao, Ahalada. 2014. 'Employee Participation, Valuation of Human Resources and Creation of Intangible Assets', *International Journal of Business and Administration Research Review*, July–September, 3 (6): 47, www.ijbarr.com/downloads/0111201419.pdf
7 Infosys. 2011. 'Human Resource Valuation', Annual Report 2010–11, www.infosys.com/investors/reports-filings/annual-report/annual/Documents/AR-2011/ai_20.html (accessed on 1 October 2016).

Part VII

Strategic finance

23 Mergers and acquisitions

Every organisation wants to grow big over a period of time. There are two ways by which a company can grow its size: first, by eating the market share of the competitor; second, by eating the competitor itself. In other words, growth may be attained either organically or inorganically. *Organic growth* is increasing the profit base of the organisation through capital investment process. *Inorganic growth, or external growth*, is accomplished through various business combinations, namely, mergers and acquisitions (M&A). These business combinations are an important feature of 'corporate restructuring' and have played an important role in the external growth of number of leading companies over the world. The type of approach to be used by the organisation depends upon various factors, such as growth cycle of the business, time period, resources available and of course the risk factor.

Types of combinations

Business combinations can be categorised as follows.

I Merger

Merger means 'combination of two things'. In business sense, the term 'merger' refers to a fusion between two or more enterprises, which results in the emergence of a single enterprise. Such a process involves the transfer of assets and liabilities of the merging companies to the merged (combined) company. The shareholders of the merging company/companies become the shareholders in the merged company.

   The basic objective of merger is to improve the operational efficiency of merging entities. The companies that transfer their assets to the other company are termed as *transferor or merging companies*, and the company to which such assets are transferred is known as *transferee or the merged company.*

Box 23.1   Merger vs. absorption vs. amalgamation

Absorption is merger with an existing company, where all other firms are absorbed into the surviving firm. *For example*, absorption of Hutchinson Essar Ltd. by Vodafone Plc. Vodafone, an acquiring company (a buyer), survived after merger while Hutch, an acquired company (a seller), ceased to exist. Hutch transferred its assets, liabilities and shares to Vodafone.

Amalgamation/consolidation implies that all the firms are combined to form a new entity through the transfer of all their property to such a new corporation. In this case, the other companies lose their existence. *For example*, the merger of Hero Group and Honda Motor Company Ltd. into an entirely new company called 'Hero Honda Ltd.'

The term 'merger' is used interchangeably with these terms.

II *Acquisition*

An 'acquisition or takeover' refers to acquiring of effective working control by one company over another. The control may be acquired either through purchase of majority of shares carrying voting rights or controlling the composition of the board of directors of the other company. The company acquiring shares is termed as the *holding company*, while the company in which the shares are acquired is termed as the *subsidiary company.*

In an acquisition, two or more companies may remain independent, separate legal entities, but there may be a change in control of the companies.

Box 23.2   Acquisitions vs. takeovers

Though acquisition and takeover have a similar connotation in corporate restructuring, but acquisitions basically are willingly done, whereas takeovers are hostile. A 'forced' acquisition is called a takeover.

Types of mergers

Mergers are of the following types.

1. *Horizontal merger*

This is a combination or joining of two or more firms in the same area of business. In a horizontal merger, both the merging firm(s) and the merged firm(s) produce and sell identical or similar products in the same geographic area. A merger of firms which are in direct competition with each other is called horizontal merger.

> *For example*, the merger of Reliance Communications Ltd. with Aircel and the acquisition of Daksh by IBM are examples of horizontal merger.

The advantages of horizontal merger are:

- Elimination or reduction in competition
- End to price wars
- Economies of scale in operations.

2. *Vertical merger*

This is a combination of two or more firms involved in different stages of the production or distribution. A combination of two or more firms that fall in the same industry but operate at different stages of production-distribution chain is termed as vertical merger.

> *One example* of such merger is between Time Warner Incorporated, a major cable operation, and the Turner Corporation, which produces CNN, TBS and other programming.

Vertical merger may take the form of 'forward' or 'backward integration'. When a company combines with the supplier of material, it is called *backward integration (merger)*, for example a tyre manufacturer integrates with a rubber manufacturing firm. It is an upstream merger.

When a firm combines with the buyer or customer, it is known as *forward integration (merger)*, for example a tyre manufacturing firm combines with a two-wheeler manufacturing firm. It is downstream merger.

The advantages of a vertical merger are:

- Reduction in cost of production
- Optimisation of resources
- Better service resulting from supply chain integration.

3. Conglomerate merger

This is a combination of two or more firms which are engaged in unrelated lines of business activity. It is a type of combination in which firm(s) established in one industry combine with other firm(s) in unrelated industry. It generally involves diversification of business activities and therefore is considered to pose no threat to competition.

> *For example*, merging of different businesses, like manufacturing of cement products and electronics products. The merger between the Walt Disney Company and the American Broadcasting Company is an example of conglomerate merger.

The advantages of such a merger are:

- Market expansion or product extension
- Mitigation of risk.

A brief explanation of each form of combination is given in Figure 23.1.

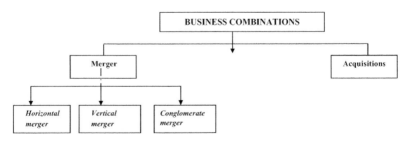

Figure 23.1 Forms of business combinations

Motives of mergers and acquisitions

The key goal of merger and acquisition is believed to be 'the maximisation of the shareholders' wealth'. In general, mergers and acquisitions are done for the following motivations:

1   **Synergies:** This is the most common reason for a merger. The value of the new entity will be more than the combined value of two separate companies. Generally, there are two types of synergies that are aimed for:

    • *Operating synergies*: These are the synergies that result in economies of scale due to increase in the scale of operations of the combined firm. Such an optimal utilisation of resources brings down the cost per unit of output. Operating economies also accrue in specific management functions such as R&D, production, marketing or finance.
    • *Financial synergies*: These are the synergies that increase the capacity of the combined firm to mobilise financial resources at a lower cost. They further increase the overall revenue through expansion in markets, products cross-selling and an increase in prices.

2   **Profitability:** Operational synergies enhance operational efficiency and economies of scale of the acquiring company. Duplication of resources can be avoided by the combined firm, which may bring down the cost of operations and lead to higher profits. The financial synergies can lead to access of cheaper funds (debt), reducing the overall cost of capital and giving a push to the profitability.

3   **Market power:** A horizontal merger in a small industry helps in increasing the market share. An increased market share will, in turn, give the power to influence prices. A vertical merger can also increase the market power by reducing the dependence on external suppliers.

4   **Reduction in competition:** Merging with (or acquiring) the competitors not only increases the market share of the acquiring company but also reduces its competition significantly. This reduction in competition is direct in case of horizontal merger and indirect in case of vertical mergers, as the benefits of upstream/downstream integration in vertical mergers provide the combined firm a significant cost advantage over its competitors.

5   **Rapid growth:** Mergers and acquisitions are a way of achieving external growth by increasing sales through external resources.

The companies which are in matured phase generally prefer to grow externally. It is less risky to have external growth. M&A results in expansion of resources thus increasing the growth rate.

6   **Diversification:** The company can diversify easily through the M&A route. This is cheaper and less stringent than the company going through the process of entering into new line of business single-handedly.

7   **Increase in EPS:** A merger deal is expected to have a positive effect on the company's earnings per share (EPS). This occurs due to increase in the profit base of the acquiring company. An increase in the current EPS of the company will lead to increase in the market price of the share.

8   **Tax saving:** Merging with firms having accumulated losses allows the merged firm to set off these accumulated losses against the post-merger profits of the merged firm. The provisions under Section 72A and 72AA of the Indian Income Tax Act, 1961 allow this facility to set off and carry forward the losses against the profits of the merged entity. Such a set-off reduces the taxable income of the merged firm resulting in tax saving for it.

9   **International goals:** International mergers and acquisitions have become more common and important in today's business world for global outreach.

Process of mergers and acquisitions

There are three important steps involved in the analysis of mergers and acquisitions:

1. Planning

The acquiring firm should review its objectives of acquisition in the context of its strengths and weaknesses and the corporate goals. This will help in identifying the product market strategies that are suitable for the firm.

Due diligence refers to the reasonable care that should be taken before entering into an agreement or a transaction. It is an investigating process or audit of a potential transaction or deal so as to find out all relevant facts pertaining to the ensuing transaction. There are various types of due diligence, such as technological due diligence, environmental due diligence, organisational due diligence, financial due diligence and so forth.

In the context of M&A, it refers to assessing the price and identifying the financial risks involved in an M&A deal. The decisions to merge/acquire/takeover are based on the due diligence report. Critical issues addressed by such an analysis from the perspective of the acquiring/merged firm may include:

(i) Value of target firm(s)
(ii) Synergies from the deal
(iii) Estimated value creation for the acquiring/merged firm from the deal and so forth

2. Search and screening

Search enables to find out suitable candidates for acquisition. Screening short-lights the candidates from the available lot and then detailed information about each of these candidates is obtained.

3. Financial evaluation

Financial evaluation of a merger is needed to find out the earnings, cash flows, areas of risk, the maximum price payable to the target company and the best method for financing the merger. This involves the application of different valuation methods.

M&A valuation methods

There are three main methods for business valuation. Among all the methods, the 'discounted-cash-flow' (DCF) method is the most commonly used valuation method in M&A. These methods are discussed below.

1. Asset based – 'net assets method'

In case of 'privately held' companies, market information is not available. So the *net assets method* is commonly used in these acquisitions. The comparative analysis is done of the target company with regard to its total assets size and its outstanding liabilities to have the net purchase price.

The total value of the assets (minus the liabilities) of the target company is computed to find out the value of the equity of its business.

Illustration 23.1: Ind Ltd. decides to acquire 100% equity of Bright Corp. Bright Corp. is a private limited company with Rs. 80 million of market value of assets and Rs. 50 million of liabilities outstanding. What is the acquisition value as per the net assets method?

Solution

Total assets of Bright Corp. =	Rs. 80 million
Less: Outstanding Liabilities =	Rs. 50 million
Acquisition Price =	Rs. 30 million

2. Income based – 'discounted cash-flow method'

The discounted cash-flow method in an M&A deal attempts to determine the value of the company by computing the present value of cash flows over the life of the company. It involves discounting the future expected cash flows over a forecast period and comparing it with the investment price to arrive at the decision. Basically, NPV approach is used here, as followed in capital budgeting decision. If the NPV of the investment is positive, it is a viable M&A decision and vice versa.

Illustration 23.2: AB Company is considering acquiring Z Ltd. for Rs. 10 million in cash @ 14% cost of capital. Z Ltd. can generate Rs. 2 million of cash inflows over the next 15 years. Using NPV, advise whether it is a viable acquisition for AB Company.

Solution:	
Initial Cash Outlay =	Rs. 10 million
Present Value of Cash Inflows of Rs. 2 million = (6.142 × 2 million)	Rs. 12.284 million
Net Present Value =	Rs. 2.284 million

Based on NPV, AB Company should acquire Z Ltd. since there is a positive NPV for this investment.

Note: 6.142 is the present value factor of annuity at 14%, 15 years.

3. Market based – 'market value method'

This method is popular in case of 'publicly held' companies. Market value (MV) is presumed to reflect the public information about the company and its industry. On average, for a profitable company mergers offer command a suitable premium over the price.

Its computation involves the following steps:

---

1. Calculate the 'value the equity' of the firm (E): Stock price × outstanding shares.
2. Calculate the 'market value of debt' (D): Price per bond × number of bonds outstanding.
3. Calculate the value the firm (V): E + D.

Illustration 23.3: New India Ltd. is a public listed company with 2,000,000 shares outstanding. The market price per share is Rs. 70 and the fair market value of its debt is Rs. 10 million. What is the market value of the firm for the proposed acquisition?

Solution

Market Value of Stock (20,00,000 × Rs. 70) =	Rs. 140 million
Market Value of Debt =	Rs. 10 million
Value of the Firm =	Rs. 150 million

Box 23.3   Enterprise value method

Enterprise value method is an extension of market value method. The 'enterprise value' is calculated as:

'Value of equity + Value of debt – Cash and cash equivalents'

Points to remember

- Growth may be attained either organically or inorganically. *Organic growth* is increasing the profit base of the organisation through capital investment process. *Inorganic growth or external growth* is accomplished through various business combinations, namely, mergers and acquisitions (M&A).

- 'Merger' refers to a fusion between two or more enterprises, which results in the emergence of a single enterprise. Such a process involves the transfer of assets and liabilities of the merging companies to the merged (combined) company. The term merger is used interchangeably with 'absorption', 'amalgamation' or 'consolidation'.

- 'Absorption' is the merger with an existing company, where all other firms are absorbed into the surviving firm. *For example*, the absorption of Hutchinson Essar Ltd. by Vodafone Plc.

- 'Amalgamation/consolidation' implies that all the firms are combined to form a new entity. *For example*, the merger of Hero Group and Honda Motor Company Ltd. into an entirely new company called 'Hero Honda Ltd.'

- 'Acquisition or takeover' refers to acquiring of effective working control by one company over another. Though acquisition and takeover have a similar connotation in corporate restructuring, *acquisitions* basically are willingly done, whereas *takeovers* are hostile.

- 'Horizontal merger' is a combination or joining of two or more firms in the same area of business. *For example*, the merger of Reliance Communications Ltd. with Aircel.

- 'Vertical merger' is a combination of two or more firms involved in different stages of the production or distribution. It can be 'forward' or 'backward'. *For example*, the merger between Time Warner Incorporated, a major cable operation, and the Turner Corporation, which produces CNN, TBS and other programming.

- 'Conglomerate merger' is a combination of two or more firms which are engaged in unrelated lines of business activity. The merger between the Walt Disney Company and the American Broadcasting Company is an example of conglomerate merger.

- The key advantages of mergers and acquisitions are *synergies, profitability, market power, reduced competition, rapid growth, diversification, increased EPS, tax benefits* and *international goals.*
- There are three important steps involved in the analysis of mergers and acquisitions: *planning, search and screening,* and *financial evaluation.*
- There are three key methods which are used for business valuation: *net assets method, discounted cash flow method* and *market value method.* Enterprise value method is an extension of market method.

24 Corporate governance

Ever since India's biggest-ever corporate fraud and governance failure unearthed at Satyam Computer Services Ltd., the concept of good corporate governance has come again into the limelight. Corporate governance has been an important area of discussion in the whole world, particularly since the last decade. It has emerged from obscurity into being a mainstream topic and moved into all sections of the corporate sector and the political scene. Corporate governance is not only important from legal point of view, but specifically from the stakeholders' value perspective. Corporate governance should be seen as practice rather an obligation from a firm's view.

Concept of corporate governance

Corporate governance is concerned with the standards of behaviour and conduct expected from directors and other senior executives (including the financial manager) in directing and controlling the affairs of a company. Corporate governance not only defines the relationships between managers and shareholders but also includes the relationships between the board, senior executives, shareholders, other stakeholders as customers, suppliers and employees, regulators and the firm's auditors

The simplest of definition of corporate governance is provided by the Cadbury Report (UK): 'Corporate governance is the system by which business are directed and controlled'.[1]

The Organisation for Economic Co-operation and Development (OECD) Principles of Corporate Governance states:

Corporate governance involves a set of relationships between a company's management, its board, its shareholders and

other stakeholders. Corporate governance also provides the structure through which the objectives of the company are set, and the means of attaining those objectives and monitoring performance are determined.[2]

SEBI (2003) states, 'The aim of good corporate governance is to enhance the long-term value of the company for its shareholders and all other partners. Corporate governance integrates all the participants involved in a process, which is economic, and at the same time social'.[3]

Need for corporate governance

The necessity for having sound corporate governance arises because of the following factors:

1 **Efficient allocation of resources.** The efficient allocation of scarce economic resources is a priority. It will be achieved if companies are accountable to those who take profit or bear the loss after all other claims on the company have been met.
2 **Wide spread of shareholders.** Today a large number of shareholders of the company spread all over the nation and even the world; a majority of shareholders are unorganised and have an indifferent attitude towards corporate affairs. In such a scenario, it is necessary that shareholders' democracy is well implemented through a code of conduct of corporate governance.
3 **Shareholders' confidence.** Corporate scams (or frauds) in several years in the past have shaken public confidence in corporate management. The need for corporate governance is, thus, imperative for maintaining the investors' confidence in the corporate sector.
4 **Societal expectations.** The society of today holds greater expectations of the corporate sector in terms of reasonable price, better quality, environmental contribution and so forth. To meet social expectations, there is a need for a code of corporate governance for the company in economic and social terms.
5 **Sound growth.** For long, quality growth, it is necessary that boards of the companies carry out the affairs of the management of the company and monitor the development with good corporate governance.
6 **Globalisation.** The globalisation of the economy has driven the largest companies to access international capital markets. Frauds on a global scale have led to greater awareness of inadequacies of governance and demand for reform in corporate practices.

Principles of corporate governance

The fundamental principles of corporate governance are described as follows.

1. Transparency

Transparency means the 'quality of something' which enables one to understand the truth easily. In the context of corporate governance, it implies an accurate, adequate and timely disclosure of relevant information about the operating results and other information of the corporate enterprise to the stakeholders.

In fact, transparency is the foundation of corporate governance; which helps to develop a high level of public confidence in the corporate sector. For ensuring transparency in corporate management, a company should publish relevant information about corporate affairs timely.

2. Accountability

Accountability is a liability to explain the results of one's decisions taken in the interest of others. In the context of corporate governance, accountability implies the responsibility of the chairman, the board of directors and the chief executive for the use of company's resources (over which they have authority) in the best interest of company and its stakeholders.

3. Independence

Good corporate governance requires independence on the part of the top management of the corporation, that is the board of directors must be free from all biases so that they can take all corporate decisions objectively.

Box 24.1   OECD principles of corporate governance

Originally developed by the OECD in 1999, then updated in 2004, the 2015 revision of the Principles of Corporate Governance addresses these and other emerging issues that are increasingly relevant. These Principles provide an indispensable and globally recognised benchmark for assessing and improving corporate governance.

The Principles have been adopted as one of the Financial Stability Board's key standards for sound financial systems, and have been used by the World Bank Group in more than 60 country reviews worldwide. They also serve as the basis for the guidelines on corporate governance of banks issued by the Basel Committee on Banking Supervision.[4]

These are:

I   *Ensuring the basis for an effective corporate governance framework*

II   *The rights and equitable treatment of shareholders and key ownership functions*

III   *Institutional investors, stock markets, and other intermediaries*

IV   *The role of stakeholders in corporate governance*

V   *Disclosure and transparency*

VI   *The responsibilities of the board*[5]

Evolution of corporate governance

A. Foreign

I US

The US is known for its shareholder-oriented or market-based model to corporate governance with features like *active institutional investors, an open market for corporate control, independent outside directors on the board, long-term equity-based compensation for executives* and *gatekeepers who monitor the process of market disclosure.*

However, scandals like Enron in 2000 generated criticism and lead to substantial changes in the corporate regulation through the Sarbanes-Oxley (SOX) legislation.

The Sarbanes-Oxley Act of 2002 (SOX) introduced major changes to the regulation of financial practice and corporate governance to protect investors from the possibility of fraudulent accounting activities by corporations.

II UK

The first version of the UK Corporate Governance Code (the Code) was produced in 1992 by the 'Cadbury Committee'. In 2012, they came out with the new Code which applies to all listed companies regardless of whether they are incorporated in the UK or elsewhere. The UK Corporate Governance Code is a set of principles of good corporate governance aimed at companies listed on the London Stock Exchange.

It sets standards of good practice in relation to board leadership and effectiveness, remuneration, accountability and relations with shareholders.

B. India

Corporate governance was guided by *Clause 49* of the Listing Agreement before introduction of the Companies Act of 2013. As per the new provision, Securities and Exchange Board of India (SEBI) has also approved certain amendments in the Listing Agreement so as to improve the transparency in transactions of listed companies and giving a bigger say to minority stakeholders in influencing the decisions of management. These amendments became effective 1 October 2014.

1. Desirable Code Of Corporate Governance – Voluntary Code by CII (1998)

Corporate governance in India gained prominence in the wake of liberalisation during the 1990s and was introduced, by the industry association Confederation of Indian Industry (CII), as a voluntary measure to be adopted by Indian companies. The first major initiative was undertaken by the CII in 1998 in the form of the *'Desirable Code of Corporate Governance – Voluntary Code'*.

2. The Kumar Mangalam Birla Committee Report (2000)

Consequently, the second major corporate governance initiative in the country was undertaken by SEBI. In early 1999, it set up a committee under Kumar Mangalam Birla to promote and raise the standards of good corporate governance. In early 2000, the SEBI board accepted ratified the key recommendations of the Birla Committee, which were incorporated into Clause 49 of the Listing Agreement of the Stock Exchanges. It soon acquired a mandatory status in early 2000s through the introduction of Clause 49 of the Listing Agreement, as all companies (of a certain size) listed on stock exchanges were required to comply with these norm.

3. The Naresh Chandra Committee report (2002)

The Naresh Chandra Committee was appointed in August 2002 by the Department of Company Affairs (DCA) under the Ministry of Finance and Company Affairs, to examine various corporate governance issues. The Committee submitted its report in December 2002. It made recommendations in terms of two key aspects of corporate governance: financial and non-financial disclosures, and independent auditing and board oversight of management.

4. The N. R. Narayana Murthy committee report (second report of the SEBI Committee) (2003)

With an objective to improving corporate governance standards in India, SEBI once again constituted a committee in 2002 under the chairmanship of N. R. Narayana Murthy to review the existing code on corporate governance. Some of the major recommendations of the committee primarily related to audit committees, audit reports, independent directors, related party transactions, risk management, directorships and director compensation, codes of conduct and financial disclosures.

5. Dr. J. J. Irani Committee report (2005)

India's corporate governance reform efforts did not cease after the adoption of Clause 49. In parallel, the review and redrafting of the Companies Act, 1956 was taken up by the Ministry of Corporate Affairs (MCA). The government constituted an Expert Committee on Company Law under the Chairmanship of Dr. J. J. Irani on 2 December 2004 to offer advice on a new Companies Bill. Based, among other things, on the recommendations of the Irani Committee, the Government of India introduced the Companies Bill, 2008, in the Indian Parliament for introducing the best international corporate practices that foster entrepreneurship and investment. This finally became the Companies Act, 2013.

Corporate governance regulation in India

The Indian legal framework has, by and large, been in consonance with the international best practices of corporate governance. Broadly speaking, the corporate governance mechanism for companies in India is regulated by the following regulations.

1. The Companies Act, 2013

The Companies Act, 2013 ('New Companies Act'), replaces the erstwhile Companies Act, 1956 with its applicability still in place. The Companies Act is the principal legislation governing companies in India.

It contains provisions relating to board constitution, board meetings, board processes, independent directors, general meetings, audit committees, related party transactions, disclosure requirements in financial statements and so forth.

The New Act covers corporate governance through its following provisions:

- The companies should have adequate composition of the boards of directors.
- Every company is required to appoint one resident director on its board.
- The New Companies Act for the first time codifies the duties of directors.
- Listed companies and certain other public companies shall be required to appoint at least one woman director on its board.
- A class action suit was introduced for minority shareholders.
- The New Companies Act mandates following committees to be constituted by the board for prescribed class of companies:

  - *Audit committee*
  - *Nomination and remuneration committee*
  - *Stakeholders relationship committee*
  - *Corporate social responsibility committee.*

Box 24.2   Corporate social responsibility (CSR) obligations

India is the only country in the world with codified corporate social responsibility (CSR) obligations. The Companies Act, 2013 requires specified companies to spend at least 2% of the average net profits made during the three immediately preceding financial years on prescribed CSR activities. This provision operates on a 'comply or explain' basis, and the board of directors must provide an explanation in the directors' report if the company does not spend the requisite amount on CSR.

This requirement is applicable to companies which have:

(i)   A net worth of at least Rs. 5 billion during any financial year
(ii) A turnover of at least Rs. 10 billion during any financial year
(iii) A net profit of at least Rs. 50 million during any financial year.

Every company which fulfils the above threshold requirements must constitute a corporate social responsibility committee, formulate a CSR policy and make recommendations on CSR to the board. The CSR activities must be performed within India and are not permitted to be for the exclusive benefit of the company's employees or their family members.

2. SEBI's revised Clause 49 of listing agreement of stock exchanges

SEBI is a regulatory authority having jurisdiction over listed companies and which issues regulations, rules and guidelines to companies to ensure protection of investors. *SEBI has amended the Listing Agreement with effect from 1 October 2014 to align it with the New Companies Act.*

Revised Clause 49 (2014) and the First Clause 49 (2005) of the Listing Agreement can be said to be a bold initiative towards strengthening corporate governance among the listed companies. This clause intends to put a check over the activities of companies in order to save the interest of the shareholders.

In addition to the Companies Act, companies are governed by the Securities and Exchange Board of India Act 1992 (SEBI Act) and various regulations notified under the SEBI Act, particularly the SEBI (Listing Obligations and Disclosure Requirements) Regulations 2015. Companies are also bound by the standard listing agreement of BSE/NSE.

Broadly, Revised Clause 49 provides for the following:

1. Board of directors

The board of directors shall have an optimum combination of executive and non-executive directors with not less than 50% of the board of directors comprising of non-executive directors.

(a) Where the *chairman* of the board is a *non-executive director*, at least one-third of the board should comprise of independent directors and in case the *chairman is an executive director*, at least half of the board should comprise of independent directors.
(b) If the non-executive chairman is a promoter of the company or is related to any promoter or person occupying management positions at the board level or at one level below the board, at least one-half of the board of the company shall consist of independent directors of such number of minimum independent directors, as prescribed.

Box 24.3   Independent directors

Independent director is any non-executive director who possesses relevant expertise and integrity and in no way is related to the company.

---

2. Audit Committee

The audit committee to be set up comprises a minimum of three directors as members, two-thirds of whom shall be independent.

3. Disclosure requirements

Periodical disclosures relating to the financial and commercial transactions, remuneration of directors and so forth need to done by the company to ensure transparency.

4. CEO/CFO certification

The CEO and the CFO shall certify to the board that they have reviewed the financial statements and the same are fair and in compliance with the laws/regulations and accept responsibility for internal control systems.

5. Report and compliance

A separate section in the annual report should on 'compliance with corporate governance'. Also, a quarterly compliance report needs to be submitted to the stock exchange signed by the compliance officer or CEO.

Points to remember

- Corporate governance is the system by which business are directed and controlled (Cadbury Report, UK).
- The necessity for having sound corporate governance arises because of these factors: *efficient allocation of resources, wide spread of shareholders, shareholders' confidence, societal expectations, sound growth* and *globalisation*.
- The fundamental principles of corporate governance are *transparency, accountability* and *independence*.
- The OECD Principles of Corporate Governance were originally developed in 1999, then updated in 2004, and the 2015 revision of the Principles of Corporate Governance provide an indispensable and globally recognised benchmark for assessing and improving corporate governance.
- In the US, *the Sarbanes-Oxley Act of 2002 (SOX)* introduced major changes to the regulation of financial practice and corporate governance to protect investors from the possibility of fraudulent accounting activities by corporation.
- The first version of the UK Corporate Governance Code (the Code) was produced in 1992 by the 'Cadbury Committee'. In 2012, they came out with the new Code which applies to all listed companies regardless of whether they are incorporated in the UK or elsewhere.
- Indian corporate governance is guided by *SEBI's Revised Clause 49 of the Listing Agreement* and the *Companies Act of 2013*.
- The Revised Clause 49 provides for the following: board of directors, audit committee, disclosure requirements, CEO/CFO, and certification report and compliance.

Notes

1 Report of the Committee on the Financial Aspects of Corporate Governance. 1992. December, www.ecgi.org/codes/documents/cadbury.pdf (accessed on 5 October, 2016).
2 OECD Principles of Corporate Governance. 2004. www.oecd.org/corporate/ca/corporategovernanceprinciples/31557724.pdf (accessed on 5 October 2016).
3 SEBI. 2003. 'Report of the Committee on Corporate Governance', 8 February.
4 OECD, 'G20/OECD Principles of Corporate Governance', www.oecd.org/corporate/principles-corporate-governance.htm (accessed on 5 October 2016).
5 OECD Library, 'G20/OECD Principles of Corporate Governance', www.oecd-ilibrary.org/governance/g20-oecd-principles-of-corporate-governance-2015_9789264236882-en (accessed 5 October 2016).

Part VIII
Tax planning

25 Direct taxation
Income tax

Taxes are the largest source of income for the government. This money is deployed for various purposes and projects for the development of the nation. India has a well-developed and a continuously evolving tax structure drawn from the Constitution of India. For every tax, there needs to be an accompanying law that is passed in either the Parliament or the State Legislature. Direct tax collection of Indian government has grown by 18% to cross Rs. 10.02 lakh crore in the fiscal year ending on 31 March 2018.[1] For healthy tax planning by taxpayers, due diligence and complete awareness about the tax laws and corresponding rules and regulations is required. The present chapter discusses income tax in India. Goods and Services Tax is discussed in the next chapter.

Indian tax structure

The tax structure in India is a three-tier federal structure: the central government, state governments, and local municipal bodies. There are two types of taxes – *direct and indirect tax*. Direct taxes are paid by the assessee while indirect taxes are levied on goods and services. The Indian taxation system has witnessed several modifications over the years. There has been standardization of income tax rates with simpler governing laws for the understanding of the common man. The net result has been ease of paying taxes, improved compliance and enhanced enforcement of the laws.

Revenue authority

These revenue authorities are a part of the Department of Revenue under the Ministry of Finance, Government of India. They are classified as follows:

I Central Board of Direct Taxes (CBDT)

The CBDT provides inputs for policy and planning of direct taxes in India and is responsible for the administration of direct tax laws through the Income Tax Department.

II Central Board of Indirect Taxes & Customs (CBIC)

The CBIC is responsible for the formulation of policy concerning levy and collection of customs, GST, central excise, service tax, and narcotics in India and their administration.

Direct vs. indirect tax

Direct tax is levied directly on individuals and corporate entities and cannot be transferred to others. Examples of direct tax include income tax, wealth tax, gift tax, and capital gains tax.

Box 25.1   Income tax

This is the largest form of direct tax. It is applicable to both individuals and companies. As per the Income Tax Act, 1961 every assessee whose total income exceeds the maximum exempt limit is liable to pay this tax. The tax structure rates and revisions are annually prescribed by the Parliament in the Finance Act, commonly known as the Annual Budget. This tax is imposed during each assessment year, which commences on 1 April and ends on 31 March.

The total income is calculated under one or more of the following heads: salary, house property, business or profession, capital gain, and other sources.[2]

Indirect taxes are indirectly levied on the public through goods and services. The sellers of the goods and services collect the tax, which is then deposited to the government bodies.

As a significant step towards the reform of indirect taxation in India, the Central Government had introduced the goods and service tax (GST) on July 1, 2017. GST is a comprehensive indirect tax on the manufacture, sale and consumption of goods and services throughout India and incorporates many indirect taxes levied by the central and state governments.

GST has replaced excise, service tax and various other indirect taxes in India. Now, there are majorly two types of indirect taxes exist in India – GST and customs.

Basic terminologies (Income Tax Act, 1961)

1 **Assessment Year [Sec. 2(9)]:** This is the year in which income is taxable and refers to the period of 12 months starting from April 1 and ending on March 31 of the next year. For example, the assessment year of 2019–20 will commence on 1 April 2019 and will end on 31 March 2020.
2 **Previous Year [Sec. 3]:** It is the year in which income is earned and means 'the financial year immediately preceding the assessment year'. The income earned in the previous year is taxable in the next year, i.e. assessment year. So, the income earned during the previous year 2018–19 is taxable in the assessment year 2019–20.
3 **Assessee [Sec. 2(7)]:** This means a person by whom any tax or any other sum of money is payable under the Income Tax Act, 1961.
4 **Person [Sec. 2(31)]:** The term 'person' includes:

   (i)   an individual (e.g. Ram, Mohan, Jack);
   (ii) a Hindu undivided family (HUF) (e.g. joint family business of Mr A, Mrs A and their sons);
   (iii) a company (e.g. Reliance Industries Ltd., ONGC Ltd.);
   (iv) a firm (e.g. AB and Co., Amit and Associates);
   (v)   an association of persons or a body of individuals, whether incorporated or not (e.g. X and Y, the legal heirs of their father, decide to carry on his business);
   (vi) a local authority (e.g. North Delhi Municipal Corporation); and
   (vii) every artificial juridical person not falling within any of the preceding sub-clauses (e.g. Shri Ram College of Commerce).

5 **Income [Sec. 2(24)]:** The term 'income' includes:

   (i)   profits and gains;
   (ii) dividend;
   (iii) voluntary contributions received by a trust created wholly or partly for charitable or religious purposes or by an institution established wholly or partly for such purposes or by an association or institution, or by a fund or trust or institution or by any university or other educational institution or by any hospital or other institution or by an electoral trust;
   (iv) the value of any perquisite or profit in lieu of salary;

(v) any special allowance or benefit, specifically granted to the assessee to meet expenses wholly, necessarily and exclusively for the performance of his duties;

(vi) any allowance granted to the assessee either to meet his personal expenses at the place where he performs his duties or to compensate him for the increased cost of living;

(vii) the value of any benefit or perquisite, whether convertible into money or not, obtained from a company either by a director or by a person who has a substantial interest in the company, or by a relative of the director or such person;

(viii) the value of any benefit or perquisite, whether convertible into money or not, obtained by any representative assessee or beneficiary and any sum paid by the representative assessee in respect of any obligation which, but for such payment, would have been payable by the beneficiary ;

(ix) any sum chargeable to income-tax under clauses (ii), (iii), (iiia), (iiib), (iiic), (iv) and (v) of section 28 or clauses (ii) and (iii) of section 41 or section 59;

(x) any capital gains;

(xi) the profits and gains of any business of insurance carried on by a mutual insurance company or by a cooperative society;

(xii) the profits and gains of any business of banking carried on by a cooperative society;

(xiii) any winnings from lotteries, crossword puzzles, races including horse races, card games and other games of any sort or from gambling or betting of any form or nature whatsoever;

(xiv) any sum received by the assessee from his employees as contributions to any provident fund or superannuation fund or any fund set up under the provisions of the Employees' State Insurance Act 1948 (34 of 1948), or any other fund for the welfare of such employees;

(xv) any sum received under a Keyman insurance policy including the sum allocated by way of bonus on such policy;

(xvi) any sum referred to in clause (va) of section 28.[3]

Box 25.2   PAN and TAN

PAN (permanent account number) is a ten-digit unique alphanumeric number issued by the Income Tax Department in the form of a laminated plastic card. It enables the department to identify/

link all transactions of the PAN holder with the department. Every assessee has to obtain PAN.

TAN or tax deduction and collection account number is a 10 digit alpha numeric number required to be obtained by all persons who are responsible for deducting or collecting tax. Under Section 203A of the Income Tax Act, 1961, it is mandatory to quote TAN allotted by the Income Tax Department on all TDS returns.

6   **Residence in India [Sec. 6]:** The related provisions are as follows:

(1) An individual is said to be resident in India in any previous year, if he:

   (i) is in India in that year for a period or periods amounting in all to 182 days or more; or

   (ii) having within the four years preceding that year been in India for a period or periods amounting in all to 365 days or more, is in India for a period or periods amounting in all to 60 days or more in that year.

(2) A Hindu undivided family, firm or other association of persons is said to be resident in India in any previous year in every case except where during that year the control and management of its affairs is situated wholly outside India.

(3) A company is said to be a resident in India in any previous year, if:

   (i) it is an Indian company; or

   (ii) its place of effective management, in that year, is in India.

(4) Every other person is said to be resident in India in any previous year in every case, except where during that year the control and management of his affairs is situated wholly outside India.

(5) If a person is resident in India in a previous year relevant to an assessment year in respect of any source of income, he shall be deemed to be resident in India in the previous year relevant to the assessment year in respect of each of his other sources of income.

A person is said to be 'not ordinarily resident' in India in any previous year if such person is:

(a) an individual who has been a non-resident in India in nine out of the ten previous years preceding that year, or has during the seven previous years preceding that year been in India for a period of, or periods amounting in all to, 729 days or less; or

(b) a Hindu undivided family whose manager has been a non-resident in India in nine out of the ten previous years preceding that year, or has during the seven previous years preceding that year been in India for a period of, or periods amounting in all to, 729 days or less.[4]

Income tax

According to Section 14 of the Income Tax Act, 1961, for the purposes of charge of income tax and computation of total income all income is classified under the following heads of income:

A. Salaries
B. Income from house property
C. Profits and gains of business or profession
D. Capital gains
E. Income from other sources

A. Salaries [Sec. 15]

The following income shall be chargeable to income tax under the head 'Salaries':

(a) any salary due from an employer or a former employer to an assessee in the previous year, whether paid or not;

(b) any salary paid or allowed to him in the previous year by or on behalf of an employer or a former employer though not due or before it became due to him;

(c) any arrears of salary paid or allowed to him in the previous year by or on behalf of an employer or a former employer, if not charged to income tax for any earlier previous year.[5]

Salary [Sec. 17] includes:

(i)   wages;

(ii)   any annuity or pension;

(iii)   any gratuity;

(iv)   any fees, commissions, perquisites or profits in lieu of or in addition to any salary or wages;

(v)   any advance of salary;

(vi)   any payment received by an employee in respect of any period of leave not availed of by him;

(vii)   the annual accretion to the balance at the credit of an employee participating in a recognised provident fund;

(viii) the aggregate of all sums that are comprised in the transferred balance of an employee participating in a recognised provident fund; and

(ix)   the contribution made by the Central Government or any other employer in the previous year, to the account of an employee under a pension scheme referred to in section 80CCD.[6]

B. Income from house property [Sec. 22]

The annual value of property consisting of any buildings or lands of which the assessee is the owner, not occupied for the purposes of any business or profession carried on by him the profits of which are chargeable to income tax, shall be chargeable to income tax under the head 'Income from house property'.[7]

C. Profits and gains of business or profession [Sec. 28]

The following income shall be chargeable to income-tax under the head 'Profits and gains of business or profession':

(i)   the profits and gains of any business or profession that was carried on by the assessee at any time during the previous year;

(ii) any compensation or other payment due to or received by:

(a) any person, managing the whole or substantially the whole of the affairs of an Indian company;

(b) any person, managing the whole or substantially the whole of the affairs in India of any other company;

(c) any person, holding an agency in India for any part of the activities relating to the business of any other person;

(d) any person, for or in connection with the vesting in the government, or in any corporation owned or controlled by the government, under any law for the time being in force, of the management of any property or business.[8]

D. Capital gains [Sec. 45]

Any profits or gains arising from the transfer of a capital asset effected in the previous year shall, save as otherwise provided in sections 54, 54B, 54D, 54E, 54EA, 54EB, 54F, 54G and 54H, be chargeable to income tax under the head 'Capital gains', and shall be deemed to be the income of the previous year in which the transfer took place.[9]

Income from capital gains is classified as 'Short-term capital gains' and 'Long-term capital gains'.

(a) *Short-term capital asset.* Any capital asset held by the taxpayer for a period of not more than 36 months immediately preceding the date of its transfer will be treated as short-term capital asset.

(b) *Long-term capital asset.* Any capital asset held by the taxpayer for a period of more than 36 months immediately preceding the date of its transfer will be treated as long-term capital asset.

However, in respect of certain assets like share (equity or preference) which are listed in a recognised stock exchange in India, units of equity oriented mutual funds, listed securities like debentures and government securities, units of UTI and Zero Coupon Bonds, the period of holding to be considered is 12 months instead of 36 months.[10]

E. Income from other sources [Sec. 56]

Income of every kind under the Act shall be chargeable to income tax under the head 'Income from other sources', if it is not chargeable to income tax under any of the heads specified in Section 14, items A to E.

In particular, the following incomes shall be chargeable to income tax under the head 'Income from other sources', namely:

(i)   dividends;

(ii)   income referred to in sub-clause (viii), (ix), (x) and (xi) of clause (24) of Section 2;

(iii)   income by way of interest on securities;

(iv)   income from machinery, plant or furniture belonging to the assessee and let on hire;

(v) where an assessee lets on hire machinery, plant or furniture belonging to him and also buildings, and the letting of the buildings is inseparable from the letting of the said machinery, plant or furniture, the income from such letting;

(vi) where any sum of money exceeding Rs. 25,000 is received without consideration by an individual or a Hindu undivided family from any person on or after 1 September 2004 but before 1 April 2006, the whole of such sum;

(vii) where any sum of money, the aggregate value of which exceeds Rs. 50,000, is received without consideration, by an individual or a Hindu undivided family, in any previous year from any person or persons on or after 1 April 2006 but before 1 October 2009, the whole of the aggregate value of such sum;

(viii) where an individual or a Hindu undivided family receives, in any previous year, from any person or persons on or after 1 October 2009 [but before 1 April 2017]:

(a) any sum of money, without consideration, exceeding Rs. 50,000,

(b) any immovable property,

(c) any property, other than immovable property.

(ix) where a firm or a company not being a company in which the public are substantially interested, receives, in any previous year, from any person or persons, on or after 1 June 2010 [but before 1 April 2017], any property, being shares of a company not being a company in which the public are substantially interested;

(x) where a company, not being a company in which the public are substantially interested, receives, in any previous year, from any person being a resident, any consideration for issue of shares that exceeds the face value of such shares, the aggregate consideration received for such shares as exceeds the fair market value of the shares;

(xi) income by way of interest received on compensation or on enhanced compensation referred to in clause (b) of Section 145A;

(xii) any sum of money received as an advance or otherwise in the course of negotiations for transfer of a capital asset.[11]

Computation of total tax liability

After ascertaining the total income for the year, as discussed above, the tax liability of the taxpayer is computed. Table 25.1 provides an overview of the computation of tax liability for the year.

Table 25.1 Computation of total income and tax liability for the year

Particulars	Amount
Income from salary	XXXXX
Income from house property	XXXXX
Profits and gains of business or profession	XXXXX
Capital gains	XXXXX
Income from other sources	XXXXX
Gross total income	*XXXXX*
Less: Deductions under Chapter VI-A (i.e., under Section 80C to 80U)	(XXXXX)
Total income (i.e. taxable income)	*XXXXX*
Tax on total income to be computed at the applicable rates	XXXXX
Less: Rebate under Section 87A	(XXXXX)
Tax liability after rebate	*XXXXX*
Add: Surcharge	XXXXX
Tax liability after surcharge	*XXXXX*
Add: Education Cess @ 2% on tax liability after surcharge	XXXXX
Add: Secondary and Higher Education Cess @ 1% on tax liability after surcharge	XXXXX
Tax liability before rebate under Sections 86, Section 89, Sections 90, 90A and 91 (if any) (*)	XXXXX
Less: Rebate under Sections 86, Section 89, Sections 90, 90A and 91 (if any) (*)	(XXXXX)
Tax liability for the year before pre-paid taxes	XXXXX
Less: Prepaid taxes in the form of TDS, TCS and advance tax	(XXXXX)
Tax payable/refundable	*XXXXX*

Source: www.incometaxindia.gov.in/Pages/faqs.aspx?k=FAQs%20on%20Computation%20of%20tax (accessed on 26 August 2018).

(*) Rebate under Section 86 is available to a member of association of persons (AOP) or body of individuals (BOI) in respect of income received by such member from the AOP/BOI.

Rebate (i.e. relief) under section 89 is available to a salaried employee in respect of sum received towards arrears of salary, gratuity, etc.

Rebate under sections 90, 90A and 91 is available to a taxpayer in respect of double taxed income, i.e. income that is taxed in India as well as abroad.

1. Individual Tax

For individuals, the tax to be paid by them depends on the tax bracket they fall in. This bracket or slab determines the tax to be paid based on the annual income of the assessee and ranges from zero tax to 30% tax for the high income groups.

The government fixes different taxes slabs for various groups of individuals under the Finance Act every year: general taxpayers, senior citizens (people aged between 60 and 80), and super senior citizens (people aged over 80).

Box 25.3   Gross total income vs. total income

Gross total income is the sum of your (i) income from salary, (ii) income from house property, (iii) profits or gains from business or profession, (iv) capital gains and (v) income from other sources. It is the total amount of money you have earned from all your sources of income

Total income or taxable income is basically your gross total income minus deductions under Section 80C to Section 80U.

The tax rates for Assessment Year 2018–19 are given in Table 25.2.

Table 25.2 Tax rates for individual for assessment year 2018–19

(i) In case of an individual (resident or non-resident) or HUF or association of person or body of individual or any other artificial juridical person

Taxable income	Tax rate
Up to Rs. 2,50,000	Nil
Rs. 2,50,000 to Rs. 5,00,000	5%
Rs. 5,00,000 to Rs. 10,00,000	20%
Above Rs. 10,00,000	30%

Less: Rebate under Section 87A
Add: Surcharge and Education Cess

(Continued)

Table 25.2 (Continued)

(ii) In case of a resident senior citizen (who is 60 years or more at any time during the previous year but less than 80 years on the last day of the previous year)

Taxable income	Tax rate
Up to Rs. 3,00,000	Nil
Rs. 3,00,000 to Rs. 5,00,000	5%
Rs. 5,00,000 to Rs. 10,00,000	20%
Above Rs. 10,00,000	30%

Less: Rebate under Section 87A
Add: Surcharge and Education Cess

(iii) In case of a resident super senior citizen (who is 80 years or more at any time during the previous year)

Taxable income	Tax rate
Up to Rs. 5,00,000	Nil
Rs. 5,00,000 to Rs. 10,00,000	20%
Above Rs. 10,00,000	30%

Add: Surcharge and Education Cess (see note)

Source: www.incometaxindia.gov.in/charts%20%20tables/tax%20rates.htm (accessed on 26 August 2018).

Notes
(a) *Surcharge:*
  (i) at the rate of 10% of such tax, where total income exceeds Rs. 50 lakh but does not exceed Rs. 1 crore.
  (ii) at the rate of 15% of such tax, where total income exceeds Rs. 1 crore.
(b) *Education Cess:* at the rate of 2% of such income-tax and surcharge.
(c) *Secondary and Higher Education Cess:* at the rate of 1% of such income-tax and surcharge.
(d) *Rebate under Section 87A:* The rebate is available to a resident individual if his total income does not exceed Rs. 3,50,000. The amount of rebate shall be 100% of income tax or Rs. 2,500, whichever is less.

Illustration 25.1: Mr Amit is 40 years old and employed in ABC Ltd. The details of his income and investment during financial year 2017–18 are as follows:

Basic pay	Rs. 4,00,000
Incentives	Rs. 1,00,000
House rent allowance	Rs. 1,50,000
Contribution by Amit to Provident Fund	Rs. 36,000
Amount deposited in PPF account	Rs. 50,000
House rent paid for residence in Delhi	Rs. 84,000

LIC premium paid	Rs. 14,000
Medical insurance premium paid	Rs. 20,000
Interest received from Saving Bank Account	Rs. 10,000

Calculate income tax liability of Amit for assessment year 2018–19.

Solution

Computation of taxable income

Income from salary:			
Basic Pay		Rs. 4,00,000	
Incentives		Rs. 1,00,000	
House Rent Allowance	Rs. 1,50,000		
Less: Exemption (see note 1)	Rs. 44,000	<u>Rs. 1,06,000</u>	Rs. 6,06,000
Income from other sources:			
Interest received from saving bank account			Rs. 10,000
Gross Total Income			**Rs. 6,16,000**
Less: **Deduction under Chapter VI-A**			
Under Section 80C			
Contribution to Provident Fund	Rs. 36,000		
Deposit in PPF Account	Rs. 50,000		
LIC Premium paid	<u>Rs. 14,000</u>	Rs. 1,00,000	
Under Section 80D			
Medical Insurance Premium Paid		Rs. 20,000	
Under Section 80TTA			
Interest from saving bank account		Rs. 10,000	Rs. 1,30,000
Taxable Income			**Rs. 4,86,000**
Income tax payable on Rs. 4,86,000/=		Rs.	11,800
Add: Education Cess @ 2%		Rs.	236
Add: Secondary & Higher Education Cess @ 1%		Rs.	118
Total Tax Liability		Rs.	12,154

Notes:
1 Amount of HRA exemption is the least of following:

(i) Actual HRA received	Rs. 1,50,000
(ii) Rent paid – 10% of salary, i.e. (84,000–40,000)	Rs. 44,000
(iii) 50% of salary	Rs. 2,00,000

2 Medical Insurance Premium is allowed up to Rs. 25000 as deduction under Section 80D.
3 Deduction under Section 80TTA is allowed up to Rs. 10,000 in respect of interest received from saving bank accounts.
4 A rebate of income tax is not allowed under Section 87A since the taxable income in above case is more than Rs. 3,50,000. [The amount of rebate is actual income tax payable or Rs. 2,500, whichever is less if the taxable income is up to Rs. 3,50,000.]

2. Cooperative society tax

A cooperative society is taxed as per the slabs. For the assessment year 2018–19, its taxation is given in Table 25.3.

Table 25.3 Tax rates for cooperative society for assessment year 2018–19

Taxable income	Tax rate
Up to Rs. 10,000	10%
Rs. 10,000 to Rs. 20,000	20%
Above Rs. 20,000	30%

Add surcharge: at the rate of 12% of such tax, where total income exceeds Rs. 1 crore.

Source: www.incometaxindia.gov.in/charts%20%20tables/tax%20rates.htm(accessed on 26 August 2018).

3. Partnership firm tax

The partnership firm is taxed at flat rate. For the assessment year 2018–19, a partnership firm (including LLP) is taxable at 30%.

Add:

(a) *Surcharge:* at the rate of 12% of such tax, where total income exceeds Rs. 1 crore.
(b) *Education Cess:* at the rate of 2% of such income tax and surcharge.
(c) *Secondary and Higher Education Cess:* at the rate of 1% of such income tax and surcharge.[12]

4. Local authority tax

The local authority's taxation is also at flat rate. For the assessment year 2018–19, a local authority is taxable at 30%.

Add:

(a) *Surcharge:* at the rate of 12% of such tax, where total income exceeds Rs. 1 crore.
(b) *Education Cess:* at the rate of 2% of such income tax and surcharge.
(c) *Secondary and Higher Education Cess:* at the rate of 1% of such income tax and surcharge.[13]

5. Corporate tax

Corporate tax is the income tax that is paid by companies from the revenue they earn. The imposition of such a tax varies from a domestic company to a foreign organization. For the assessment year 2018–19, following are the rates of corporate tax, which is levied on different companies:

1. Domestic company

Domestic companies are taxable at 30%. However, the tax rate would be 25% where turnover or gross receipt of the company does not exceed Rs. 50 crores in the previous year 2015–16. Tax rate (25% or 30%) for assessment year 2018–19 will be determined based on the turnover for previous year 2015–16.

Add:

(a) *Surcharge:* at the rate of 7% of such tax, where total income exceeds Rs. 1 crore but not exceeding Rs. 10 crores and at the rate of 12% of such tax, where total income exceeds Rs. 10 crores.
(b) *Education Cess:* at the rate of 2% of such income tax and surcharge.
(c) *Secondary and Higher Education Cess:* at the rate of 1% of such income tax and surcharge.

Box 25.4   Minimum alternate tax (MAT)

MAT stands for 'minimum alternate tax' and AMT stands for 'alternate minimum tax'. MAT is the minimum tax to be paid by companies, which currently stands at 18.5%.

Initially the concept of MAT was introduced for companies and progressively it has been made applicable to all other taxpayers in the form of AMT.

Background of MAT

It is possible that a taxpayer, being a company, may have earned income during the year, but by taking the advantage of various provisions of income tax law (such as exemptions, deductions, depreciation, etc.), it may have reduced its tax liability or may not have even paid any tax. Due to increase in the number of zero-taxpaying companies, MAT was introduced by the Finance Act, 1987, with effect from assessment year 1988–89. Later on, it was withdrawn by the Finance Act, 1990, and then reintroduced by Finance (No. 2) Act, 1996.

Objective of MAT

The objective of introduction of MAT is to bring into the tax net 'zero tax companies' which, in spite of having earned substantial book profits and having paid handsome dividends, do not pay any tax due to various tax concessions and incentives provided under the Income Tax Act.

Basic provisions of MAT

Since the introduction of MAT, several changes have been introduced in the provisions of MAT and today it is levied on companies as per the provisions of Section 115JB.

As per the concept of MAT, the tax liability of a company will be the higher of the following:

- Tax liability of the company computed as per the normal provisions of the Income Tax Act, i.e. tax liability by applying the tax rate applicable to the company. Tax computed in above manner can be termed as normal tax liability.
- Tax computed @ 18.5% (plus surcharge and cess as applicable) on book profit (book profit means net profit as shown in the statement of profit and loss prepared in accordance with Schedule III to the Companies Act, 2013) is MAT.[14]

Illustration 25.2: The taxable income of MG Metals Pvt. Ltd. computed as per the provisions of Income Tax Act is Rs. 8,40,000. Book profit of the company computed as per the provisions of section 115JB is Rs. 18,40,000.

What will be the tax liability of the company (ignore cess and surcharge)?

Solution

The tax liability of a company will be the higher of: (i) normal tax liability, or (ii) MAT.

Normal tax rate applicable to an Indian company is 30%*(plus cess and surcharge as applicable).

Tax @ 30% on Rs. 8,40,000 = Rs. 2,52,000 (plus cess).

Book profit of the company is Rs. 18,40,000.

MAT liability (excluding cess and surcharge) @ 18.50% on Rs.18,40,000 = Rs. 3,40,400.

Thus, the tax liability of MG Metals Pvt. Ltd. = Rs. 3,40,400 (plus cess as applicable) being higher than the normal tax liability.

2. Foreign company

The nature of income and tax rates for foreign companies for the assessment year 2018–19 are given below.

Nature of income	Tax rate
Royalty received from the government or an Indian concern in pursuance of an agreement made with the Indian concern after 31 March 1961, but before 1 April 1976, or fees for rendering technical services in pursuance of an agreement made after 29 February 1964 but before 1 April 1976 and where such agreement has, in either case, been approved by the central government	50%
Any other income	40%

Add:

(a) *Surcharge:* at the rate of 2% of such tax, where total income exceeds Rs. 1 crore but not exceeding Rs. 10 crores and at the rate of 5% of such tax, where total income exceeds Rs. 10 crores.

(b) *Education Cess:* at the rate of 2% of such income tax and surcharge.

(c) *Secondary and Higher Education Cess:* at the rate of 1% of such income tax and surcharge.[15]

Illustration 25.3: Young Ltd. is a company engaged in the business of manufacturing readymade shirts and trousers for men. For the accounting year ended 31 March, 2017, business sales were Rs. 70 lakhs. Total expenses excluding income tax were Rs. 20 lakhs. The company has a business loss of Rs. 10 lakhs brought forward from the previous year.

The company sold off land in February 2017 for Rs. 30 lakhs which was purchased for Rs. 14 lakhs the previous year in February.

Compute the total income for the relevant year.

Solution

Computation of total income of Young Ltd. for AY 2017–18

Particulars	Rs.
Net profit (Rs. 70 lakhs – Rs. 20 lakhs)	50,00,000
Less: Business loss brought forward from the previous year	10,00,000
Business income	40,00,000
Capital gains (see note)	16,00,000
Total income	56,00,000

Note:
Sale proceeds of land   = Rs. 30,00,000
Less: Cost of acquisition = Rs. 14,00,000
Short-term capital gains   = Rs. 16,00,000
(since the period of holding is less than 36 months)

> *Points to remember*
>
> - The tax structure in India is a three-tier federal structure: the central government, state governments, and local municipal bodies.
> - *Direct tax* is levied directly on individuals and corporate entities and cannot be transferred to others, like income tax, wealth tax, gift tax, and capital gains tax. *Indirect taxes* are indirectly levied on the public through goods and services.
> - Assessment year is the year in which income is taxable and refers to the period of twelve months starting from April 1 and ending on March 31 of the next year.
> - Previous year is the year in which income is earned and means 'the financial year immediately preceding the assessment year'.
> - Assessee means a person by whom any tax or any other sum of money is payable under Income Tax Act, 1961.

- The term 'person' includes: an individual, a Hindu undivided family, a company, a firm, an association of persons or a body of individuals, a local authority, every artificial juridical person not falling within any of the preceding subclauses.
- The term 'income' includes: (i) profits and gains; (ii) dividend; (iii) voluntary contributions received by a trust; (iv) the value of any perquisite or profit in lieu of salary; (v) any special allowance or benefit, (vi) any allowance granted to the assessee; (vii) the value of any benefit or perquisite obtained, (viii) any sum chargeable to income tax under Section 28, Section 41 or Section 59; (ix) any capital gains; (x) the profits and gains of any business of insurance and banking; (xi) any winnings from lotteries, crossword puzzles, etc.; (xii) any sum received by the assessee from his employees as contributions to any provident fund or superannuation fund or any fund; (xiii) any sum received under a Keyman insurance policy; (xiv) any sum referred to in clause (va) of Section 28.
- PAN (permanent account number) is a ten-digit unique alphanumeric number issued by the Income Tax Department in the form of a laminated plastic card. TAN or tax deduction and collection account number is a ten-digit alphanumeric number required to be obtained by all persons who are responsible for deducting or collecting tax.
- An *individual* is said to be resident in India in any previous year, if he (a) is in India in that year for 182 days or more; or (b) having within the four years preceding that year been in India for 362 days or more. A *Hindu undivided family, firm or other association of persons* is said to be resident in India in any previous year in every case except where during that year the control and management of its affairs is situated wholly outside India. A *company* is said to be a resident in India in any previous year, if (i) it is an Indian company; or (ii) its place of effective management, in that year, is in India. Every *other person* is said to be resident in India in any previous year in every case, except where during that year the control and management of his affairs is situated wholly outside India.
- According to Section 14 of the Income Tax Act, 1961, for the purposes of charge of income tax and computation of total

income all income is classified under the following heads of income: (i) Salaries, (ii) Income from house property, (iii) Profits and gains of business or profession, (iv) Capital gains, (v) Income from other source.

- For individuals, the tax to be paid by them depends on the tax bracket they fall in. This bracket or slab determines the tax to be paid based on the annual income of the assessee and ranges from zero tax to 30% tax for the high-income groups.
- Cooperative societies are taxed as per the slabs.
- Partnership firms are taxed at a flat rate.
- Local authority taxation is also at a flat rate.
- Corporate tax varies from a domestic company to a foreign organization.
- MAT stands for 'minimum alternate tax' and AMT stands for 'alternate minimum tax'. MAT is the minimum tax to be paid by the companies which currently stands at 18.5%. Initially the concept of MAT was introduced for companies and progressively it has been made applicable to all other taxpayers in the form of AMT.

Notes

1 Direct tax collections surge 18% to Rs. 10.02 lakh crore in FY18: Jaitley, April 4 2018, https://timesofindia.indiatimes.com/business/india-business/direct-tax-collections-surge-18-to-rs-10-02-lakh-crore-in-fy18-jaitley/articleshow/63608704.cms (accessed on 26 August 2018).
2 Tax Structure and Taxation System in India, www.hdfclife.com/insurance-knowledge-centre/tax-saving-insurance/Tax-Structure-in-India (accessed on 20 August 2018).
3 Section 2, Income Tax Act, 1961–2018, www.incometaxindia.gov.in/Pages/acts/income-tax-act.aspx (accessed on 20 August 2018).
4 Section 6, Income Tax Act, 1961–2018, www.incometaxindia.gov.in/Pages/acts/income-tax-act.aspx (accessed on 20 August 2018).
5 Section 15, Income Tax Act, 1961–2018, www.incometaxindia.gov.in/Pages/acts/income-tax-act.aspx (accessed on 20 August 2018).
6 Section 17, Income-tax Act, 1961–2018, www.incometaxindia.gov.in/Pages/acts/income-tax-act.aspx (accessed on 20 August 2018).
7 Section 22, Income Tax Act, 1961–2018, www.incometaxindia.gov.in/Pages/acts/income-tax-act.aspx (accessed on 20 August 2018).
8 Section 28, Income Tax Act, 1961–2018, www.incometaxindia.gov.in/Pages/acts/income-tax-act.aspx (accessed on 20 August 2018).

9 Section 45, Income Tax Act, 1961–2018, www.incometaxindia.gov.in/Pages/acts/income-tax-act.aspx (accessed on 20 August 2018).

10 Tax on long-term capital gains, www.incometaxindia.gov.in/tutorials/15-%20ltcg.pdf (accessed on 26 August 2018).

11 Section 56, Income Tax Act, 1961–2018, www.incometaxindia.gov.in/Pages/acts/income-tax-act.aspx (accessed on 20 August 2018).

12 Tax rates, www.incometaxindia.gov.in/charts%20%20tables/tax%20rates.htm (accessed on 26 August 2018).

13 Tax rates, www.incometaxindia.gov.in/charts%20%20tables/tax%20rates.htm (accessed on 26 August 2018).

14 MAT and AMT, www.incometaxindia.gov.in/tutorials/10.mat-and-amt.pdf (accessed on 26 August 2018).

15 Tax rates, www.incometaxindia.gov.in/charts%20%20tables/tax%20rates.htm (accessed on 26 August 2018).

26 Indirect taxation
Goods and Services Tax

Indirect taxes form a sizeable portion of the government income. These taxes are levied by adding them to the price of the product or service, which increases their cost. As an indirect tax, Goods and Services Tax (GST) has brought in 'one nation, one tax' system, and is structured for efficient tax collection, reduction in corruption, easy interstate movement of goods and many more. It applies on all types of businesses, small or large. This is a new chapter in the process of tax reforms in the country. Collections from the levy of the Goods and Services Tax stood at a provisional Rs. 7.41 lakh crore for the year ending 31 March 2018.[1]

Concept of Goods and Services Tax (GST)

Goods and Services Tax (GST) is an 'indirect tax' that has replaced many central and state indirect taxes (like central sales tax, excise duty, service tax, and value addition tax) levied on goods and services in India.

The Goods and Service Tax Act was passed in the Parliament on 29 March 2017. The Act came into effect on 1 July 2017. Goods and Services Tax law in India is a comprehensive, multi-stage, and destination-based tax that is levied on every value addition. It is considered to be the biggest tax reform in the Indian tax structure, which is oriented to simplify the current taxation system.

> In simple words, Goods and Services Tax (GST) is 'one indirect tax for the entire country'. It means tax on supply of goods and services.

VAT (value-added tax)[2] and GST (Goods and Services Tax) are used interchangeably as the latter denotes comprehensiveness of VAT by coverage of goods and services. France was the first country to implement

VAT in1954. Presently, more than 160 countries have implemented GST/VAT in some form or the other. The most popular form of VAT is where taxes paid on inputs are allowed to be adjusted in the liability at the output. The VAT or GST regimes in practice varies from one country to another in terms of their technical aspects such as 'definition of supply', 'extent of coverage of goods and services', 'treatment of exemptions and zero rating', etc. However, at a broader level, they has one common principle, each is a 'destination-based consumption tax'.[3]

Key features of GST

1. Dual system

GST is applicable on both goods and services and India follows a 'dual system' of GST to keep both the centre and state independent of each other.

There are two types of GST structure in the world. These are:

(i)   Single GST
(ii) Dual GST

India has adopted the dual GST system, like Canada, wherein both centre and states administer tax independently. In this, central GST and state GST are levied on the taxable value of every transaction of supply of goods and services. The threshold limit for exemption is to be Rs. 20 lac (Rs. 10 lac for special category states except J&K). The government has decided four different tax slab rates: 5%, 12%, 18%, 28% for various items, with some goods and services exempted. There is a separate tax rate (3% or 0.5%) for precious metals/stones.

Box 26.1   Items outside GST

1   *Alcohol for human consumption.* Power to tax remains with the state.
2   *Five petroleum products – crude oil, diesel, petrol, natural gas and ATF.* GST Council to decide the date from which GST will be applicable.
3   *Tobacco.* Part of GST but power to levy additional excise duty with central government.
4   *Entertainment tax levied by local bodies.* Power to tax remains with local bodies.[4]

2. Comprehensive

GST is one tax that replaces the following indirect taxes earlier levied by the centre and the state:

(i)   Taxes levied and collected by the centre:

1   Central excise duty
2   Additional duties of excise
3   Excise duty levied under Medicinal & Toilet Preparation Act
4   Additional duties of customs
5   Service tax
6   Surcharges and cesses

(ii) Taxes levied and collected by the state:

1   State VAT/sales tax
2   Central sales tax
3   Purchase tax
4   Entertainment tax
5   Luxury tax
6   Entry tax
7   Taxes on lottery, betting and gambling
8   Surcharges and cesses

3. Multi-stage

Under the GST regime, the tax will be levied at every point of sale, i.e. on each stage of the value chain, from the procurement of raw material to the sale of the finished product to the end consumer whenever there is value addition and transfer of ownership.

In case of intrastate sales, CGST and SGST will be charged. Interstate sales will be chargeable to Integrated GST.

There are multiple change-of-hands an item goes through along its supply chain: from manufacture to final sale to the consumer.

Let us consider the following chain:

- Purchase of raw materials
- Production or manufacture
- Sale to wholesaler
- Sale of the product to retailer
- Sale to the end consumer

Goods and Services Tax is levied on each of these stages which makes it a 'multi-stage tax'.

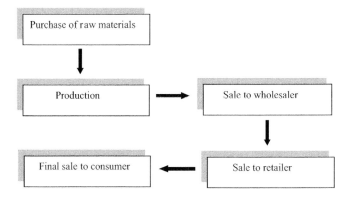

Figure 26.1 Supply chain

4. *Value-addition*

GST is levied on the supply of goods and services at every stage of value addition. This is presented in Figure 26.2.

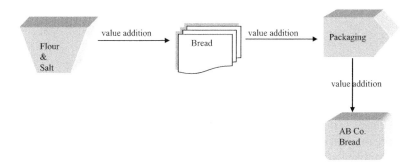

Figure 26.2 Value addition

In Figure 26.2:

1   The manufacturer who makes bread buys flour, salt and other material. The value of the inputs increases when the salt and flour are mixed and baked into bread.
2   The manufacturer then sells the bread to the packaging agent who packs large quantities of bread. That is another addition of value, after which it is sold it to the retailer.
3   The retailer packages the bread in smaller quantities and labels it as 'AB Co. Bread' after due marketing, thus increasing its value.

GST will be levied on these value additions, i.e. the monetary worth added at each stage to achieve the final sale to the end customer.

5. Destination-based

GST is destination-based because the final purchase is the place whose government collects GST. Considering the above example, bread is manufactured in Delhi and is sold to the final consumer in Uttar Pradesh. Since GST is levied at the point of consumption, in this case, the entire tax revenue will go to Uttar Pradesh and not Delhi.

6. Compensation to states

The Goods and Services Tax (Compensation to States) Act, 2017 provides for compensation to the states for the loss of revenue arising on account of implementation of the GST. The compensation will be provided to a state for a period of five years from the date on which the state brings its SGST Act into force. For the purpose of calculating the compensation amount in any financial year, year 2015–16 will be taken as the base year for calculating the revenue to be protected.[5]

7. Anti-profiteering mechanism

Implementation of GST in many countries was coupled with increase in inflation and the prices of the commodities. This happened in spite of the availability of the tax credit. This happened because the supplier was not passing on the benefit to the consumer and thereby indulging in illegal profiteering. Any reduction in rate of tax or the benefit of increased 'input tax credit' should be passed on to the recipient by way of commensurate reduction in prices.

The National Anti-Profiteering Authority (NAPA) has been constituted under GST by the central government to examine the complaints of non-passing the benefit of reduced tax incidence.[6]

GST and cascading effect

In the pre-GST regime, every buyer including the end-consumer paid tax on tax. This tax on tax is called the 'cascading effect of taxes.' GST avoids this cascading effect as the tax is calculated only on the value-add at each stage of transfer of ownership.

Taking the above example further and assigning some numbers, the tax computation pre and post GST is explained below.

Tax calculation earlier:

Transaction	Cost	10% tax (VAT)	Total
Manufacturer	1,000	100	1,100
Packaging agent repacks @ 200	1,300	130	1,430
Retailer advertises and labels @ 400	1,830	183	2,013
Total	1,600	413	2,013

It can be seen that earlier, the tax liability was passed on at every stage of the transaction and the final liability comes on the customer. This is called the 'cascading effect of taxes' where a tax is paid on tax and the value of the item keeps increasing every time.

Tax calculation under GST:

Transaction	Cost	10% tax	Actual liability	Total
Manufacturer	1,000	100	100	1,100
Packaging agent repacks @ 200	1,200	120	20	1,320
Retailer advertises and labels @ 400	1,600	160	40	1,760
Total	1,600		160	1,760

In case of GST, someone can claim credit for tax paid in acquiring input when they submit their taxes.

In the end, every time an individual claims 'input tax credit', the sale price is reduced and the ultimately the cost price for buyer is reduced because of a lower tax liability. The final value of the bread is therefore reduced from Rs. 2,013 to Rs. 1,760, thus reducing the tax burden on the final customer.

GST mechanism

There are three taxes applicable under this system: CGST, SGST and IGST.

* **CGST (Central Goods and Services Tax)** is collected by the central government on an intrastate sale of goods and services (in the above example: transaction happening within Delhi). The revenue collected under CGST is for the central government.

    However, input tax credit on CGST is given partly to the centre and partly to the states as it will be utilized against the payment of both CGST and IGST.

- **SGST (State Goods and Services Tax)** is collected by the state government on an intrastate sale of goods and services (in the above example: transaction happening within Delhi).

> State GST (state tax/SGST) would be called UTGST (Union Territory Goods and Services Tax) in Union territories without legislature. CGST and SGST/UTGST shall be levied on all taxable intrastate supplies.

- **IGST (Integrated Goods and Services Tax)** is collected by the central government for interstate sale of goods and services (in the above example: transaction happening from Delhi to Uttar Pradesh). IGST will also be applicable on the import of goods.

  The IGST is CGST plus SGST on all interstate supply of goods or services or both. The interstate supplier will pay IGST on value addition after adjusting available credit of IGST, CGST and SGST on his purchases. The 'exporting state' will transfer to the centre the credit of SGST used in payment of IGST. The person based in the 'destination state' will claim credit of IGST while discharging his output tax liability in his own state. The centre will transfer to the 'importing state' the credit of IGST used in payment of SGST.[7]

In the GST regime, the tax structure will be as shown in Table 26.1.

Table 26.1 Tax structure under GST

Transaction	Tax	Revenue sharing
Sale within the state	CGST + SGST	Revenue will be shared equally between the centre and the state
Sale to another state	IGST	There will only be one type of tax (central) in case of interstate sales. The centre will then share the IGST revenue based on the destination of goods.

Illustration 26.1: Dealer 'A' in Rajasthan sells the goods to dealer 'B' in Rajasthan worth Rs. 10,000. Further dealer 'B' in Rajasthan resells goods to dealer 'C' in Punjab for Rs. 20,000. Finally, dealer 'C' in Punjab sells goods to end-consumer 'D' in Punjab for Rs. 25,000. GST @ 18% comprises of SGST @ 9% and CGST @ 9%.

The tax implication at every stage is depicted as follows:

Figure 26.3 Tax implication under GST

- In the above case, the dealer 'A' has to charge Rs. 1,800 as GST. Out of this Rs. 900 revenue will go to the central government and Rs. 900 will go to the Rajasthan government as the sale is 'within the state'.
- Then dealer 'B' will charge Rs. 3,600 from dealer 'C', which will go to central government as the sale is 'interstate'.
- Finally, dealer 'C' charges Rs. 4,500 as GST from the end-consumer. Out of this Rs. 2,250 revenue will go to the central government and Rs. 2,250 will go to the Punjab government as the sale is one again 'within the state'.

The tax settlement for the above is presented in Table 26.2.

Advantages of GST

GST will have a multiplier effect on the economy and its benefits in various forms and to different sectors are discussed below.

1 *Single tax.* By subsuming multiple taxes, GST has led to a harmonized system of indirect taxes. GST avoids the cascading effect of tax as the tax is calculated only on the value-addition by persons whenever the ownership gets transferred, as discussed above.

2 *Lower cost of goods and services.* GST removes the cascading effect on the sale of goods and services, which directly impacts the cost of goods. Since tax on tax is eliminated in this process, the cost of goods decreases.

3 *Benefits to exporters.* GST reduces the cost of locally manufactured goods. This will increase the competiveness of Indian goods in the international markets, thereby giving a boost to Indian exports.

Table 26.2 Tax statement under GST

Stage	Parties	Sale Price (Rs.)	Tax Amount Received (Rs.)		
			Rajasthan govt.	Punjab govt.	Central govt.
I	A to B	10,000	10,000*9% = 900	—	10,000*9% = 900
II	B to C	20,000	—	—	20,000*IGST @18% 3,600 (-) CGST credit 900 (-) SGST credit 900 Net 1,800
III	C to D	25,000	—	25,000*SGST @9% 2,250 (-) IGST credit balance (3,600-2,250) 1,350 Net 900	25,000*CGST @9% 2,250 (-) IGST credit** 2,250 Net 0
Total Receipt			900	900	2,700
IV	Adjustment		(-) 900 going to centre	(+) 1,350 coming from centre	(+) 1,350
Final			0	2,250	2,250

Notes:

1. ** IGST credit is applied to set off in this order:
   first set off against IGST liability,
   then CGST, and
   the balance credit is used to set off SGST.

2. GST being a consumption-based tax, the state where the goods were consumed (Punjab) will receive GST. So, Rajasthan (where goods were sold) will not get any taxes.
   Punjab government and central government will get (25,000*9%) = Rs. 2,250 each.
   Thus, Rajasthan (exporting state) will have to transfer credit of SGST of Rs. 900 (used in payment of IGST) to the centre.
   In turn, central government will transfer to Punjab (importing state) Rs. 1,350 IGST.

4   *Increased efficiency.* GST is mainly technologically driven. All activities like registration, return filing, application for refund and response to notice are done online on the GST Portal. This speeds up the processes.

5   *Higher collection.* This indirect tax system under GST improves the collection of taxes as well as boost the development of Indian economy by removing the indirect tax barriers between states and integrating the country through a uniform tax rate.

6   *Ease of doing business.* GST has resulted in simpler tax regime, avoiding multiplicity of taxes and reduction in the compliance cost. All interaction is through the common GSTN portal, therefore, less public interface between the taxpayer and the tax administration. This makes business in India easier and simplified.

Box 26.2   Benefits of GST

GST offers multiple benefits to the Indian nation, as discussed above. Following is the snapshot of its benefits:

A. Indian economy

- Unified common national market for India
- Boost to foreign investment and "Made in India" campaign
- Boost to exports
- Substantive economic growth
- Better employment opportunities
- Reduction in tax evasion
- Better compliance

B. Consumers

- Reduction in prices of goods and services
- Transparency in taxation system

C. Business houses/traders

- Single tax and reduction in multiplicity of taxes
- Simpler tax system
- Input tax credit
- Increase in exports

Key terms under GST

1. Taxable person

He is a person who carries out any business at any place in India and is registered or required to be registered under the GST Act.

Amongst others, GST registration is mandatory for:

- Any business whose turnover in a financial year exceeds Rs. 20 lakhs (Rs. 10 lakhs for North Eastern and hill states)
- An input service distributor
- An e-commerce operator or aggregator
- A person who supplies via e-commerce aggregator
- An NRI doing business in India

2. GSTN

The Goods and Services Tax Network (GSTN) has been set up by the government as a private company under Section 8 of the Companies Act, 2013. It would provide three front-end services to the taxpayers, namely registration, payment and return.

3. GSTIN

This refers to the unique 'GST identification number' that every business will be allotted. Every taxpayer will be allotted a state-wise, PAN-based 15-digit Goods and Services Taxpayer Identification Number.

4. Reverse charge

Generally, when the supplier supplies goods, the tax is levied upon the supplier. In certain cases, the tax is levied upon the buyer of the goods. This is called 'reverse charge' as the chargeability of tax gets reversed. This is applicable on goods and services both.

5. Composition scheme

This is an alternative method of levying tax meant for small taxpayers with low turnover, i.e. taxpayers whose aggregate turnover does not exceed Rs. 1.5 crores threshold in a financial year. In case of special category states, this limit is Rs. 75 lakhs. The objective of this scheme is to make compliance easier and cost effective for the taxpayers.

GST composition scheme rate is given in Table 26.3.

Table 26.3 GST composition scheme tax rate

Sl. no.	Category of registered persons	Rate of tax
1	Manufacturers of goods (other than those specifically notified by govt.)	1% of the turnover
2	Suppliers making supplies referred to in clause (b) of paragraph 6 of Schedule II	2.5% of the turnover
3	Any other supplier eligible for composition levy under Section 10 and these rules	0.5% of the turnover

Source: Composition Rules, www.cbic.gov.in/resources//htdocs-cbec/gst/gst-31.03.17-composition-rules.pdf;jsessionid=83DB3C1C7B34EA22CE92246283EF8ECA (accessed on 2 September 2018).

6. E-way bill

This refers to the electronic way bill or electronic permit required for movement of goods exceeding Rs. 50,000 in value. This bill is required in both interstate (between different states) and intrastate (within a state) movement of goods.

Invoices under GST

There are two types of invoices under the new regime:

- Tax invoice
- Bill of supply

1. Tax invoice

This is issued by a registered supplier when supplying taxable goods or services. Following are the rules regarding the use and contents of the invoice:

- *Serial number of the invoice:* Serial numbers are consecutive and consist of letters, numbers, special characters, or any combination thereof; they are unique for each financial year.
- *Billing and shipping address:* This information is required as it will ultimately determine the 'place of supply' and the taxation of such transaction accordingly.
- *GSTIN/unique ID:* A GST identification number is required for the receiver.
- *HSN code/accounting code:* The notified person must include an HSN code for the goods and an accounting code for the services supplied.

2. Bill of supply

The bill of supply is issued by a registered supplier when:

- The goods or services supplied are exempt
- The supplier decides to pay taxes under the composition scheme

The bill of supply must contain the following details:

- *Serial number:* It should be a consecutive number consisting of letters and/or numbers and should be unique for one financial year.
- *Details of receiver:* These are required only if the receiver is registered: name, address, and GSTIN/unique ID of the receiver.
- *Particulars of goods:* The value of supply of goods or services or both taking into account discount or abatement.

Points to remember

- Goods and Services Tax (GST) is an 'indirect tax' that has replaced many central and state indirect taxes (like central sales tax, excise duty, service tax, and value addition tax) levied on goods and services in India. The Goods and Service Tax Act came into effect on 1 July 2017.
- Key features of GST: (i) *Dual system:* India has adopted the dual GST system, like Canada, wherein both centre and states administer tax independently. The government has decided on four different tax slab rates: 5%, 12%, 18%, 28% for various items, with some goods and services exempted. (ii) *Comprehensive:* It is one tax that replaces the following indirect taxes earlier levied by the centre and the state. (iii) *Multi-stage:* Under the GST regime, the tax will be levied at every point of sale, i.e. on each stage of the value chain. (iv) *Value-addition:* It is levied on the supply of goods and services at every stage of value addition. (v) *Destination-based:* It is destination-based because the final purchase is the place whose government collects GST. (vi) *Compensation to states:* The Goods and Services Tax (Compensation to States) Act, 2017 provides for compensation to the states for the loss of revenue arising on account of implementation of the GST. (vii) *Anti-profiteering mecha-*

nism: The National Anti-Profiteering Authority (NAPA) has been constituted under the GST by the central government to examine the complaints of non-passing the benefit of reduced tax incidence.

- In the pre-GST regime, every buyer including the end-consumer paid tax on tax. This tax on tax is called the 'cascading effect of taxes.' GST avoids this cascading effect as the tax is calculated only on the value-add at each stage of transfer of ownership.
- There are three taxes applicable under this system: CGST, SGST and IGST. *CGST (Central Goods and Services Tax)* is collected by the central government on an intrastate sale of goods and services. *SGST (State Goods and Services Tax)* is collected by the state government on an intrastate sale of goods and services. *IGST (Integrated Goods and Services Tax)* is collected by the central government for interstate sale of goods and services.
- GST will have a multiplier effect on the economy and its benefits in various forms and to different sectors are: (i) single tax, (ii) lower cost of goods and services (iii), benefits to exporters, (iv) increased efficiency, (v) higher collection, and (vi) ease of doing business.
- 'Taxable person' is a person who carries out any business at any place in India and is registered or required to be registered under the GST Act.
- The Goods and Services Tax Network (GSTN) has been set up by the government as a private company under erstwhile Section 25 of the Companies Act, 1956 to provide three front end services to the taxpayers, namely registration, payment and return.
- 'GSTIN' refers to the unique 'GST identification number' that every business will be allotted. Every taxpayer will be allotted a state-wise, PAN-based 15-digit Goods and Services Taxpayer Identification Number.
- 'Reverse charge' is the tax levied upon the buyer of the goods. This is applicable on goods and services both.
- 'Composition scheme' is an alternative method of levying tax meant for small taxpayers with low turnover, i.e. taxpayers whose aggregate turnover does not exceed Rs. 1.5 crores threshold in a financial year. In case of special category states, this limit is Rs. 75 lakhs.

- The 'e-Way bill' is the electronic way bill or electronic permit required for movement of goods exceeding Rs. 50,000 in value.
- There are two types of invoices under the new regime: tax invoice and bill of supply. *Tax invoice* is issued by a registered supplier when supplying taxable goods or services. *Bill of supply* is issued by a registered supplier when the goods or services supplied are exempt and the supplier decides to pay taxes under the composition scheme.

Notes

1 GST collections for 2017–18 at Rs. 7.41 lakh crore, www.thehindubusinessline.com/economy/policy/gst-collections-for-2017-18-at-741-lakh-crore/article23702170.ece (accessed on 27 August 2018).
2 Value-added tax (VAT) is a consumption tax levied on a product whenever value is added at each stage of the supply chain, from production to the point of sale.
3 Goods and Services Tax (GST) – Concept & Status, p. 7, www.cbic.gov.in/resources//htdocs-cbec/gst/01082018_GST_Concept_Status.pdf (accessed on 2 September 2018).
4 GST – An Update (As on 1st August 2018), www.cbic.gov.in/resources//htdocs-cbec/gst/01082018_GST_PPT_An%20Update.pdf;jsessionid=8C61 4EACB1B8460270E15455EB3D180B(accessed on 2 September 2018).
5 Goods and Services Tax (GST) – Concept & Status, p. 28, www.cbic.gov.in/resources//htdocs-cbec/gst/01082018_GST_Concept_Status.pdf (accessed on 2 September 2018).
6 Goods and Services Tax (GST) – Concept & Status, p. 29, www.cbic.gov.in/resources//htdocs-cbec/gst/01082018_GST_Concept_Status.pdf (accessed on 2 September 2018).
7 Goods and Services Tax (GST) – Concept & Status, p. 27, www.cbic.gov.in/resources//htdocs-cbec/gst/01082018_GST_Concept_Status.pdf (accessed on 2 September 2018).

Appendix I

Future/Compound value factor of a lump sum (FVIF/CVIF) of Re 1, FVIF(i, n)

Period	1%	2%	3%	4%	5%	6%	7%	8%	9%	10%	11%	12%	13%	14%	15%	16%	17%	18%	19%	20%
1	1.010	1.020	1.030	1.040	1.050	1.060	1.070	1.080	1.090	1.100	1.110	1.120	1.130	1.140	1.150	1.160	1.170	1.180	1.190	1.200
2	1.020	1.040	1.061	1.082	1.103	1.124	1.145	1.166	1.188	1.210	1.232	1.254	1.277	1.300	1.323	1.346	1.369	1.392	1.416	1.440
3	1.030	1.061	1.093	1.125	1.158	1.191	1.225	1.260	1.295	1.331	1.368	1.405	1.443	1.482	1.521	1.561	1.602	1.643	1.685	1.728
4	1.041	1.082	1.126	1.170	1.216	1.262	1.311	1.360	1.412	1.464	1.518	1.574	1.630	1.689	1.749	1.811	1.874	1.939	2.005	2.074
5	1.051	1.104	1.159	1.217	1.276	1.338	1.403	1.469	1.539	1.611	1.685	1.762	1.842	1.925	2.011	2.100	2.192	2.288	2.386	2.488
6	1.062	1.126	1.194	1.265	1.340	1.419	1.501	1.587	1.677	1.772	1.870	1.974	2.082	2.195	2.313	2.436	2.565	2.700	2.840	2.986
7	1.072	1.149	1.230	1.316	1.407	1.504	1.606	1.714	1.828	1.949	2.076	2.211	2.353	2.502	2.660	2.826	3.001	3.185	3.379	3.583
8	1.083	1.172	1.267	1.369	1.477	1.594	1.718	1.851	1.993	2.144	2.305	2.476	2.658	2.853	3.059	3.278	3.511	3.759	4.021	4.300
9	1.094	1.195	1.305	1.423	1.551	1.689	1.838	1.999	2.172	2.358	2.558	2.773	3.004	3.252	3.518	3.803	4.108	4.435	4.785	5.160
10	1.105	1.219	1.344	1.480	1.629	1.791	1.967	2.159	2.367	2.594	2.839	3.106	3.395	3.707	4.046	4.411	4.807	5.234	5.695	6.192
11	1.116	1.243	1.384	1.539	1.710	1.898	2.105	2.332	2.580	2.853	3.152	3.479	3.836	4.226	4.652	5.117	5.624	6.175	6.777	7.430
12	1.127	1.268	1.426	1.601	1.796	2.012	2.252	2.518	2.813	3.138	3.498	3.896	4.335	4.818	5.350	5.936	6.580	7.288	8.064	8.916
13	1.138	1.294	1.469	1.665	1.886	2.133	2.410	2.720	3.066	3.452	3.883	4.363	4.898	5.492	6.153	6.886	7.699	8.599	9.596	10.699
14	1.149	1.319	1.513	1.732	1.980	2.261	2.579	2.937	3.342	3.797	4.310	4.887	5.535	6.261	7.076	7.988	9.007	10.147	11.420	12.839
15	1.161	1.346	1.558	1.801	2.079	2.397	2.759	3.172	3.642	4.177	4.785	5.474	6.254	7.138	8.137	9.266	10.539	11.974	13.590	15.407
16	1.173	1.373	1.605	1.873	2.183	2.540	2.952	3.426	3.970	4.595	5.311	6.130	7.067	8.137	9.358	10.748	12.330	14.129	16.172	18.488
17	1.184	1.400	1.653	1.948	2.292	2.693	3.159	3.700	4.328	5.054	5.895	6.866	7.986	9.276	10.761	12.468	14.426	16.672	19.244	22.186

(Continued)

(Continued)

Period	1%	2%	3%	4%	5%	6%	7%	8%	9%	10%	11%	12%	13%	14%	15%	16%	17%	18%	19%	20%
18	1.196	1.428	1.702	2.026	2.407	2.854	3.380	3.996	4.717	5.560	6.544	7.690	9.024	10.575	12.375	14.463	16.879	19.673	22.901	26.623
19	1.208	1.457	1.754	2.107	2.527	3.026	3.617	4.316	5.142	6.116	7.263	8.613	10.197	12.056	14.232	16.777	19.748	23.214	27.252	31.948
20	1.220	1.486	1.806	2.191	2.653	3.207	3.870	4.661	5.604	6.727	8.062	9.646	11.523	13.743	16.367	19.461	23.106	27.393	32.429	38.338
25	1.282	1.641	2.094	2.666	3.386	4.292	5.427	6.848	8.623	10.835	13.585	17.000	21.231	26.462	32.919	40.874	50.658	62.669	77.388	95.396
30	1.348	1.811	2.427	3.243	4.322	5.743	7.612	10.063	13.268	17.449	22.892	29.960	39.116	50.950	66.212	85.850	111.065	143.371	184.675	237.376
35	1.417	2.000	2.814	3.946	5.516	7.686	10.677	14.785	20.414	28.102	38.575	52.800	72.069	98.100	133.176	180.314	243.503	327.997	440.701	590.668
40	1.489	2.208	3.262	4.801	7.040	10.286	14.974	21.725	31.409	45.259	65.001	93.051	132.782	188.884	267.864	378.721	533.869	750.378	1,051.668	1,469.772
50	1.645	2.692	4.384	7.107	11.467	18.420	29.457	46.902	74.358	117.391	184.565	289.002	450.736	700.233	1,083.657	1,670.704	2,566.215	3,927.357	5,988.914	9,100.438

Appendix II

Future/Compound value factor of an annuity (FVIFA/CVIFA) of Re 1, FVIFA(i, n)

Period	1%	2%	3%	4%	5%	6%	7%	8%	9%	10%	11%	12%	13%	14%	15%	16%	17%	18%	19%	20%
1	1.000	1.000	1.000	1.000	1.000	1.000	1.000	1.000	1.000	1.000	1.000	1.000	1.000	1.000	1.000	1.000	1.000	1.000	1.000	1.000
2	2.010	2.020	2.030	2.040	2.050	2.060	2.070	2.080	2.090	2.100	2.110	2.120	2.130	2.140	2.150	2.160	2.170	2.180	2.190	2.200
3	3.030	3.060	3.091	3.122	3.153	3.184	3.215	3.246	3.278	3.310	3.342	3.374	3.407	3.440	3.473	3.506	3.539	3.572	3.606	3.640
4	4.060	4.122	4.184	4.246	4.310	4.375	4.440	4.506	4.573	4.641	4.710	4.779	4.850	4.921	4.993	5.066	5.141	5.215	5.291	5.368
5	5.101	5.204	5.309	5.416	5.526	5.637	5.751	5.867	5.985	6.105	6.228	6.353	6.480	6.610	6.742	6.877	7.014	7.154	7.297	7.442
6	6.152	6.308	6.468	6.633	6.802	6.975	7.153	7.336	7.523	7.716	7.913	8.115	8.323	8.536	8.754	8.977	9.207	9.442	9.683	9.930
7	7.214	7.434	7.662	7.898	8.142	8.394	8.654	8.923	9.200	9.487	9.783	10.089	10.405	10.730	11.067	11.414	11.772	12.142	12.523	12.916
8	8.286	8.583	8.892	9.214	9.549	9.897	10.260	10.637	11.028	11.436	11.859	12.300	12.757	13.233	13.727	14.240	14.773	15.327	15.902	16.499
9	9.369	9.755	10.159	10.583	11.027	11.491	11.978	12.488	13.021	13.579	14.164	14.776	15.416	16.085	16.786	17.519	18.285	19.086	19.923	20.799
10	10.462	10.950	11.464	12.006	12.578	13.181	13.816	14.487	15.193	15.937	16.722	17.549	18.420	19.337	20.304	21.321	22.393	23.521	24.709	25.959
11	11.567	12.169	12.808	13.486	14.207	14.972	15.784	16.645	17.560	18.531	19.561	20.655	21.814	23.045	24.349	25.733	27.200	28.755	30.404	32.150
12	12.683	13.412	14.192	15.026	15.917	16.870	17.888	18.977	20.141	21.384	22.713	24.133	25.650	27.271	29.002	30.850	32.824	34.931	37.180	39.581
13	13.809	14.680	15.618	16.627	17.713	18.882	20.141	21.495	22.953	24.523	26.212	28.029	29.985	32.089	34.352	36.786	39.404	42.219	45.244	48.497
14	14.947	15.974	17.086	18.292	19.599	21.015	22.550	24.215	26.019	27.975	30.095	32.393	34.883	37.581	40.505	43.672	47.103	50.818	54.841	59.196
15	16.097	17.293	18.599	20.024	21.579	23.276	25.129	27.152	29.361	31.772	34.405	37.280	40.417	43.842	47.580	51.660	56.110	60.965	66.261	72.035
16	17.258	18.639	20.157	21.825	23.657	25.673	27.888	30.324	33.003	35.950	39.190	42.753	46.672	50.980	55.717	60.925	66.649	72.939	79.850	87.442

(*Continued*)

(Continued)

Period	1%	2%	3%	4%	5%	6%	7%	8%	9%	10%	11%	12%	13%	14%	15%	16%	17%	18%	19%	20%
17	18.430	20.012	21.762	23.698	25.840	28.213	30.840	33.750	36.974	40.545	44.501	48.884	53.739	59.118	65.075	71.673	78.979	87.068	96.022	105.93
18	19.615	21.412	23.414	25.645	28.132	30.906	33.999	37.450	41.301	45.599	50.396	55.750	61.725	68.394	75.836	84.141	93.406	103.74	115.27	128.12
19	20.811	22.841	25.117	27.671	30.539	33.760	37.379	41.446	46.018	51.159	56.939	63.440	70.749	78.969	88.212	98.603	110.28	123.41	138.17	154.74
20	22.019	24.297	26.870	29.778	33.066	36.786	40.995	45.762	51.160	57.275	64.203	72.052	80.947	91.025	102.44	115.38	130.03	146.63	165.42	186.69
25	28.243	32.030	36.459	41.646	47.727	54.865	63.249	73.106	84.701	98.347	114.41	133.33	155.62	181.87	212.79	249.21	292.10	342.60	402.04	471.98
30	34.785	40.568	47.575	56.085	66.439	79.058	94.461	113.28	136.31	164.49	199.02	241.33	293.20	356.79	434.75	530.31	647.44	790.95	966.71	1,181.9
35	41.660	49.994	60.462	73.652	90.320	111.43	138.24	172.32	215.71	271.02	341.59	431.66	546.68	693.57	881.17	1,120.7	1,426.5	1,816.7	2,314.2	2,948.3
40	48.886	60.402	75.401	95.026	120.80	154.76	199.64	259.06	337.88	442.59	581.83	767.09	1,013.7	1,342.0	1,779.1	2,360.8	3,134.5	4,163.2	5,529.8	7,343.9
50	64.463	84.579	112.80	152.67	209.35	290.34	406.53	573.77	815.08	1,163.9	1,668.8	2,400.0	3,459.5	4,994.5	7,217.7	10,436	15,090	21,813	31,515	45,497

Appendix III

Present value factor of a lump sum (PVIF) of Re 1, PVIF(i, n)

Period	1%	2%	3%	4%	5%	6%	7%	8%	9%	10%	11%	12%	13%	14%	15%	16%	17%	18%	19%	20%
1	0.990	0.980	0.971	0.962	0.952	0.943	0.935	0.926	0.917	0.909	0.901	0.893	0.885	0.877	0.870	0.862	0.855	0.847	0.840	0.833
2	0.980	0.961	0.943	0.925	0.907	0.890	0.873	0.857	0.842	0.826	0.812	0.797	0.783	0.769	0.756	0.743	0.731	0.718	0.706	0.694
3	0.971	0.942	0.915	0.889	0.864	0.840	0.816	0.794	0.772	0.751	0.731	0.712	0.693	0.675	0.658	0.641	0.624	0.609	0.593	0.579
4	0.961	0.924	0.888	0.855	0.823	0.792	0.763	0.735	0.708	0.683	0.659	0.636	0.613	0.592	0.572	0.552	0.534	0.516	0.499	0.482
5	0.951	0.906	0.863	0.822	0.784	0.747	0.713	0.681	0.650	0.621	0.593	0.567	0.543	0.519	0.497	0.476	0.456	0.437	0.419	0.402
6	0.942	0.888	0.837	0.790	0.746	0.705	0.666	0.630	0.596	0.564	0.535	0.507	0.480	0.456	0.432	0.410	0.390	0.370	0.352	0.335
7	0.933	0.871	0.813	0.760	0.711	0.665	0.623	0.583	0.547	0.513	0.482	0.452	0.425	0.400	0.376	0.354	0.333	0.314	0.296	0.279
8	0.923	0.853	0.789	0.731	0.677	0.627	0.582	0.540	0.502	0.467	0.434	0.404	0.376	0.351	0.327	0.305	0.285	0.266	0.249	0.233
9	0.914	0.837	0.766	0.703	0.645	0.592	0.544	0.500	0.460	0.424	0.391	0.361	0.333	0.308	0.284	0.263	0.243	0.225	0.209	0.194
10	0.905	0.820	0.744	0.676	0.614	0.558	0.508	0.463	0.422	0.386	0.352	0.322	0.295	0.270	0.247	0.227	0.208	0.191	0.176	0.162
11	0.896	0.804	0.722	0.650	0.585	0.527	0.475	0.429	0.388	0.350	0.317	0.287	0.261	0.237	0.215	0.195	0.178	0.162	0.148	0.135
12	0.887	0.788	0.701	0.625	0.557	0.497	0.444	0.397	0.356	0.319	0.286	0.257	0.231	0.208	0.187	0.168	0.152	0.137	0.124	0.112
13	0.879	0.773	0.681	0.601	0.530	0.469	0.415	0.368	0.326	0.290	0.258	0.229	0.204	0.182	0.163	0.145	0.130	0.116	0.104	0.093
14	0.870	0.758	0.661	0.577	0.505	0.442	0.388	0.340	0.299	0.263	0.232	0.205	0.181	0.160	0.141	0.125	0.111	0.099	0.088	0.078

(Continued)

(Continued)

Period	1%	2%	3%	4%	5%	6%	7%	8%	9%	10%	11%	12%	13%	14%	15%	16%	17%	18%	19%	20%
15	0.861	0.743	0.642	0.555	0.481	0.417	0.362	0.315	0.275	0.239	0.209	0.183	0.160	0.140	0.123	0.108	0.095	0.084	0.074	0.065
16	0.853	0.728	0.623	0.534	0.458	0.394	0.339	0.292	0.252	0.218	0.188	0.163	0.141	0.123	0.107	0.093	0.081	0.071	0.062	0.054
17	0.844	0.714	0.605	0.513	0.436	0.371	0.317	0.270	0.231	0.198	0.170	0.146	0.125	0.108	0.093	0.080	0.069	0.060	0.052	0.045
18	0.836	0.700	0.587	0.494	0.416	0.350	0.296	0.250	0.212	0.180	0.153	0.130	0.111	0.095	0.081	0.069	0.059	0.051	0.044	0.038
19	0.828	0.686	0.570	0.475	0.396	0.331	0.277	0.232	0.194	0.164	0.138	0.116	0.098	0.083	0.070	0.060	0.051	0.043	0.037	0.031
20	0.820	0.673	0.554	0.456	0.377	0.312	0.258	0.215	0.178	0.149	0.124	0.104	0.087	0.073	0.061	0.051	0.043	0.037	0.031	0.026
25	0.780	0.610	0.478	0.375	0.295	0.233	0.184	0.146	0.116	0.092	0.074	0.059	0.047	0.038	0.030	0.024	0.020	0.016	0.013	0.010
30	0.742	0.552	0.412	0.308	0.231	0.174	0.131	0.099	0.075	0.057	0.044	0.033	0.026	0.020	0.015	0.012	0.009	0.007	0.005	0.004
35	0.706	0.500	0.355	0.253	0.181	0.130	0.094	0.068	0.049	0.036	0.026	0.019	0.014	0.010	0.008	0.006	0.004	0.003	0.002	0.002
40	0.672	0.453	0.307	0.208	0.142	0.097	0.067	0.046	0.032	0.022	0.015	0.011	0.008	0.005	0.004	0.003	0.002	0.001	0.001	0.001
50	0.608	0.372	0.228	0.141	0.087	0.054	0.034	0.021	0.013	0.009	0.005	0.003	0.002	0.001	0.001	0.001	0.000	0.000	0.000	0.000

Appendix IV

Present value factor of an annuity (PVIFA) of Re 1, PVIFA(i, n)

Period	1%	2%	3%	4%	5%	6%	7%	8%	9%	10%	11%	12%	13%	14%	15%	16%	17%	18%	19%	20%
1	0.990	0.980	0.971	0.962	0.952	0.943	0.935	0.926	0.917	0.909	0.901	0.893	0.885	0.877	0.870	0.862	0.855	0.847	0.840	0.833
2	1.970	1.942	1.913	1.886	1.859	1.833	1.808	1.783	1.759	1.736	1.713	1.690	1.668	1.647	1.626	1.605	1.585	1.566	1.547	1.528
3	2.941	2.884	2.829	2.775	2.723	2.673	2.624	2.577	2.531	2.487	2.444	2.402	2.361	2.322	2.283	2.246	2.210	2.174	2.140	2.106
4	3.902	3.808	3.717	3.630	3.546	3.465	3.387	3.312	3.240	3.170	3.102	3.037	2.974	2.914	2.855	2.798	2.743	2.690	2.639	2.589
5	4.853	4.713	4.580	4.452	4.329	4.212	4.100	3.993	3.890	3.791	3.696	3.605	3.517	3.433	3.352	3.274	3.199	3.127	3.058	2.991
6	5.795	5.601	5.417	5.242	5.076	4.917	4.767	4.623	4.486	4.355	4.231	4.111	3.998	3.889	3.784	3.685	3.589	3.498	3.410	3.326
7	6.728	6.472	6.230	6.002	5.786	5.582	5.389	5.206	5.033	4.868	4.712	4.564	4.423	4.288	4.160	4.039	3.922	3.812	3.706	3.605
8	7.652	7.325	7.020	6.733	6.463	6.210	5.971	5.747	5.535	5.335	5.146	4.968	4.799	4.639	4.487	4.344	4.207	4.078	3.954	3.837
9	8.566	8.162	7.786	7.435	7.108	6.802	6.515	6.247	5.995	5.759	5.537	5.328	5.132	4.946	4.772	4.607	4.451	4.303	4.163	4.031
10	9.471	8.983	8.530	8.111	7.722	7.360	7.024	6.710	6.418	6.145	5.889	5.650	5.426	5.216	5.019	4.833	4.659	4.494	4.339	4.192
11	10.368	9.787	9.253	8.760	8.306	7.887	7.499	7.139	6.805	6.495	6.207	5.938	5.687	5.453	5.234	5.029	4.836	4.656	4.486	4.327
12	11.255	10.575	9.954	9.385	8.863	8.384	7.943	7.536	7.161	6.814	6.492	6.194	5.918	5.660	5.421	5.197	4.988	4.793	4.611	4.439
13	12.134	11.348	10.635	9.986	9.394	8.853	8.358	7.904	7.487	7.103	6.750	6.424	6.122	5.842	5.583	5.342	5.118	4.910	4.715	4.533
14	13.004	12.106	11.296	10.563	9.899	9.295	8.745	8.244	7.786	7.367	6.982	6.628	6.302	6.002	5.724	5.468	5.229	5.008	4.802	4.611
15	13.865	12.849	11.938	11.118	10.380	9.712	9.108	8.559	8.061	7.606	7.191	6.811	6.462	6.142	5.847	5.575	5.324	5.092	4.876	4.675
16	14.718	13.578	12.561	11.652	10.838	10.106	9.447	8.851	8.313	7.824	7.379	6.974	6.604	6.265	5.954	5.668	5.405	5.162	4.938	4.730
17	15.562	14.292	13.166	12.166	11.274	10.477	9.763	9.122	8.544	8.022	7.549	7.120	6.729	6.373	6.047	5.749	5.475	5.222	4.990	4.775

(Continued)

(Continued)

Period	1%	2%	3%	4%	5%	6%	7%	8%	9%	10%	11%	12%	13%	14%	15%	16%	17%	18%	19%	20%
18	16.398	14.992	13.754	12.659	11.690	10.828	10.059	9.372	8.756	8.201	7.702	7.250	6.840	6.467	6.128	5.818	5.534	5.273	5.033	4.812
19	17.226	15.678	14.324	13.134	12.085	11.158	10.336	9.604	8.950	8.365	7.839	7.366	6.938	6.550	6.198	5.877	5.584	5.316	5.070	4.843
20	18.046	16.351	14.877	13.590	12.462	11.470	10.594	9.818	9.129	8.514	7.963	7.469	7.025	6.623	6.259	5.929	5.628	5.353	5.101	4.870
25	22.023	19.523	17.413	15.622	14.094	12.783	11.654	10.675	9.823	9.077	8.422	7.843	7.330	6.873	6.464	6.097	5.766	5.467	5.195	4.948
30	25.808	22.396	19.600	17.292	15.372	13.765	12.409	11.258	10.274	9.427	8.694	8.055	7.496	7.003	6.566	6.177	5.829	5.517	5.235	4.979
35	29.409	24.999	21.487	18.665	16.374	14.498	12.948	11.655	10.567	9.644	8.855	8.176	7.586	7.070	6.617	6.215	5.858	5.539	5.251	4.992
40	32.835	27.355	23.115	19.793	17.159	15.046	13.332	11.925	10.757	9.779	8.951	8.244	7.634	7.105	6.642	6.233	5.871	5.548	5.258	4.997
50	39.196	31.424	25.730	21.482	18.256	15.762	13.801	12.233	10.962	9.915	9.042	8.304	7.675	7.133	6.661	6.246	5.880	5.554	5.262	4.999

Appendix V
List of corporates and business organisations

Apollo Tyres Ltd. – Tyre sector
Ashok Leyland Ltd. – Automobile sector
Bajaj Auto Ltd. – Automobile sector
Bharat Electronics Ltd. – Electronics sector
Bharti Airtel Ltd. – Telecommunications sector
Colgate Palmolive India Ltd. – Fast-moving consumer goods (FMCG) sector
Dabur India Ltd. – Fast-moving consumer goods (FMCG) sector
DLF Ltd. – Realty sector
Emami – Fast-moving consumer goods (FMCG) sector
GlaxoSmithKline Consumer Healthcare – Fast-moving consumer goods (FMCG) sector
Godrej Consumer Products Limited (GCPL) – Fast-moving consumer goods (FMCG) sector
Hindustan Construction Company Ltd. (HCC) – Construction sector
Hindustan Unilever Ltd. (HUL) – Fast-moving consumer goods (FMCG) sector
ICICI Bank – Banking sector
Idea Cellular Ltd. – Telecommunications sector
Infosys Ltd. – IT sector
ITC Ltd. – Conglomerate sector
Larsen and Toubro Ltd. (L&T) – Infrastructure sector
Marico – Fast-moving consumer goods (FMCG) sector
Maruti Suzuki Ltd. – Automobile sector
Nestle India Ltd. – Fast-moving consumer goods (FMCG) sector
NHPC Ltd. – Power sector
NTPC Ltd. – Power sector
P&G Hygiene and Health Care Ltd. – Fast-moving consumer goods (FMCG) sector

Parsvnath Developers Ltd. – Realty sector
Power Grid Corporation of India Ltd. – Power sector
State Bank of India (SBI) – Banking sector
Tata Power Ltd. – Power sector
Torrent Power Ltd. – Power sector
Unitech Ltd. – Realty sector

Glossary

Absorption   It is the merger with an existing company, where all other firms are absorbed into the surviving firm.

Absorption Costing   It is the practice of 'charging all costs' – both variable and fixed to operations, products or processes.

Accounting   It is the art of recording, classifying and summarising in significant manner and in terms of money, transactions and events which are, in part, at least of a financial character and interpreting the results thereof.

Accounting Concepts   These are the basic assumptions or postulates which need to be followed by business firms in preparing financial statements.

Accounting Conventions   These are the accounting principles which are pursued by business firms as practice and therefore are included.

Accounting Period Principle   It requires that every business organisation must report the results of a business at regular intervals.

Accounting Principles   There are basic accounting principles and guidelines that govern the field of accounting. These are referred to as 'generally accepted accounting principles' (GAAP).

Accounting Rate of Return (ARR) (or average rate of return)   It is the ratio of the average net income from the project to the average book value of assets of the project.

Accounting Standards   These are legalistic accounting rules which are mandatory in nature.

Accrual Basis of Accounting   Under this basis, income is recorded when a sale is made, irrespective of the receipt and expenses are recorded when they are incurred, without being paid.

Acquisition   It refers to acquiring of effective working control by one company over another.

Aggressive Beta   This is beta more than 1 and is more risky.

Aggressive Working Capital Policy   It involves keeping a low amount of current assets by the enterprise. It finances the current assets by short-term sources.

Alternate Minimum Tax (AMT)   This is the minimum tax made applicable to all other taxpayers except companies.

Amalgamation   (or consolidation) This implies that all the firms are combined to form a new entity through the transfer of all their property to such a new corporation.

American Depositary Receipts (ADRs)   These depositary receipts are issued by non-US companies to raise capital in the US equity market from US investors.

Amortisation   It is used for writing off and replacing intangible assets.

Annuity   If same amount is invested every year, it is termed as 'annuity'.

Assessee   This means a person by whom any tax or any other sum of money is payable under the Income Tax Act, 1961.

Assessment Year   This is the year in which income is taxable and refers to the period of 12 months starting from April 1 and ending on March 31 of the next year.

Assets   They are resources that are owned by a business having commercial value and which are used for generating return.

Asset Management Companies (AMCs)   These are the companies that operate the mutual funds.

Assets Turnover Ratio (ATR)   It is a measure of how efficient the company has been in generating sales from the assets at its disposal.

Associate Company   An associate company is one whose 20% or more shares are owned by a holding company.

Authorised Share Capital   It is the maximum limit which the company is registered with the Registrar of Companies to raise.

Average Collection Period (ACP)   This ratio indicates the number of days taken by the firm in collecting its receivables.

Average Holding Period (AHP)   It indicates the number of days the company holds its inventory.

Average Payment Period (APP)   This ratio indicates the average number of days in which the company makes payments to its suppliers.

Backward Integration   When a company combines with the supplier of material, it is called backward integration (merger).

Balanced Mutual Funds   These funds invest in a mix of equities and fixed income securities.

Balance Sheet   (or position statement) It depicts the economic resources owned by an entity and the claims against those resources, that is liabilities and owners' equity.

Bank Finance   It refers to the finance raised from commercial banks.

Bank Rate   It is the rate of interest which a central bank charges on the loans and advances to a commercial bank.

Batch Costing   It is a type of specific order costing, wherein a quantity of identical articles are produced as a single job in the form of a batch.

Beta (β)   It is a measure of the volatility or sensitivity of a security's return in relation to changes in the return of the stock market.

Bid Rate   The buying rate in the forex market is known as the 'bid rate'.

Bills of Exchange (or discounted bills)   These are short-term, negotiable, and liquidating instruments with low risk.

Bookkeeping   It refers to the recording of business transactions only. It is a part of accounting.

Book Value per Share (BV)   It measures the net worth to be enjoyed by the ordinary shareholders of the company after all debts are paid.

Bonus Shares   Bonus shares are also called a 'stock dividend', as these are shares which issued free of cost to the shareholders of a company, by capitalising a part of the company's reserves.

Borrowed Funds   They refer to the borrowings of a business firm.

Bottom Line   It is the net profit of the company, left for distribution to shareholders and reinvestment for future growth.

Break-even Point   It is the volume of sales or production where there is neither profit nor loss.

Budget   It is 'a plan expressed in numerical or financial terms'.

Budgeting   It is the act of building budgets and with their help coordinates the various departments of the firm.

Budgetary Control   This technique is used as a tool for planning and control with the help of which the management is able to assess the performance of each and every individual/unit/department in the organisation.

Business Entity Principle   It states that all business transactions of the firm should be considered separate from the business owner's personal transactions.

Business Organisation   (also known as business enterprise, business undertaking, business firm or business concern). It is an enterprise which makes, distributes or provides any article or service which the other members of the community need and are able and willing to pay for.

Call Money   It is the money lent by a bank which is repayable on demand.

Call Option It gives the buyer the right but not the obligation to buy a certain quantity of the underlying asset, at a given price on or before the specified date in future.

Capital It is the money contributed by owners. It is shareholders' funds in a business.

Capital Analysis This provides information about the funds required to start the project and keep it running until it is self-sustaining.

Capital Asset Pricing Method (CAPM) It is used to calculate cost of equity, based on the 'risk-return' trade-off for securities.

Capital Budgeting Decision It pertains to investment in fixed assets/long-term assets whose returns are expected over a long period of time.

Capital Market (or stock market) It is a market for long-term funds, that is funds more than one year.

Capital Structure It is the composition of debt and equity. It is the total of the long-term funds of an enterprise.

Cash Basis of Accounting In a cash accounting method, income and expenses are recorded only when funds are received or disbursed.

Cash Budget It is prepared to calculate budgeted cash flows (inflows and outflows) during a specific period of time.

Cash Cycle (or cash conversion cycle) It denotes the actual cash requirement to run the business operations.

Cash Dividend It is the dividend which is paid in cash in the form of final dividend or interim dividend.

Cash Reserve Ratio (CRR) It refers to the cash that banks are required to maintain with RBI as a certain percentage of their demand and time liabilities (DTL).

Called-up Share Capital It is that part of subscribed share capital which is called up by the company.

Capital Work-In-Progress (CWIP) This includes under-construction or under-completion of fixed assets.

Cash Flow Statement It describes the enterprise's cash flows position during the time period.

Cash Inflows These are expected returns from the operating activities.

Cash Outflows These are outlays that result from investment activities.

CCIL The Clearing Corporation of India Ltd. (CCIL) was set up on the initiative by RBI to provide guaranteed clearing and settlement functions for transactions in money, G-Secs, foreign exchange and derivative markets.

Central Board of Direct Taxes (CBDT) This provides inputs for policy and planning of direct taxes in India and is responsible for the administration of direct tax laws through the Income Tax Department.

Central Board of Indirect Taxes & Customs (CBIC) This is responsible for the formulation of policy concerning levy and collection of customs, GST, central excise, service tax, and narcotics in India and their administration.

Central Goods and Services Tax (CGST) This is collected by the central government on an intra-state sale of goods and services.

Certificate of Deposits (CODs) A short-term bank deposit.

Close-Ended Mutual Funds These are funds with a pre-specified life and are redeemable at the end. These are listed in the stock exchanges and traded like stocks.

Commercial Paper (CPs) Commercial Paper is the short term unsecured debt instrument note issued by corporate and financial institutions at a discounted price.

Committed Fixed Cost It is unavoidable in the short run if the organisation has to function.

Common-size Analysis (or vertical analysis) It is the analysis of financial statements on vertical basis to determine the contribution of each item of financial statement in total resources or with regard to a common base.

Composition Scheme An alternative method of levying tax meant for small taxpayers with low turnover, i.e. taxpayers whose aggregate turnover does not exceed Rs. 1.5 crores threshold in a financial year.

Compounding It refers to the future value of a present sum of money.

Conglomerate Merger This is a combination of two or more firms which are engaged in unrelated lines of business activity.

Conservative Beta (or defensive beta) This is beta less than 1 and is less risky.

Consistency Principle This principle is based on the assumption that, once you adopt an accounting principle or method, you should continue to use it until a better principle or method is warranted.

Conservatism Principle It states 'anticipate no profits but provide for possible losses'.

Conservative Working Capital Policy In this policy, current assets are financed by long-term sources and keep a safety net for future uncertainty.

Constant Dividend Payout Policy A constant dividend payment ratio policy whereby a corporation establishes a certain dividend payout ratio and applies this to earnings.

Constant Dividend per Share Policy   In this policy, the companies payout a constant DPS irrespective of their EPS, that is a change in their PAT (whether increase or decrease) would not affect the dividend paid out to shareholders.

Contract Costing   It is a bigger form of job costing.

Contribution   It is the difference between sales and variable cost. It contributes toward fixed cost and profit.

Contribution Margin   (or P/V ratio) It is the contribution per rupee of sales.

Controllable Cost   This cost can be influenced by the action of a manager of a cost centre and is dependent on his activity.

Conversion Cost   It is the cost of transforming direct materials into the finished products exclusive of direct material cost.

Convertible Debentures   These debentures are convertible into shares after a specified period of time.

Convertible Preference Shares   These preference shares are convertible into equity shares after a specified period of time.

Corporate Governance   It is the system by which business are directed and controlled.

Cost of Debt   It is an explicit cost in the form of interest paid by the company on the loan amount.

Cost of Equity Capital (COCE)   It is an implicit cost as there is no assured/coupon rate of return involved here. It is the rate of return that the firm must earn to meet shareholders' expectations and thereby increase shareholders' wealth.

Cost of Preference Capital It is an explicit cost in the form of fixed dividend paid by the company to preference shareholders.

Cost of Retained Earnings It is an implicit cost with no explicit obligation to pay a return. It is the cost of re-earning forgone by the shareholders.

Cost-Volume-Profit Analysis (CVP Analysis)   It is a technique for studying the relationship between cost, volume and profit at different levels of sales or production.

Cooperative Organisation   A cooperative society is a voluntary association of persons who join hands together to carry on a commercial activity.

Cost   It means 'the amount of expenditure (actual or notional) incurred on, or attributable to, a given thing'.

Cost Accounting It is the formal mechanism by means of which costs of products or services are ascertained and controlled.

Cost Analysis. This analysis determines the possible cost structure of the project.

Cost Centres   These are the segments of activity or area of responsibility for which costs are accumulated.

Cost Sheet   It is the 'cost statement' which is prepared internally to show the cost structure of the total output produced during the period.

Cost Unit   It is the 'quantitative unit' of a product or service, in relation to which cost is ascertained.

Cost of Goods Sold (COGS)   It means the cost, to the company, of the merchandise that is sold to customers.

Cost of Sales   (or total cost) It is the final cost of goods or services, which is arrived at after adding the selling and distribution overheads to office cost.

Cost Principle   According to this principle, the items are shown in the financial statements at historical cost.

Credit   It is the portion of transaction that accounts for the increase in income, liabilities and equity, and the decrease in assets and expenses.

Creditors Turnover Ratio (CTR)   This ratio is used to measure a company's ability to get trade credit and the speed at which it pays off its suppliers.

Cumulative Fixed Deposits   These are the deposits where the interest accumulates with principal so as to earn higher returns when compared to a non-cumulative plan.

Cumulative Preference Shares These preference shares are those where dividend is accumulated and paid in total if not paid in a specific year.

Current Assets   These are meant for current use, for day-to-day operations and are for less than a year.

Current Budgets   The period for these budgets is usually of months and weeks.

Current Liability   These liabilities are for less than a year.

Current Ratio   It indicates the ability of a company to pay its short-term creditors from the realisation of its current assets.

Debentures   (or bonds) They are known as creditorship securities because debenture holders are the creditors of a company.

Debit   It is the portion of transaction that accounts for the increase in assets and expenses, and the decrease in liabilities, equity and income.

Debt-Equity Ratio (D/E)   It indicates the relative proportions of debt and equity in financing the assets of a firm.

Debt Service Coverage Ratio (DCSR)   It is the amount of cash flow available to meet annual interest and principal payments on debt.

Debtors Turnover Ratio (DTR)   This ratio indicates how quickly the firm is able to sell its products and collect its debts.

Deferred Tax Assets   (or Liabilities) These are fictitious assets and arise as a part of accounting differences between Companies Act and Income Tax Act.

Demographic Analysis   This involves analysis of demographic trends that are occurring in a particular market area, based on indicators, like age, education, and income level.

Departmental Undertaking   It is a public sector enterprise which is managed by government officials under the supervision of the head of the department concerned.

Dependent Projects   (*or contingent projects*) In this case, the acceptance of one proposal is contingent upon the acceptance of other proposals.

Depletion   It refers to the process of writing off and replacing natural resourses.

Depository Receipts These are owned securities of domestic companies issued in the foreign country in its currency.

Depreciation   It means 'the reduction in or loss of quality or value of a fixed asset through physical wear and tear in use or passage of time or from any other cause'. It is basically used for tangible assets.

Depreciation Accounting It is the process of writing off the fixed asset during its life and providing funds for its replacement when it becomes unproductive.

Derivatives   These are instruments whose value is derived from the price of some underlying asset like securities, commodities, bullion, currency, interest level, stock market index and so forth.

Direct Cost   It is a cost that can be specifically identified with a cost object. This includes direct material, direct labour and direct expenses.

Direct Expenses These are 'chargeable expenses' to the product, other than direct material and direct labour which are directly incurred on a specific product or job.

Direct Labour   It takes an active part in the production process of goods and services.

Direct Material   It is one which forms an integral part of the product.

Direct Quotations   The exchange quotation which gives the price for the foreign currency in terms of the domestic currency is known as 'direct quotation'.

Direct Tax   Tax that is levied directly on individuals and corporate entities and cannot be transferred to others.

Discounted Cash-Flow Method of Valuation (DCF)   It attempts to determine the value of the company by computing the present value of cash flows over the life of the company. It is widely used in capital investment decisions.

Discounted Payback Period   It is an improved version of the payback method as it considers the time value of money.

Discounting   It denotes the present value of a future sum of money.

Discretionary Fixed Cost   It is the cost which is set at a fixed amount for specific time periods by management in the budgeting process.

Diversification Investment Decision   It is deciding to entering into new lines of business either product-wise or territory-wise.

Diversifiable Risk   (or unsystematic risk or internal risk) It is the risk which is controllable and can be managed by the firm, such as management policies, strikes and so forth.

Dividend   It is the amount of profits distributed to the shareholders as 'return'. It could be annual dividend or/and interim dividend.

Dividend Decision   It is the decision about distributing net profit to shareholders and retaining for future growth.

Dividend Payout Ratio (D/P Ratio)   It refers to the amount of dividend paid per share with respect to the earnings per share.

Dividend per Share (DPS)   It is defined as the portion of company's profit distributed to each common shareholder.

Dividend Policy   It is the policy of the management about the profits to be distributed as cash dividends and part to be reinvested for future growth.

Dividend Yield Ratio (D/Y)   It refers to the amount of dividend paid per share with respect to the market price per share.

Double Declining Balance Method of Depreciation   Here, the depreciation expense is computed by multiplying the asset cost less accumulated depreciation by twice the straight line rate expressed in percentage.

Double Entry System of Accounting   It is the system wherein every transaction is considered to have two effects and recorded in two accounts.

Dual Aspect Principle   It is the underlying basis for double entry accounting system and states that every transaction has two aspects: debit and credit.

Due Diligence   It is an investigating process or audit of a potential transaction or deal so as to find out all relevant facts pertaining to the ensuing transaction.

DuPont Analysis   It is used to find out the factors responsible for performance of shareholders' value in terms of 'ROE'.

Earnings before Interest, Tax and Depreciation and Amortisation (EBITDA)   This is the amount of profit earned from the core activities of business, excluding finance costs, tax and depreciation provisioning.

EBITDA Margin   It measures the profitability of a concern after meeting other line of expenses, including office and selling expenses but excluding non-cash expense of depreciation.

Earnings before Interest and Tax (EBIT)   (operating profit) This represents operating profit earned during the normal course of operations after adjusting non-cash expenses of depreciation and amortisation.

Earnings per Share (EPS)   It is defined as the portion of company's profit allocated to each outstanding share of a common stock.

EBIT Margin   (or operating profit ratio) It measures the profitability of a concern after charging non-cash expense of depreciation.

Economic Value added (EVA)   It is the financial performance measure that captures the true economic profit of an enterprise. It is the profits generated by any economic entity over its cost of capital employed.

Economic Value Method of Human Valuation   (or discounted net present value of future earnings method). Under this method, human asset is valued on the basis of the contribution they will make to the organisation till their retirement from the job.

Efficiency Ratios   (or turnover ratios) These are computed to find out the efficiency of the management in utilisation of resources, both long-term and short-term.

Enterprise Value Method of Valuation   The 'enterprise value' is the total of value of equity and debt minus cash and cash equivalents.

Environmental Analysis   This consists of analysing the environmental impacts of the business.

Equity Linked Saving Schemes (ELSS)   They are an equity mutual fund which is qualified for tax exemption under Section 80C of the Income Tax Act.

Equity Shares   (or ordinary shares or common shares) These are those shares which do not carry any special or preferential rights in the payment of annual dividend or repayment of capital.

E-Way Bill   The Electronic Way Bill or electronic permit required for movement of goods exceeding Rs. 50,000 in value.

Expansion Investment Decision   It is a decision regarding whether the firm should increase its production capacity and operations by adding new products, additional machines, and so on.

Expenses   These are the costs which are incurred to run and maintain a business.

Explicit Costs   These are the costs that are paid by the firm to procure a source of finance. These are fixed and visible.

Factory Cost   It is the total of prime cost and factory overheads.

Feasible Business Venture   It is one where the business will generate adequate cash flow and profits, withstand the risks it will encounter, remain viable in the long-term and meet the predetermined goals.

Financial Accounting   It is mainly concerned with the financial performance of an organisation and involves the preparation of financial statements of profit and loss account and the balance sheet.

Financial Analysis   (or financial appraisal) It is the process of analysing the financial statements information and interpreting the meaning of those numbers with the help of financial tools.

Financial Feasibility   (or economic feasibility) This determines the commercial viability of the project, that is if its probable revenues exceed the total costs.

Financial Forecasting   It is the process adopted by the firms for planning their future financial activities.

Financial Leverage   It is the use of fixed financing costs by a firm to magnify EPS.

Financial Leverage Ratio   It is the degree of total debt involved in the financial structure of a firm.

Financial Management   It is the process of acquiring and disbursement of funds. It includes all the activities relating to planning, organising, directing and controlling the funds of the enterprise.

Financial Market   It is a marketplace where buyers and sellers come together and take part in the trade of assets, such as equities, bonds and derivatives.

Financial Ratio   It is a relationship between two financial elements that indicates information about business activities.

Financial Statements   These are financial reports in a prescribed format required to be prepared by an entity to meet the information needs of various stakeholders.

Financial Structure   It refers to the total amount of funds of an enterprise, both short term and long term.

Financial Synergies   These are the synergies that increase the capacity of the combined firm to mobilise financial resources at a lower cost.

Financing Decision   It refers to the process of raising funds from various sources.

Fixed Assets   (or non-current assets) They are long-term resources, more than a year and are used for long-term growth and expansion of a business.

Fixed Budget   (or static budget) It is a budget which does not change with the change in the output or any activity.

Fixed Capital   It refers to the investment in the fixed assets from firm's capital.

Fixed Cost   This cost remains constant al different levels of output. It is independent of any changes in the volume of activity.

Flexible Budget   This budget is flexible enough to adapt the changes which occur due to change in the output or any other factor.

Forex Market   The forex market or 'foreign exchange market' is the market which brings the participants across the globe together to buy, sell, exchange and speculate on currencies.

Forwards   A forward contract is a contract between two parties, where settlement takes place on a specific date in future at today's pre-agreed price.

Forward-Forward Swap   Here, both the deals are in the forward, that is one buys two months forward and sells three months forward, each deal cancelling the other or vice versa.

Forward Integration   When a firm combines with the buyer or customer, it is known as forward integration (merger).

Forward Market   It is the place where the transactions for the exchange of currencies take place at a specified future after the spot date.

Full Disclosure Principle   It states that the company must disclose fully and fairly all the information to the stakeholders which they have to report.

Functional Budgets   They relate to various functions of the firm.

Futures   A future is a contract between two parties to buy or sell an asset in future at a specific price.

Global Depositary Receipts (GDRs)   These represent depository receipts issued outside the US.

Going Concern Principle   This accounting principle assumes that a company will continue to exist *for an indefinite period of life* to carry out its objectives and commitments and will not liquidate in the near future.

Goods and Services Tax (GST)   An 'indirect tax' that has replaced many central and state indirect taxes levied on goods and services in India.

Goods and Services Tax Network (GSTN)   It has been set up by the government as a private limited company under Section 8 of the Companies Act, 2013 to provide three front end services to the taxpayers, namely registration, payment and return.

Government Company   It is a company in which not less than 51% of the paid-up share capital is held by the central government or by one or more state governments or jointly by the central and state governments.

Government Securities (G-Secs)   They refer to government and semi-government debt securities issued by the Reserve Bank of India (RBI).

Gross Profit   The gross profit represents the amount of direct profit associated with the actual manufacturing of goods.

Gross Profit Ratio   This indicates the margin generated out of sales after meeting production expenses.

Gross Working Capital   It refers to the firm's investment in 'total current assets' needed to operate over a normal business cycle.

Growth Mutual Funds   These predominantly invest in equities. These funds aim to grow faster than other funds, so there is usually a higher risk.

GST Identification Number (GSTIN)   This refers to the unique PAN-based, 15-digit Goods and Services Taxpayer Identification Number.

Historical Cost Method of Human Valuation   Under this method, all actual costs incurred on recruitment, training, selection and so forth are capitalised. Then, the capitalised cost is amortised (written off) over the period an employee serves in the organisation.

Holding Company   It is the parent company which owns 20% or more shares of another company.

Horizontal Merger   This is a combination or joining of two or more firms in the same area of business.

Human Resource Valuation (HRV)   (or human resource accounting [HRA]) It is the process of identifying and measuring data about human resources and communicating this information to interested parties.

Hybrid Dividend Policy   Using this approach, companies will generally have one set dividend, which is set as a relatively small portion of yearly income. On top of this set dividend, these companies will offer another extra dividend paid only when income exceeds general levels.

Implicit Costs   They are not an assured cost but an opportunity cost of funds.

Income Mutual Funds   These are primarily a debt fund. They invest in securities that pay a fixed rate of return like government bonds and corporate bonds.

Incremental Cash Flows   These are the cash flows that are affected, or change, if the asset is purchased.

Independent Directors   Independent director is any non-executive director who possesses relevant expertise and integrity and in no way is related to the company.

Independent Projects The project whose acceptance does not affect the acceptance of any other project is an independent project.

Index Mutual Funds These funds invest in a specific set of stocks of an index like BSE Sensex or NSE Nifty.

Indirect Cost It is a cost which cannot be directly identified with a single product or service. They are the common cost of support centres.

Indirect Expenses 'Overheads'. They could be manufacturing overheads, office overheads or/and selling overheads.

Indirect Labour It is the supporting staff which carries out tasks incidental to providing goods and services.

Indirect Material It is the additional material used on the product.

Indirect Quotations The exchange quotation which gives the quantity of foreign currency per unit of domestic currency is known as 'indirect quotation'.

Indirect Taxes These taxes are indirectly levied on the public through goods and services.

Industry Analysis This analysis examines and identifies industries trends that are presently occurring in the market place.

Industry-Specific Mutual Funds They focus upon specific industries, such as construction, pharmaceuticals or banking.

Inorganic Growth (or external growth) It is accomplished through various business combinations, namely, mergers and acquisitions (M&A).

Institutional Finance It refers to the finance raised from financial institutions, both central and state level financial institutions.

International Financial Reporting Standards (IFRS) These are global standards for the preparation of financial statements by public companies as a part of harmonisation of global reporting.

Intangible Fixed Assets These fixed assets are those which are not visible.

Integrated Goods and Services Tax (IGST) This is collected by the central government for inter-state sale of goods and services.

Inter-Corporate Deposits (ICDs) These are usually an unsecured inter-corporate loan.

Interest Coverage Ratio (ICR) It is the ratio which gives an idea about a company's ability to pay interest on its overdue debt.

Internal Rate of Return (IRR) It is the rate of return at which NPV is zero, that is the rate at which present value of cash inflows is equal to present value of cash outflows.

Inventory Turnover Ratio (ITR) This ratio measures the velocity of conversion of inventory in generating sales over a period.

Investment Decision   It implies the allocation of funds in various assets. The investment in fixed assets is called 'capital budgeting decision'. The investment in current assets is called a 'working capital decision'.

Irredeemable Debentures   These debentures are issued for perpetuity.

Irredeemable Preference Shares   These preference shares are issued for perpetuity.

Issued Share Capital   It represents that amount actually offered to the public for subscription.

Job Costing   It is a form of specific order costing which is used in those business concerns where production is carried out as per specific order and customer specifications.

Joint Hindu Family Business   It may be defined as a form of business organisation in which all the male members of a Hindu undivided family carry on business under the management and control of the head of the family called 'Karta'.

Joint Sector Enterprise   It consists of those business undertakings wherein the ownership, management and control are shared jointly by the government, private entrepreneurs and the public.

Joint Stock Company   It is an association of persons having a separate legal existence, perpetual succession and common seal and incorporated under the Companies Act, 1956.

Leverage   It is the employment of an asset or source of funds for which the firm has to pay a fixed cost or return.

Leverage Ratio   This ratio is used to calculate the amount of fixed obligations involved in a company's structure and its ability to meet those obligations.

Lev and Schwartz Model of Human Valuation   It values human resources in the form of discounted present values of all future payments to the employees. Here, 'the human resource of a company is the summation of value of all the net present value (NPV) of expenditure on employees'.

Liability   It is a debt or outstanding balance owed to another party requiring a future cash flow for payment

Limited Liability Partnership (LLP)   It is a corporate structure that combines the flexibility of a partnership on the basis of a mutually arrived agreement, and the advantages of limited liability of a company.

Liquidity   It is the availability of cash or near cash funds for meeting day-to-day expenses of the firm.

Liquid Ratio   (or acid-test ratio or quick ratio) It assesses the company's short-term financial health based on more liquid assets, excluding stock.

Liquidity Ratios   These ratios provide information about a firm's ability to meet its short-term financial obligations.

Long-Run Residual Dividend Policy   Such a policy is created by the corporation by first forecasting the relevant variables, such as earnings, investment needs, interest charges and taxation, for a given period and then dividends are determined.

Long-term Budgets   They range from a period of five to ten years.

Long-term Finance   It refers to that category of funds whose repayment is generally more than a ten-year period.

Long-term Liability   (or non-current liability) These liabilities are for more than a year.

Management Accounting   It is the accounting which provides necessary information to the management for taking various decisions.

Marginal Cost   It is the change in the total cost with the change in the quantity produced, that is it is the cost of producing additional unit of a good.

Marginal Costing   This is a technique of costing where those expenses are allocated to production which arise as a result of production.

Market Feasibility   It is conducted to determine the viability of a proposed product in the marketplace.

Market Ratios   These ratios are used to determine the market performance of company in the stock market.

Market Value Added (MVA)   It is the market value created by the firm over its capital employed.

Market Value Method of Valuation (MV)   It is presumed to reflect the public information about the company and its industry; it values the company as per the current price prevailing in the market.

Margin of Safety   It implies the 'cushion' over break-even sales.

Master Budget   This budget is for the whole organisation. It covers all the information of an organisation in a summarised manner.

Matching Principle   This principle requires that expenses should be matched with revenues of the same year.

Matching Working Capital Policy   (or hedging working capital policy) This policy is an arrangement where the current assets of the business are used perfectly to match the current liabilities. It is a medium-risk proposition.

Materiality Principle   This principle allows accountants to use their discretion in the treatment of an item as significant or insignificant in the books of accounts.

Medium-term Finance   (or intermediate-term finance) It is that category of finance whose repayment can be projected within a planning cycle of reasonable length of time.

Merger It refers to a fusion between two or more enterprises, which results in the emergence of a single enterprise.

Merged Company (or the transferee company) This is the company to which assets are transferred.

Merging Company (or the transferor company) These are the companies that transfer their assets to the other company.

Minimum Alternate Tax (MAT) The minimum tax to be paid by the companies.

Money Market It is a market for short-term funds, that is funds up to one year.

Money Market Mutual Funds These funds invest in short-term fixed income securities, such as treasury bills, commercial paper and certificates of deposit.

Money Measurement Principle It states that accounting records only those transactions that can be expressed in money.

Mutual fund It is a pool of money mobilised from numerous investors and invested on their behalf in several securities in the market.

Mutually Exclusive Projects These are the projects wherein the decision to invest in one project affects other projects because only one project can be purchased.

National Anti-Profiteering Authority (NAPA) This is a body constituted under the GST by the central government to examine the complaints of non-passing the benefit of reduced tax incidence.

Negative Working Capital It occurs when current liabilities exceed current assets.

Net Assets Method of Valuation Under this, the total value of the assets (minus the liabilities) of the target company is computed to find out the value of the equity of its business

Net Asset Value (NAV) Net asset value of a fund is the total of the market value of the assets (securities) that comprise its portfolio, net of any liabilities at that time. Net asset value of a unit is the NAV of fund divided by the number of units outstanding.

Net Operating Profit after Tax (NOPAT) It is the profits generated from the core operations of the company after tax.

Net Present Value (NPV) It is the difference between the present value of net cash inflows and present value of cash outflows.

Net Profit Margin (or PAT margin) It measures the net margin of profitability on sales.

Net Working Capital It represents the difference between current assets and current liabilities.

Net Worth It represents the shareholders' funds in a company, as the total of share capital and reserves and surplus.

Neutral Beta   (or average beta) This is beta equal to 1.

Non-Convertible Debentures   These debentures are not convertible into equity shares.

Non-Convertible Preference Shares   These preference shares are those which are not convertible into equity shares.

Non-Cumulative Fixed Deposits   These deposits pay off the interest earned on investment on regular basis.

Non-Cumulative Preference Shares   These preference shares do not have a cumulative advantage of dividend.

Non-Diversifiable Risk   (or systematic risk or market risk) It is the risk which is non-controllable and cannot be managed by the firm, such as interest tare changes, inflation and so forth.

Non-Operating Expenses   These are related to the non-core activities of the business.

Non-Operating Revenue   It is the income which comes from non-core activities of the business.

Offer Rate   The selling rate in the forex market is known as the 'offer rate'.

Office Cost   (or cost of production) It is the total of factory cost and office overheads.

Open-Ended Mutual Funds   They are irredeemable and open for investment and redemption throughout the year.

Operating Expenses   These are the core expenses of business.

Operating Leverage   It is the use of fixed operating costs by a firm to magnify EBIT.

Operating Leverage Ratio   It is the degree of fixed operating costs involved in a project.

Operating Ratio   It analyses the profitability of the firm with regard to coverage of expenses.

Operating Revenue   It refers to the core income of business, that is 'turnover' or 'sales and services'.

Opportunity Cost   It is the cost of next best alternative (return) sacrificed in decision-making.

One Person Company (OPC)   It is a company with only one person as its member.

Operating Cycle   It is the number of days taken by a company in realising its inventories in cash.

Operating Synergies   These are the synergies that result in economies of scale due to increase in the scale of operations of the combined firm.

Opportunity Cost Method of Human Valuation   This method is used to value those employees who possess specific skills and, thus, are rare in availability. A 'bid price' is offered by the managers for acquiring such scarce employees. This bid price becomes the investment in such employees.

Options   An option gives the contract holder the right to buy or sell on a specified date in the future, but they are under no obligation.

Organic Growth   It is increasing the profit base of the organisation through the capital investment process.

Organisational Feasibility   (or managerial feasibility) It involves determining the managerial capability to undertake the project.

Organisation Structure Analysis   This study identifies the proposed legal structure of the business with all the stakeholders involved.

Out-of-Pocket Cost   It is a cost that will result in a necessary outflow of cash.

Over-The-Counter Market (OTC Market)   An 'over-the-counter market' means that there is no single market or stock exchange but an electronic market where trading takes place.

Owned Funds   They refer to the funds provided by the owners.

Paid-up Share Capital   It is the actual amount paid up by shareholders on subscription.

Partnership   In this form of ownership, two or more persons enter into a contract to carry on some lawful business jointly and to share its profits.

Payback Period   It is defined as 'the time period required to recover the initial investment of the project'.

Performance Analysis   This is the formal review process of the project with all parties involved at periodic interval for achieving the desired results of the project.

Period Cost   It is a cost which is associated with time period rather than the unit of output or manufacturing activity.

Permanent Account Number (PAN)   A ten-digit unique alphanumeric number issued by the Income Tax Department in the form of a laminated plastic card.

Permanent Working Capital   (or core working capital) It refers to the core current assets which are essential to run a business.

Person   The term 'person' includes an individual, a Hindu undivided family, a company, a firm, an association of persons or a body of individuals, a local authority, and every artificial juridical person.

Positive Working Capital   It occurs when current assets exceed current liabilities.

Preference Shares   These shares carry certain special or preferential rights in the payment of dividend and repayment of capital as compared to equity shareholders.

Previous Year   The year in which income is earned and means 'the financial year immediately preceding the assessment year'.

Price to Book Ratio (P/B)   It is a valuation ratio expressed as a multiple (i.e. how many times a company's stock is trading per share as compared to the company's book value per share).

Price to Earnings Ratio (P/E Multiple)   It is a market prospect ratio that calculates the market value of a stock relative to its earnings.

Primary Market   (or new issue market) It is a market which refers to first time issue of securities, i.e. 'Initial Public Offering (IPO)'.

Prime Cost   It is the direct cost which is also known as basic or flat cost.

Private Company   It is a form of company which is prohibited from issuing shares to the public.

Private Enterprise   It is owned, managed and controlled exclusively by private businessmen. There is no participation by the central or state governments in its establishment and ownership.

Private Placement   It is the process where securities are issued to selected mature and sophisticated institutional investors as opposed to general public.

Process Costing   This method is used in those industries where a product passes through different stages of production and each stage is distinct and well-defined.

Product Cost   It is a cost which is associated with unit of output. It is regarded as a part of inventory.

Profit   It is the excess of income over expenses.

Profit Before taxes (EBT)   This is the amount of profit earned by the business before taxes.

Profit After taxes (PAT)   This is the 'bottom line' earnings of the business.

Profitability Index (PI)   (or benefit-cost ratio ([B/C ratio])) It is the ratio of present value of cash inflows and the present value of cash outflows at the required rate of return.

Profitability Ratios   These ratios are used to analyse the profitability of a company in total and return generated for shareholders.

Project Feasibility   (or project appraisal) It is 'assessing, in advance, whether a project is worthwhile and therefore if it should be undertaken or not'.

Public Company   It is a form of company which is free to invite the general public to subscribe to its shares and debentures.

Public Deposits   They refer to the deposits received by a company from the public as loan or debt.

Public Enterprise   It may be defined as an enterprise which may be owned by the state, managed by the state, or owned and managed by the state.

Put Option   It gives the buyer the right, but not the obligation to sell a certain quantity of the underlying asset at a given price on or before the specified date.

Ratio Analysis   It involves computing 'financial ratios' and analysing the business performance based on them.

Redeemable Debentures   These debentures are repaid within the life-time of the company.

Redeemable Preference Shares   These preference shares are refund-able during the lifetime of the company.

Replacement Cost Method of Human Valuation   This method values the human resource on the basis of his replacement cost, that is the cost of recruitment, training and development, opportunity cost for the period till the new recruit attains the same efficiency level as of the old (to be replaced) employee.

Replacement Investment Decision   It involves decision concerning whether an existing asset should be replaced by a newer one of the same type or with a different type of machine with the same operational use.

Repo Rate   It is the rate at which banks can acquire funds from RBI by selling the securities and at the same time agreeing to repur-chase them at a later date at a predetermined price.

Reserve Bank of India (RBI)   It is the apex bank of India and regu-lates banking and financial companies in India.

Reserves and Surplus   (or retained earnings) This represents the amount of profit undistributed to the shareholders and kept aside for future growth.

Resource Analysis   This provides the information about the opera-tions of your business about the inputs needed to produce a prod-uct or service.

Responsibility Centres   These are the cost centres allotted to different persons and each person is held responsible for the control of cost of the centre under him.

Retail Sales Analysis   Retail sales analysis focuses on purchasing trends of the existing population within a market area and whether there is an opportunity for new retail to capture a portion of the existing market.

Return on Capital Employed (ROCE)   It measures whether or not a company is generating adequate profits in relation to the funds invested in it.

Return on Equity (ROE)   It indicates whether or not a company is generating enough return for them.

Revenue   (or income) It is the money that comes in on account of sales of goods or provision of services.

Revenue Analysis   'Revenue projection' is done here to find out the expected revenue, profit margin and expected net profit of the project.

Revenue Recognition Principle   This states that accounting transactions should be recorded in the accounting period when they actually occur, rather than in the period when they are realised.

Reverse Charge   The tax levied upon the buyer of the goods.

Reverse Repo Rate   It is the rate which is paid by RBI to banks on deposit of funds with RBI.

Rights Issue   It is the process when securities are exclusively offered to the existing shareholders.

Secondary Market   It is a market which refers to the trading of existing securities.

Secured Debentures   These debentures are secured against the assets of the company.

Secured Loan   It is the loan is taken by company against an asset as security.

Securities and Exchange Board of India (SEBI)   It is the stock market regulator of India.

Semi-Variable Cost   (or semi-fixed cost) It refers to cost which is partly fixed and partly variable.

Share   It is one of the units into which the share capital of a company can be divided.

Share Capital   The share capital of company represents the funds of a company raised through issue of shares, either common or preference shares.

Share Buyback   Share repurchase occurs when a company buys back its own shares from the market and reduces the number of shares outstanding.

Shareholders Wealth Maximisation (SWM)   Wealth maximisation is a combination of regular return to shareholders in the form of dividend and appreciating market returns.

Short-term Budgets   They are generally for one or two years.

Short-term Finance   It is that category of finance which is employed by an enterprise for day-to-day operations.

Shut Down Cost   It is the cost of an idle plant.

Single Entry System of Accounting   It is the system wherein only one aspect of a transaction is recognised.

Sole Proprietorship   In this form of a business enterprise, one person provides the entire capital, bears all the risks and manages the business.

Solvency   It implies the long-term soundness of the firm, that is its ability to pay interest on long-term loans and repay these loans at regular intervals.

Solvency Ratios   (or leverage ratios) These ratios are used to find out how financially sound a company is to meet its long-term obligations.

Spot-Forward Swap   In this swap, one deal is done in the spot market and another in the forward market, that is one buys in the spot and sells in the forward or vice versa.

Spot Market   It *is* the market where transactions for the exchange (purchase and sale) of currencies take place two days after the date of the contact.

Spread   In the forex market, the difference between the 'bid rate' and the 'offer rate' is the gross profit for the bank and is known as the spread.

Standard Costing   It is a system under which the cost of the product is determined in advance on certain predetermined standards.

State Goods and Services Tax (SGST)   This is collected by the state government on an intra-state sale of goods and services.

Statement of Profit and Loss   (or income statement) It is a summary of an entity's revenues generated and expenses incurred during a period whose net result is either profit or loss.

Statutory Corporation   (or a public corporation) It is a body set up under a special Act of Parliament or of a state legislature.

Statutory Liquidity Ratio (SLR)   It refers to the liquid reserve which is required to be maintained by banks in the form of cash and cash deposits.

Straight Line Method of Depreciation (SLM)   (or fixed instalment method) In this method, depreciation is charged at fixed amount throughout the life of an asset.

Stock Exchange   These are marketplace where buyers and sellers come together to trade in a firm's shares and other securities.

Stock Split   A stock split is a division of the stock into multiple shares with a lower face value.

Subscribed Share Capital   It is that part of the issued share capital which is subscribed by the investors.

Subsidiary Company   A company is called to be subsidiary if 50% shares are owned by a holding company.

Sum-of-the-Years-Digits Method of Depreciation   Here, depreciation is calculated by adding up the number of years of the useful economic life.

Sunk Cost These costs are historical or past costs.

Super-Quick Ratio   (or cash ratio) It is the closest indicator of liquidity of a firm as it focuses only on 'cash and bank balances' availability to meet current liabilities.

Swap Market   It is a combination of a spot and a forward transaction. The term 'swap' implies a temporary exchange of one currency for another with an obligation to reverse it at a specific future date.

SWIFT   It is an acronym for 'Society for Worldwide Interbank Financial Telecommunications'. It is a communications network for international financial market transactions which links effectively more than 25,000 financial institutions throughout the world who have been allotted bank-identified codes.

Synergies   This refers to the value addition to the new entity due to combination of two separate companies.

Systematic Investment Plan (SIP)   It involves investing a fixed amount in a mutual fund at regular intervals, monthly or quarterly over a period of time, thereby averaging out the cost of investing and yielding the benefit from power of compounding.

Takeover   A 'forced' acquisition is called a takeover.

Tangible Fixed Assets   These include physical fixed assets, which are visible.

Tax Deduction and Collection Account Number (TAN)   A ten-digit alphanumeric number required to be obtained by all persons who are responsible for deducting or collecting tax.

Taxable Person   A person who carries out any business at any place in India and is registered or required to be registered under the GST Act.

Technical Feasibility   It identifies the technical requirements of men, machines and materials of the proposed project.

Technology Analysis   This is assessing the type of technology required for the project and the constraints involved in the implementation.

Time Value of Money (TVM)   It describes the relationship between the value of a rupee today and the value of a rupee in future.

Temporary Working Capital   (or variable capital) It is the extra working capital needed to support the changing production and sales activities.

Terminal Cash Flows   These are the cash flows that occur only at the end of the life of the asset.

Term Loans   These are long-term loans provided by central and state level financial institutions to the business firms.

Top Line   It refers to the total income generated by the company.

Trading on Equity   It is the ability of the firm to use the debt financing to magnify the shareholders' return.

Treasury Bills (T-bills) These are short-term government securities issued by RBI on behalf of the central government.

Trend Analysis It takes the base year as hundred and express the respective years in percentage to find out the growth pattern of a company.

Turnover It refers to the firm's sales from goods or services.

Two-Way Quotations It means the rate quoted by the bank will indicate two prices, one at which it is willing to buy the foreign currency, and the other at which it is willing to sell the foreign currency.

Uncontrollable Cost It is a cost that is beyond the control of a manager.

Unsecured Debentures These are simple debentures and have no security.

Unsecured Loan It is a loan is taken by company without any security.

Value-Added Tax (VAT) A consumption tax levied on a product whenever value is added at each stage of the supply chain, from production to the point of sale.

Value Creation It is a corporation's raison d'être, the ultimate measure by which it is judged.

Variable Cost This cost changes with the changes in the volume of output.

Vertical Merger This is a combination of two or more firms involved in different stages of the production or distribution.

Weighted Average Cost of Capital (WACC) (or cost of capital employed) It is the total cost of raising the funds for investment purposes.

Working Capital This means 'the capital used to carry out the day to day operations of a business'.

Working Capital Management It is concerned with the problems that arise in attempting to manage the current assets, current liabilities and the inter-relationship that asserts between them.

Working Capital Turnover Ratio (WCTR) This ratio is used to measure the company's ability to utilise its working capital efficiently to generate revenue.

Written-Down-Value Method of Depreciation (WDV) (or diminishing balance method or reducing balance method) In this method, depreciation is charged at fixed rate on the reducing balance (i.e. cost less depreciation) every year.

Zero Based Budgeting (ZBB) It is starting from 'scratch'. Here, every year is taken as a new year and previous year is not taken as a base.

Zero Coupon Bonds (or deep discount bonds) These bonds are issued at substantial discount but redeemed at full.

Index